This book is due for return on or before the last date shown below.

E ─────────────────────────────────── S

1 6 JUN 2005   2 1 NOV ...

1 2 DEC 2005   2 1 NOV 2007

0 3 JAN 2006   1 8 JAN 2008

                        − 6 JAN 2010

17 FEB 2006

1 5 MAR 2006

1 3 APR 2006

1 1 JAN 2007

2 6 JUN 2007

intellect™
Bristol, UK
Portland, OR, USA

intellect – European Studies Series

General Editor – Keith Cameron

First Published in Hardback in 2003 by
Intellect Books, PO Box 862, Bristol BS99 1DE, UK

First Published in USA in 2003 by
Intellect Books, ISBS, 5804 N.E. Hassalo St, Portland, Oregon 97213–3644, USA

A catalogue record for this book is available from the British Library

ISBN 1-84150-014-3

Series Editor:	Keith Cameron
Copy Editor:	Holly Spradling

The cover photograph shows *Allegory to Sports – 1896* (Olympic Museum, Lausanne) by Charles de Coubertin, father of the founder of the modern Olympic Games.

Printed and bound in Great Britain by Antony Rowe, Eastbourne

Contents

Contributors

Arnd Krüger is Head of the Department of Sports Science at Georg-August University, Gottingen, Germany. Born in the German Democratic Republic of a runner-wrestler father, he emigrated as a boy to West Germany where he became 11-time German champion at 800 and 1500m, reaching the Olympic semi-finals in 1968. Author of many seminal works, Professor Kruger is the founding President of the Committee on European Sports History (CESH).

James Riordan studied at Birmingham, London and Moscow universities before becoming Professor of Russian Studies in Britain. Until recently he was Head of the Department of Linguistic and International Studies at the University of Surrey. He is currently Honorary Professor in Sports Studies at Stirling University. Much of his research has been on communist sport; he lived and worked for five years in Moscow, playing football for Moscow Spartak.

Marc Keech is Senior Lecturer in Sport and Leisure Studies at the Chelsea School, University of Brighton, England. His research publications range from sport and diplomacy in apartheid South Africa, leisure culture, and sport and social exclusion. His football career was curtailed by injury; he now dreams of seeing England win the World Cup instead of watching re-runs of 1966.

Ian Thomson has lectured and worked in Scottish sport for most of his life – at Jordanhill College, Dunfermline College and Stirling University where he was the first Director of Physical Recreation. He has also been county advisor for community education in Midlothian and advisor to the Scottish Sports Council. A former soccer and squash player, he is now to be found mostly on St Andrews Golf Course.

Else Trangbaek is Associate Professor at the Institute of Exercise and Sports Sciences, University of Copenhagen. Her main scholarly writing is on the history of gymnastics, physical education and women. One-time Danish gymnastics champion (six-time all-round national champion), she took part in the Nordic, European and World championships, as well as the 1968 Olympic Games.

Hart Cantelon is Associate Professor in Sociology and Physical and Health Education at Queen's University, Kingston, Canada. He pioneered the study of Soviet ice hockey, spending time in Moscow during the 1970s. He has written extensively on ice hockey, the Olympics and working class culture. Professor Cantelon holds high-level coaching certificates in ice hockey and Canadian football.

Thierry Terret was a school PE teacher for seven years before becoming Professor of Sports Studies at the University of Lyon in 1992. He now lectures in sports history and manages an interdisciplinary research centre on 'Sport and Integration'. He is currently

President of the International Society for the History of PE and Sport and former President of the French Association for Sports Sciences. He spends his free time playing village rugby, feeding his three cats, goat (Mister B) and Josephine the Frog.

Teresa Gonzalez Aja is Professor of Sports History at the Instituto Nacional de Educacion Fisica , Technical University of Madrid. With a PhD in Sport and Art, she has written widely on Spanish sports history. She is currently President of the Committee on European Sports History and a member of the Spanish Olympic Academy. Her active sporting pursuits are golf and the Spanish folk game of *Mus*.

Patrick Stumm obtained his PhD at Georg-August University, Gottingen, before embarking on research into sporting trends in Germany, Italy and Spain. He has studied in Mannheim, Gottingen and Padua (Italy), and spent a few years in Madrid and Rome on sports research. A former German professional sprinter (100m) and long jumper, he now devotes much of his leisure time to inline skating and fitness sport.

Angela Teja is Professor of Sports History at the University of Cassino, Rome. She is a founding member and current General Secretary of CESH, and has written widely on Italian sports history, particular the military and women during the fascist period. A top-level runner at Rome's Federal Athletics Centre, she now mainly confines her energies to modern rhythmic gymnastics.

Marco Impiglia, one-time lecturer in Sports History at the University of Cassino, Rome, is now a freelance journalist writing on sports history for major Italian sports periodicals. His particular area of expertise is football to which he has dedicated virtually all his physical and mental energy over the last decade.

Introduction

James Riordan and Arnd Krüger

Modern sport and gymnastics had their origins in Europe during the last two centuries. Organised competitive sports, like football, rugby and athletics, emerged in the nineteenth century as the private domain of the new social class born of industrialisation and urbanisation. They were a social innovation, confined to class and national boundaries; in the main they excluded manual workers, women and certain ethnic minorities (e.g. Jews and Gypsies). Essentially, these sports were a private initiative, in no way associated with the state or politics, let alone foreign policy.

Not so gymnastics. The various schools of physical exercises – associated with Jahn in Germany, Nachtegall in Denmark, Ling in Sweden, Lesgaft in Russia – developed as pedagogical, political and military instruments for building a national identity. And that involved everybody: man and woman, squire and peasant, factory owner and worker. To learn to put one's body at the service of the nation emanated from a policy of acculturation of the common people in the same way as learning one's national language.

In much of Europe, sport and gymnastics contended for influence, with enthusiasts for one refusing to recognise or engage in the other. At the turn of century, particularly after the 1914-18 World War, however, competitive sports started to prevail. This was encouraged by the new international contests, especially the modern Olympic Games (brainchild of the French aristocrat Baron Pierre de Coubertin) inaugurated at Athens in 1896. Sport and sporting spectacle rapidly spread throughout Europe and, from Europe, to the rest of the world.

As international competition grew, states began to perceive the potential political benefits to be gained from sporting victory. With the coming to power of totalitarian regimes (Soviet Communism from 1917, Italian Fascism from 1922, German Nazism from 1933, Spanish Fascism from 1936, East European State Socialism from 1945) private clubs and associations in these countries gave way to state direction of sport, elevating sport to a high priority on the political agenda.

The growing internationalisation and politicisation of sport inevitably raised broader issues, like religion, social class, gender and race. Sometimes this caused a split in the movement, with various groups playing among themselves – like socialist and communist workers who formed their own sports associations and Olympics.

In the second half of the twentieth century, a mounting tension developed between amateur-elitist sport for wealthy, privileged males and commercial spectator sport for the mainly middle classes, as well as worker and female sport, with commercial sport prevailing. After the Second World War, sport became further politicised with the Cold War rivalry between capitalist and communist states, utilising sports victories as evidence of political superiority. At the same time, erstwhile underprivileged groups –

blacks, women, disabled, the gay community – were struggling for recognition and sometimes integration.

All these developments are apparent, in varying degrees, in every European nation. Yet each country also possesses its own specifics, and each sees the concepts of 'sport' and 'gymnastics' differently. Thus, French sport still bears the imprint of the French Revolution of 1789, the educational philosophy of Jean-Jacques Rousseau and the noble aspirations of Coubertin; Germany's recent history includes Jahn's 'gymnastics' (for national regeneration after Napoleonic occupation), the Nazi-controlled sports system, the division of Germany into capitalist West and communist East, and subsequent reunification; Russia, at the back end of Europe, with a dozen foreign states on its borders in tsarist and Soviet times, has always had a close relationship between sport, the state and the military; Italy likewise: half its medal winners at the 1994 Summer Olympics of Atlanta were in the armed forces.

In those parts of Europe that experienced authoritarian regimes, state-centralised sport pursued certain utilitarian functions on behalf of the ruling party, above all to promote a togetherness, a 'culture of consent' among the population at home, and recognition and prestige abroad. For communist states, like the Soviet Union, East Germany, Hungary and Romania, and for fascist states, like Italy and Germany, Olympic sports were the priority. They therefore sponsored full-time 'state amateurs' to achieve these ends. The Soviet Union 'won' every Olympics, summer and winter (apart from 1964), in which it competed; Fascist Italy came second in the 1932 Los Angeles Games, and third behind the USA and Germany in the 1936 Berlin Olympics. Football was another sporting priority, particularly in Fascist Spain, which spurned the Olympics and focused attention on the Falange-controlled club Real Madrid, which duly won the European Championships from 1955 to 1960 (setting a European trend in giving top foreign players – Puskas, Kubala, Kopa, Gento, Di Stefano – Spanish citizenship to enable them to play for Real Madrid). The employment of sport for prestige abroad and unity at home is present, in varying degrees, in all nations, authoritarian or liberal, as is the promotion of a particular sport (e.g. English cricket in the British Commonwealth) for encouraging a culture of consent.

As a consequence of the above, each European nation would define sport in its own way. Germany might include naturalism and chess, Spain – bullfighting, England – cricket and croquet, France – poetry and song, Russia – paramilitary pursuits, Italy – hunting and boccia. We do not confine 'sport' or 'gymnastics' to a single, culture-specific definition. In any case, Europeanisation and, indeed, globalisation, of sport are constantly giving sport new meanings and activities, like inline skating, aerobics and synchronised swimming.

Europe as a continent is continually in flux. Its over 700 million inhabitants currently reside in over forty nations, from the 130m of Russia to the 80m of Germany, from the 1.5m of Estonia to the 0.25m of Iceland. Our book covers just eight countries and the loose geopolitical area of what was state socialist Eastern Europe (Albania, Bulgaria, Czechoslovakia, the German Democratic Republic, Hungary, Poland, Romania and Yugoslavia).

The historical period covered varies according to the emergence of modern sport and gymnastics. With France, we go back to 1789, Germany – the mid-19th century, England and Wales – the critical stage of the Industrial Revolution in the 1870s, Spain – the late 19th century, Russia – the communist revolution of 1917, Italy – the early 19th century when military physical education began to develop, Denmark – the 1850s and 1860s when gymnastics clubs emerged.

The contributors are eleven sports historians – two Germans, two Italians, two Englishmen, a Dane, Scot, Canadian, Frenchman and Spanish woman. Their intention is both to provide an insight into the unique development of sport in European society and, at the same time, to reveal the related historical processes that have shaped European sport over the last two hundred years.

England and Wales

Marc Keech

The recent historiography of sport in England and Wales has been concerned with two important issues. The first area of study has focused on the emergence of sport into recognisable modern forms, linked as it was to the social, economic, political and cultural structures of the eighteenth- and nineteenth-century society. The second, and more recent, focus has examined more contemporary aspects of the development of sport since the end of the Second World War. Here, increasing levels of state intervention have been juxtaposed against three prevailing ideologies which have shaped sport in England and Wales, amateurism, welfarism and commercialism. The chapter examines these themes through four key periods. The first, 1870-1914, examines the influence of the processes of urbanisation and industrialisation on the creation of what have become 'modern' sports. The second, 1914-1945, explores the impact of inter-war poverty and the growth of sport as a spectacle. From 1945 to 1970 the continuity of sporting practices is contrasted with the growing recognition of the professional and commercial value of sport. Since 1970, the development of sport in England and Wales has been characterised by the debates concerning whether sport is 'for all', or for 'a few'. Throughout, it is acknowledged that sport has been a predominantly male preserve, only recently reflecting upon how women can be empowered through sport.

A great deal of historical writing has concentrated on the history of sport in Britain (see Mason, 1989; Birley, 1993; 1995, Holt, 1989) and these works often incorporated some mention of sport in Scotland and also Northern Ireland. The unique constitution of the United Kingdom has been historically dominated by the English, with a larger population and significantly more resources. Until 1922 it governed the whole of Ireland as well as Scotland and Wales, hence the interchangeable and sometimes indiscriminate use of 'English' to mean 'British' which has reflected the distribution of power within the state. Only recently has devolution led to the creation of a Welsh assembly that has the power to allocate resources. Thus, it is important to acknowledge that political, economic and socio-cultural change in England was often replicated in Wales and many sporting trends followed a similar path.

1870-1914: From the old to the new

Popular recreations, medieval activities and folk games had many of their origins in the Roman occupations of Britain. Through time, activities became moulded by and rooted in the elite, agrarian or parochial identities of localised communities. Many activities were based on wagering; for example on animal baiting or cock fighting, whilst the upper classes would pursue field sports such as hunting and shooting. By the 1870s Britain was the most industrialised nation in the world; its manufacturing base was firmly located in towns and cities and it had established a reliable network of transport and communications. Prior to this period sport was not a mass participation pastime and the origins of modern sport in England and Wales were rooted in the elite educational system of the nineteenth century.

Many characteristics of modern sport in England and Wales were shaped by the extensive development of physical education and activity in public schools. Mangan (1981) provides the most comprehensive account of this period. During the latter half of the nineteenth century public schools institutionalised what were seen as two important principles. First, there was a move to competitive team games, based on the premise that these activities had an ethical basis and would teach participants to play for others and not just oneself. Second, it was believed that the moral values of physical education could be transferred beyond the playing field. Such ideologies reflected the thoughts of Jean-Jacques Rousseau, the French philosopher and in part, emerged from the innovative developments that took place through gymnastics in France and elsewhere in Europe. As Jennifer Hargreaves (1994) notes, similar values were ascribed to the development of pioneering physical education colleges for young women. By 1905 Dartford College offered the first full-time course in the theory and practice of physical education (Hargreaves, 1994: p.78). During this period middle- and some working-class girls gained their experience of physical activity through their schooling. Ideas and meanings attached to gymnastics, games, athletics, swimming and dance have had a lasting effect upon how women think about their bodies and the development of female sports became inextricably and fundamentally linked to the development of the women's physical education profession (Hargreaves, 1994: pp.86-7).

The ability of physical education to transmit moral values such as fairness, decency and, through adherence to the rules of the game, has often been questioned but the conformity of the upper classes to these values, embedded at the public schools, has had a strong legacy throughout the twentieth century. By 1906 physical education and some sporting activities were beginning to be incorporated into the state school curricula, but in public schools the amount of, and importance attached to, physical education and sport were exemplified by the number of competitions. As Holt (1981) writes, 'the full importance of games and their distinctive social function cannot be grasped without some understanding of the changing relationship within and between the middle and upper classes in nineteenth-century Britain as a whole' (p.95). By the end of the nineteenth century, Britain possessed a remarkably homogenous and cohesive elite, sharing to a high degree a common education and a common outlook and set of values (Briggs, 1965: pp.152-3, cited in Holt, 1989: p.95).

Towns and cities were rapidly growing, boosted by the manufacturing industries and whose landscapes in the latter half of the nineteenth century were dominated by large factories and crowded streets. Large swathes of the population migrated from rural communities, which had been devastated by the collapse of the common field system of farming. The provision of rational recreation activities, governed by the view and use of sport as a form of moral education which was often held by humanitarian and educational organisations, promoted a vision of society in which collective goals of improved industrial productivity and social cohesion could emerge. As Horne et al. note (1999: p.2) many activities were appropriated by the working class as their own and 'the changing society was governed by contractual relations in spheres of life such as work and the family ... it was biased toward individualism ... and rooted in factory-labour discipline rather than the social or inherited relations of the community'. John Hargreaves (1986) concluded that the rational recreation movement, which aimed to improve, educate and refine popular culture of the masses, did not engender cultural change amongst the majority of the population as cultural change takes longer to manifest itself than population migration. Throughout much of the nineteenth century the public house became a focus for a number of leisure activities including sport. For Holt (1989: p. 148) the public house and the local streets became the locations for those who learned their sports 'in the shadow of the factory'. Holt also notes that this era marks the origins of the much stronger association between sport and alcohol in England and Wales, with many participants often following their sport with a visit to their 'local', whilst 'boxers and footballers looked to the alcohol trade as a way of living after retirement'.

Modern sports in England and Wales emerged as the cultural products of a rapidly industrialising society, undergoing unprecedented levels of change. That the changing nature of society would produce markedly different sporting practices was not always evident and the time taken for that change to occur varied from sport to sport. Whilst one should not claim that sports, or sport *per se*, simply reflected the characteristics of society it is prudent to claim that they were products of the social relationships that formed within the context of societal change. However, the major issue in the development of sport during this period was the conflict between athleticism and rational recreation with the emergent forms of professional sport. The dynamics of this conflict were central to the growth of many modern sports and are critical to understanding their emergence.

The emergence of sport in the city is closely connected by population expansion in urban areas. In 1881, three quarters of the British population lived in and around towns and cities and the proportion increased as the total grew to 41 million by 1901, 33 million of whom lived in England and Wales. The introduction of the shorter working week, with cotton mills being forced to close by 2.00 p.m. on Saturdays, combined with legislation such as the Bank Holidays Act which led to the first public holiday in 1871, ensured that by the 1880s working class people in England and Wales enjoyed more leisure time than those elsewhere in Europe (Birley, 1995: p.265). Games of short duration significantly benefited from the Saturday half-day holiday particularly in heavily industrialised areas such as the Midlands and north-west of England. For example, in Birmingham the number of football clubs rose from one in 1874, to 20 in 1876 to 155 by 1880 (Birley, 1995: p. 265). To visitors from Europe the number and variety of sporting activities were surprising. The more codified versions of existing sports were suited to the limited spaces of the industrialised areas and the use of communication and transport links enabled organisations to regulate sporting forms in such ways as leagues, cup competitions and regular meetings. Two contrasting examples of this process follow.

The Rugby Football Union (RFU) was formed at a meeting in London in 1871 out of 'an urgent desire to rescue the game of rugby from the confusions of unregulated modes of play into which it was slipping'. Williams (1989: p. 309) asserts that the need for a unified code of rules was extremely pressing as the game was diffusing from its origins within the public schools and universities into wider public society. Through the latter quarter of the nineteenth century the game went through a series of rule changes to emerge in a recognisable precursor of the modern game. As with association football, clubs were often built on pre-existing formations, such as schools (in Yorkshire and Lancashire for example), or places of work (around the mines of Cornwall or the foundries of Pontypridd). In Wales, the church also had a strong influence in areas such as Llanelli, whilst the Redruth club in Cornwall, formed in 1895 from 'the usual assortment of petty bourgeoisie, managed to secure support, and a ground, from the Redruth Brewery Company' (Williams, 1989: p.311), thereby starting a pattern of patronage by local employers.

In the North of England, rugby emerged as a mass spectator sport drawing attendances in excess of 25,000. Suggestions that receipts might be spent on improving facilities for spectators or recompensing players for missing work were viewed with barely concealed suspicion by the southern-based RFU. In 1895, 22 clubs formed the Northern Union and by 1898 their number had risen to 98. The RFU's stoicism preserved the middle-class status of the sport but in doing so it led to a markedly reduced number of clubs and a loss of many of England's best players. By 1913 the Northern Union had adopted a league style structure and was benefiting from the commercial nature of the game, which was to emerge as what is now known as Rugby League. In Wales, the spread of the game relied on two factors. First, the ability of upper-middle class young men who would organise and control the sport, and second, the concomitant injection of industrialism into the southern half of Wales, which required a sizeable workforce. By 1911, the population of Wales had risen by over a million from 1871 and one in three was a miner (Williams, 1989: p.314). Rugby predated football by over 20 years and became an embodiment of the collective identity of a physically vigorous society. The Welsh Rugby Union (WRU) was formed in 1881 and retained a middle class control of the sport, but the sport remained amateur, despite the precedent set by the Northern Union.

Ex-public school and university players living and working in London formed the English Football Association (FA) in 1863. By 1880 the game had one set of rules recognised by all players and administrators. From the late nineteenth century football became the game of working-class men. Grounds were built in urban areas and the gate money charged was the catalyst for ground improvements at clubs such as Blackburn Rovers and Preston North End in the north-west. The trend was replicated most notably at cricket and horse racing venues. An important factor reflecting the growth and scope of the game was the FA knockout cup competition first competed for by 14 teams in 1871-72. The competition was replicated in Wales in the 1877-78 season. By 1885 the English FA legalised professionalism which provoked long-term contestation between the professional and amateur ethos of the game. By the 1908-09 season football had become a ritual component of many working men's lives with attendances for the English first division reaching a total of over 6 million. The number of professional football clubs in Wales quadrupled between 1906 and 1910 but the game had permeated areas in the North, closer to the English conurbations of Liverpool and Manchester, more strongly than it had in the South where rugby remained the most popular sport.

The first decade of the twentieth century set the patterns which were to become more commonplace, particularly after the Second World War. By 1901 railway lines criss-crossed the countries and the railways had become the envy of many European nations. Travelling to sport had now become habitual for some spectators and watching sport had begun to be budgeted into everyday lives as working men saved for weekly trips to popular team sports such as football. Professional sport at the beginning of the twentieth century was still in its infancy, with many sports continuing to re-evaluate their practices. Rule changes occurred almost annually; for example, until 1902 the penalty area in football was still kidney shaped when the area was re-designed into the modern size and shape. In 1908 the Olympic Games were held in London, with 2035 participants from 22 nations and were widely credited as the first Games to be well organised. In 1900 Wales began an unsurpassed run of eleven consecutive five nations rugby championships cementing rugby's place at the forefront of Welsh sporting culture. Transfer fees in football have been a source of great debate and controversy ever since Alf Common became the first £1000 player when he moved from Sunderland to Middlesborough in 1905. Furthermore, the first football disaster occurred in 1902 when 25 people died and more than 500 were injured when a wooden stand collapsed at Ibrox during the annual match between England and Scotland.

Sport in this period had undergone radical change. Upper and middle classes were in dominant positions to shape the development of amateur and professional sport and it was they, not the working classes who reconfigured sporting practices into a recognisable form, and who dominated the emergent governing bodies of sport. Sport remained governed by men with women participating for social rather than competitive reasons. Within this strongly patriarchal arena, the notion of the amateur remained strong but the professional represented the artisan, doggedly completing successive tasks and it was with the professional that the working classes identified.

1914-1945 – Poverty and spectacle

The aftermath of the Great War (1914-1918) saw England and Wales facing profound social, political and economic change. The pre-war Edwardian tranquillity of country pastimes was rapidly being replaced by the hard-headed commercial approach not just to industry, but also to sport. The War had had a profound effect on sport. Most governing bodies cancelled fixtures as soon as it started and when cricket continued with its county championship, England's greatest player of the previous forty years, W. G. Grace called upon all eligible cricketers to enlist; fixtures were cancelled soon thereafter. The decisions by the FA and the Jockey Club to continue with football and horse racing provoked outrage. Whilst footballers signed up for armed service (a footballers' battalion had its headquarters at the Richmond Athletic Ground, and they became part of the Middlesex regiment, seeing action in France in 1915), the Jockey

Club had to be asked by government to cease racing except at Newmarket, although some of the 'classics' such as the Oaks and the Derby continued. Sport became linked with the masculine pride of the nation. 'If only,' wrote the secretary of the WRU, 'every man in the first XV in Wales were to enlist, what a magnificent body there would be at the service of our country' (cited in Birley 1993: p.59). One of the few other sports to continue during the War was boxing. Jimmy Wilde, a flyweight from South Wales, won the world title in 1916 and held it for over seven years. In contrast, sport also provided one of the most symbolic moments amongst the bloodshed. A truce on Christmas Day, 1914, saw British and German infantry play football in no-man's land. When the game finished, the soldiers returned to their trenches and recommenced battle.

The inter-war period saw wildly fluctuating economic cycles and sport evolved against a background of continued economic restructuring. Following demobilisation there was an immediate boom, which was quickly followed by a punishing reduction in levels of economic activity from 1920-22. Up until 1929 there was some respite, although levels of poverty remained high. The global economic depression from 1929-1933 forced crippled economies to contract and at this time regional disparities were at their zenith. Whole communities in Wales, the north-west and north-east of England, reliant upon core industries such as coal, textiles and iron and steel, suffered mass unemployment. Conversely, new industries, based on electrical engineering and vehicle manufacturing, emerged in the South and Midlands of England. Even so, material gains tended to have clearly defined class boundaries. The overall rise in real income during this period masks inequalities of gendered access to employment, access to housing, health schemes and further conceals the quality of life endured by manual workers in the most depressed economic areas. In fourteen months at the start of the 1930s unemployment in England doubled, yet many still made it to football and cricket matches in particular. Jarrow, in the north-east of England, registered 70% unemployment whilst in London the figure hovered around 6%. Primarily for reasons around the relative prosperity of the region, London football clubs became deeply unpopular outside of the south-east. The over-riding influence of economic conditions on post-war society in England and Wales is an important consideration when one contextualises the development of sport in this period.

Sport had become a predominant leisure activity for many working-class people. The labour movement, consisting of the Trade Unions, and represented politically by the Labour Party and also the Communist Party also had a sporting wing, organised by the British Workers Sports Federation (BWSF), formed in 1923 with the aim of furthering 'the cause of peace between nations'. The BWSF lasted for over a decade and a national labour sports organisation, rooted in the origins of the London Labour Party, the National Workers Sports Association (NWSA), emerged in its place with the more sportive intention of encouraging and promoting amateur sport amongst working class organisations. Although unable to overhaul the upper- and middle-class dominance of sport, the worker sport movements provided a source of identity and a point of reference for working-class organisations and individuals and did much to cement sport's position as a mass-participation activity and pastime (Jones, 1987).

The inter-war years amplified inequities faced by women. Wages were half those of men and many had to retreat into domestic service simply in order to survive, yet the period also saw a remarkable growth in the development of women's sports. Middle-class women and working-class women who enjoyed a degree of affluence and were young and single, found sport more accessible than many poorer working-class women (Hargreaves, 1994: pp.112-113). Gradually, women, as well as men, began to attend sporting events, in part encouraged by the emergence of famous sportswomen. In tennis the appearance of France's Suzanne Lenglen and America's Helen Wills at Wimbledon challenged traditional values, whilst Kitty Godfree, who played both tennis and badminton for Britain, became symbolic of female, amateur participation (Hargreaves, 1994: pp.116-117). The growth and organisation of women's sport were strongly linked to elite girls' schools, colleges and universities. Whilst national associations for hockey and lacrosse had been formed prior to the War, a number of associations emerged in the 1920s, such as British Women's Cricket Association (BWCA) and the All England Netball Association (AENA), both of which were formed in 1926. Whilst the formation of the BWCA marked a challenge to the traditionally male preserve of cricket, the organisation of netball was significant in that the sport had been characterised as 'feminine-appropriate', played only by women and was never opposed in the manner that other team sports were (Hargreaves, 1994: p.124). The most prominent barriers to the development of women's sport during this period were the lack of resources afforded to many sports and also the struggle to obtain equality of opportunity with men in aquatic sports and especially athletics (Hargreaves, 1994: pp.125-134).

By 1920 the average working week had been reduced to 48 hours. Combined with the further growth of urban transport such as trams and buses, spectator sports expanded, with football attendances recording record figures. Football continued to be dominated by clubs from the North of England during the 1920s. However, as Birley asserts* 'the most remarkable interlopers were Cardiff City, who were at Wembley (in the FA Cup Final) twice, beating Arsenal on the second occasion in 1927 (Birley, 1995: p.182). The success of Cardiff and their closest rivals Swansea City during the 1920s suggested that a process of Anglicisation had begun to take hold of Welsh sporting culture. But, by 1929 Cardiff's time in the English first division, which had lasted since 1921, ended in relegation and Welsh football again gave way to the parochialism of rugby. In addition, football in England spread south and there were over 80 professional clubs by 1922. This growth was matched in commercial arenas, admission figures were within the budget of many working class men, and new and larger stadia were required for showpiece fixtures. In 1923, Wembley stadium, located in north-west London, hosted the FA Cup for the first time. Although the stadium had a capacity of 100,000 many more made it into the stadium with an estimated attendance in excess of 200,000. The fixture, between West Ham United and eventual winners, Bolton Wanderers became known as the White Horse Cup Final for the single mounted police officer who ensured that the crowds who had spilled on to the pitch prior to kick-off, were cleared from the playing field. Overall, there was an expansion of spectator sports, which began to emerge as an integral component of the increasingly commercialised mass-entertainment industry. Attendances at county cricket, track and field athletics and motor sports all grew whilst horse racing, swimming, boxing and newer sports such as ice hockey thrived.

According to Holt (1989: p.179) 'there was a particular cluster of popular sporting activities that middle-class society either ignored or attacked. These were sports which in one way or another involved gambling'. The prohibition of many forms of gambling meant that the 'respectable' opinion of many in the middle and upper classes saw gambling as being the twin evil of alcohol. From the 1880s, *the Sportsman, the Sporting Life* and *the Sporting Chronicle*, all newspapers that published information about horse racing meetings, the starting prices and on-course information, had augmented the culture of gambling. Horse racing became the best example of a sport that remained very exclusive in social terms but also had a huge popular following (Holt 1989: p.181). The Derby, ran at Epsom Downs, near London, epitomised popular fascination with horse racing. 'As many as a quarter of a million Londoners and others were drawn ... and not a tenth of those who came had much chance of actually seeing the race. But this hardly mattered. There was the prospect of a drink, a 'flutter', and a glimpse of the rich and high-born' (Holt, 1989: p.181). The fascination for gambling was never more acute than with the development of greyhound racing. During the 1920s the traditional racing of greyhounds was honed into an American version of dogs racing round a circuit which provided the right mixture of speed and skill to make the outcome uncertain. Tracks appeared in most of the major towns and cities, offering a cheaper alternative for those who could not afford horse racing. By 1932 there were 187 tracks and annual attendances were over 20 million people (Jones, 1987: p.46). Gambling continued to grow rapidly in the 1930s, fuelled by the introduction of the football pools, where punters would attempt to correctly predict results, usually score draws, in order to win a sum of money. By 1936, six million people regularly 'did the pools coupon' on a weekly basis.

The inter-war period witnessed an increasing commercialisation in the consumption of cultural activities. Popular leisure activities included the cinema, dance halls, the growth of excursions and longer holidays, whilst the introduction of radio broadcasts in 1922 transformed people's leisure habits. Banned by the interests of newspapers from covering sport until 1927, radio emerged as a tool through which live sport such as the Derby or the FA Cup final could be broadcast into people's homes. By the late 1920s cinema newsreels also incorporated footage of sporting events which would often be the first time that the public had witnessed a sporting event as a visually mediated sporting product.

As sport's profile continued to grow, both domestically and internationally, so too did the amount of political involvement in sporting affairs. Governments, notably Germany, used sport for political purposes, whilst the British government was involved in legislating gambling. State involvement in the provision of sport in England and Wales grew with the formation of the Central Council for Recreative Physical Training (CCRPT), which was created in 1935 through funding from the Ministry of Education. The aim of the CCPRT was to provide a national and comprehensive stimulus for post-school sport. Two years later the government passed the 1937 Physical Training and Recreation Act which paved the way for state funding for voluntary sport and recreation organisations.

The inter-war years also reflected the origins of local public intervention in sport and, gradually, a process of bureaucratisation took hold as agencies of the state were brought in not only to regulate sporting forms but also to plan and programme sporting activities and facilities. There was also the first public recognition of the lack of public facilities for the general public. Initially this reflected themes of rational recreation, wherein local health concerns could be addressed through the provision of local amenities such as wash-houses and bathing facilities. However, these concerns also reflected the origins of state intervention. From the mid-1930s the Ministry of Labour, through the Office of the Commissioner for Special Areas, was channelling funds into sport for the unemployed of South Wales and the north-east. Great importance began to be attached to physical training and recreation as one of the measures most likely to improve the physique and maintain the morale of the unemployed. Through this process links with some voluntary recreational organisations were established. Voluntarism was cemented within a collectivist approach to local sport and recreation provision, through agreements such as those between the Special Areas Office, the National Playing Fields Association and the Miners Welfare Committee, which aimed to improve provision in mining communities of South Wales (Jones, 1987: pp.133-4).

1945-1970 – Professionalisation and Politicisation
The post-war era was marked by a growth in the professionalisation of sport. The 1948 Olympics, held in London, symbolically reflected the reconstruction of the nation. The Games did much to increase the profile of sport generally, with government involvement critical to the success of the Games. However, sport remained largely controlled by amateurs and relied upon its volunteer workforce. But given the national imperative attached to sporting success, amateur values began to be challenged whilst the growing economic value of sport gradually began to be realised. Holt and Mason (2000) note that by the end of the 1950s, six main sports – boxing, cricket, cycling, golf, horse racing and football — had a professional element. Sports such as cricket and football had strong local foundations both in school and in the growing number of junior clubs. Professional football clubs often sent scouts to watch local matches in order to identify talented young people. Football and horse racing adopted apprenticeship schemes, where little formal teaching took place, but apprentices often served as cheap labour, with responsibilities such as cleaning the boots of senior professionals or cleaning stables or changing rooms. In professional sport, employers set stringent rules for behaviour and conduct, realising that 'the professional' had to perform in order to earn their wage, the levels of which differed from sport to sport but often offered an income beyond the reach of most. When Johnny Haynes became the first footballer to earn £100 a week he received seven times the average wage. The acceptance of professionals took time and when John Charles, the Welsh international footballer signed for Juventus of Italy for a then British record fee of £65,000, he said

the move was not only motivated by the promise of more money, but also the likelihood of better treatment by his employers (Holt and Mason, 2000: pp.64-87).

As the professional era dawned, amateurism began to decline. At its peak in the 1950s, amateurism represented the traditional value of sport, moulded by the spirit of fair play. However, a combination of factors, such as the growth of international competition, the expectations of the public and the state for international success, led to a decline in deference to established sporting hierarchies. In cricket falling attendances reflected a need to modernise the game whilst players could not afford to play without payment. Whilst the governing body, the MCC (Marylebone Cricket Club) strongly resisted abolishing the distinctions between amateurs and players, the inauguration of the Gillette Cup, a one day knockout competition, began a shift to a more commercial approach which resulted in the Test and County Cricket Board (TCCB) taking responsibility for the administration of the game away from the MCC in 1968. Whilst the Lawn Tennis Association attempted to preserve the sport's social status, the growth of market forces in the sport, with many foreign competitors making a living from the game, meant that in 1968 the Wimbledon championships became 'open' to professionals. In boxing, the Welsh Amateur Boxing Association was only formed in 1954, having previously been a member of its English counterpart. Whilst this may have contributed to the lack of amateur boxers in South Wales a more likely explanation is that there was a tradition of 'mountain fighters', who boxed for money and could financially support their families. This tradition quickly became replicated in the more organised forms of the sport. Howard Winstone, from Merthyr Tydfil in South Wales was amateur boxing champion at bantamweight in 1958, but he soon turned professional, holding titles for seven of his professional years up until retirement in 1968

Although television was first launched in 1936, it could only be received by people living within 20 miles of Alexandra Palace in London and television sets were expensive. When television was relaunched in 1946, sport slowly became a significant element of many schedules. The 1950s were the last decade when spectator sport was still produced for live consumption. By the end of the 1950s the regular fixed slots of Saturday afternoon (Grandstand), Wednesday night (Sportsview) and (by the early 1960s) Saturday night (football highlights) were etched into the BBC's television programming and radio commentaries such as those on cricket became woven into the fabric of the sport.

The post-war period witnessed a developing complexity in the relationship between sport and politics in British society. The Labour government of the immediate post-war period established a welfare state, based around public sector funding of health, education, social services and which also incorporated the nationalisation of selected industries. The welfare of individuals was identified as a primary concern for the state. Successive governments constructed broader leisure related policies which also witnessed the creation of the Arts Council in 1946 and the establishment of the National Parks Commission in 1949, which permitted the designation of countryside areas as protected areas designed to both conserve and provide access to the countryside for informal recreational activities. A sports policy, as such, did not exist as organisation and the first attempt at staging a meeting of sport bodies was boycotted. Not a single body turned up. The SCPR turned to the public for recognition. Working with local authorities, Festivals of Sport were organised in Edinburgh, Glasgow, Aberdeen, Inverness and Dundee. In the two largest cities 10 day events in the city centres attracted 80,000 visitors which was a huge response from the public. Governing bodies of sport agreed to stage coaching events and competitions to aid recruitment. Back in the late 1940s there had been nothing to compare with this. It helped to overcome the initial suspicion of the SCPR. Within a few years over 100 national organisations became members of the Council. In some respects it was similar to Confederations of Sports in other European countries.

The SCPR secured a donation of £120,000 from the King George Memorial Trust Fund to establish a national recreation centre. Edinburgh was the favoured site but the growing interest in outdoor activities influenced the decision to purchase a hotel in Largs which would give access to the River Clyde for canoeing and sailing. The centre was officially opened in 1958 by the Queen and Prince Philip, and is still flourishing. It was named Inverclyde after Lord Inverclyde, the first President of the SCPR.

The funding of Glenmore Lodge, the Scottish Centre for Outdoor Training came directly from the government. The SCPR recruited Lord Malcolm Douglas-Hamilton whose family had a keen interest in outdoor activities and who was aware that the Lodge would be on the market. He and other members of a deputation persuaded Tom Johnston, Secretary of State for Scotland that the Government should provide the SCPR with funds for the purchase. The Lodge was opened in 1948 by Tom Johnston himself. Thus, Scotland possessed a national centre for traditional urban sports and a centre to serve the needs of mountaineering, ski-ing and other outdoor adventurous pursuits. They became focal points of SCPR programmes and provided a meeting ground for governing bodies which traditionally had little or no contact with each other.

There was another group of interests in Scotland which needed to be brought together. These were the professional bodies representing male and female teachers of physical education, the advisers in physical education, the colleges and universities and the SCPR. May Brown went to great lengths to ensure that organisations representing teachers, lecturers and the principles of specialist colleges should meet in a common footing with each other and Her Majesty's Inspectorate. The SCPR became the link between sport and recreation on the one hand and the world of physical education on the other. In 1953 the Scottish Joint Consultative Committee on Physical Education was formed with May Brown as secretary.

The SCPR was expert in mobilising support. They latched on to a long-established tradition of royal and aristocratic patronage of Scottish sport. This ensured support from the dominant Conservative Party, the Scottish Office and the voluntary trusts which controlled substantial funds. The SCPR was itself an essentially conservative agency well suited to the role of a national voluntary organisation. From 1944 to 1948, the President was Sir Iain Colquhoun and he was followed by Lord Inverclyde. In 1953 a massive sports display was mounted in Holyrood Park in Edinburgh to celebrate the Coronation State Visit of the young Queen Elizabeth. Shortly afterwards the Queen agreed to become patron of the SCPR. Then in 1955 the Queen Mother attended the sport was still held as a voluntary activity, part of the long tradition of voluntarism in sport. Consequently, sports organisations remained concerned with preserving a large degree of autonomy. During the 1950s governing bodies of sport united under the banner of the renamed Central Council for Physical Recreation (CCPR) to call for greater resources to ensure that rising demands for sporting activities could be met.

Calls for a pattern of intervention began to gain greater weight. Sport, notably, gained support from those who saw it as a vehicle for social cohesion and integration. The Albermarle Report *'The Youth Service in England and Wales'* (1957) and the Wolfenden Report, *'Sport in the Community'* (1960) both propagated the view that the lack of sport and leisure facilities contributed to juvenile unrest and delinquency. Since these reports, successive governments have seen sport as an increasingly important mechanism of social policy through which to tackle issues concerning young people. In addition, there was a feeling that Britain, having lost much of its empire, was beginning to also lose its position in global sport. The beginnings of the post-colonial era, poor performances at the 1952 and 1956 Olympics and the defeats of the English football team by the famous Hungarian sides in the early 1950s were held as evidence of the declining cultural fabric of the international sporting nation. The period between 1945 and 1970 had marked an increasing interest in policies and programmes for sport, despite the strong interests of the voluntary sector. The concerns of 'sport for all' and international success had emerged as co-terminous themes which continue to mould increasingly complex approaches to developing sport in England and Wales. However, from 1960, government involvement in sport has been largely ad hoc, with a number of government departments having an interest. The fragmentary nature of government involvement in and responsibility for sport, which emerged during this time, has since led to an incoherent and unsystematic approach to sport.

John Hargreaves (1986) conceptualised the level of state intervention in sport in England and Wales. His 'social democratic' model viewed the state as a facilitator and provider of sporting resources rather than the state using sport as a mechanism for social control. Examples include the construction of amenities by local authorities, the role of physical education (and sport) in schools and also the lines of communication between sporting authorities and government departments. Coghlan (1990) and Houlihan (1991) provide overviews of the development of a sport development council, first suggested in the Wolfenden report, which could fund and oversee the development of both mass participation and elite sport and competition. In 1964, the Government appointed the first Minister for Sport, Lord Hailsham, whose primary responsibility was to oversee the development of the advisory sport development council, established in 1965 and members of which included esteemed sporting figures such as Roger Bannister who, in 1954, had been the first man to run a four minute mile, and Walter Winterbottom, the first England football manager. During the 1960s the case for a Sports Council, which could control and direct money for sport in local communities, was gradually accepted by the main political parties.

Post-war society remained strongly patriarchal, with women's sport suffering from negligible funding and sponsorship and militating against the growth of coaching, officiating and competition. Gender imbalances, sustained by amateurism and voluntarism were, for the most part, still underpinned by the ideologies entrenched within the development of physical education since the mid-nineteenth century. It was only in the 1960s that the entrenched ideologies began to be challenged. Sport and active leisure pursuits became a forum for the cultural politics of feminism and women were able to assert their own identity in sports parochially dominated by men, rather than pursue avenues of separate development. During this period, the formation of the Women's Football Association, in 1969, represented the organisational development of sport during this period, but inequality of opportunity, on the basis of gender, existed in a number of sports. Polley (1998: p.96) reports the 'farcical' situation of a number of women training race horses, but having to register in the names of senior stable lads, as the Jockey Club rules barred women from this position. Eventually a high court ruling in 1966 forced the Jockey Club to grant training licences to women.

Sport in Wales continued to be dominated by the collective unity engendered by rugby. Achievements on the rugby field, winning the 'Grand Slam' (beating England, Scotland, Ireland and France) in the annual five nations competition in both the 1949-50 and 1951-2 seasons did much to increase the nation's expectations. During the 1960s, increased media coverage and continued success resulted in a number of players such as Barry John obtaining celebrity status. In contrast, such was the civic pride in rugby that football players such as Ivor Allchurch made their careers outside the country, despite the Welsh team having reached the final of the World Cup for the first (and only) time in 1958. Briefly, individual achievements, such as those of Lyn Davies in the long jump during the 1960s took prominence and in 1958 Cardiff was the host for the British Empire (now Commonwealth) Games – although the event was marred by strong protests against the presence of South Africa. But the real focus was on the mythical qualities associated with rugby and Welsh identity.

1970-2001: Sport for All or Sport for a few

In 1970, the advisory Sports Council was granted executive powers and two years later received its Royal Charter, suggesting a degree of autonomy from government control. Although the Sports Council was allocated funds from central Government, and as such was not independent at all, the creation of the Sports Council represented a significant development, with the organisation becoming the conduit for the state's policies for sport. The Sports Council took over many of the responsibilities of the CCPR but more importantly, by having the power to allocate funds for sport, became the central focus for the underlying and unresolved tensions between 'sport for all' and sport for a few – the elite. The CCPR now became an independent forum, marginalised from the machinations of the Sports Council, the members of which were appointed by the Minister for Sport. At the same time, the Sports Council for Wales received its Royal Charter and received its annual grant from the Welsh Office. Lieutenant Colonel Harry Llewelyn, chair of the Sports Council for Wales was also a member of the British Sports Council to ensure continuity of policies between England and Wales. The British Sports Council, funded by different government departments, looked after the development of sport in England plus the elite concerns of British sport

The Sports Council had four main aims: first, to promote an understanding of the importance of sport and physical education; second, to increase the number of sports facilities; third, to promote wider participation in sport through the maxim of 'sport for all'; and fourth, to develop and improve the performance of elite athletes on the international stage. The Sports Council's first campaign ran from 1972 to 1977 and was called 'Sport for All', coinciding with the Council of Europe's adoption of the phrase to reflect the belief that access to sport and recreation was a fundamental right for all. 'Sport for All' reflects an ideal concerning equality of access, opportunity (to sport) and non-discrimination. It has been the focus upon which the rhetoric of sports policy has differed from the reality. In 1975 the Government published a White Paper on sport and recreation, which reflected the belief that sport could contribute to the promotion of health and social well-being. The report also echoed the welfarist sentiments of the Wolfenden and Albermarle reports insofar as it explicitly noted that sport could alleviate 'boredom, urban frustration ... hooliganism and delinquency in young people'.

The Sports Council worked, often with and sometimes against local authorities, to improve the number of leisure centres, swimming pools and other facilities such as pitches (both grass and artificial) and athletics tracks. However, a decline in the quantity and quality of physical education and sport in schools was exacerbated by a widespread 'work-to-rule' by PE teachers in 1984-5 and the educational reforms that followed. Between 1987 and 1995 over 5000 school playing fields were sold off. Young people, particularly those aged under eleven had less and less opportunity to participate. This only reinforced the folly of the Sports Council's policy, which identified the 13-24 age group as a target for its work from 1982. In attempting to address 'drop-out' rates, where people who had previously participated now ceased to, a generation of young people never began to participate in the first place. Participation levels more generally increased but often amongst those more affluent and mobile. Population groups, notably women and girls, ethnic minorities, older adults, the disabled and (during the 1980s) the unemployed, were identified as under-participating when compared to the national average. But, more critically, the under-representation of these groups in the organisation and administration of sport often prevented the development of more sensitive policies. The 1980s also witnessed the government systematically cutting grants to local authorities, with sport and recreation suffering as social and health services were prioritised. The political abandonment of welfarism in the 1980s meant that the aim of 'sport for all' was little more than a rhetorical ideal rather than reality.

When John Major, a genuine sporting enthusiast, replaced Margaret Thatcher, who had little time for sport, as Prime Minister in 1990, the Conservative government began to gradually take a more serious approach to the provision of sport. Having initially been within the remit of the (then) Department of Environment and subsequently the Department of Education and Science, sport became one area for the Department of National Heritage, created in 1992. The assumption of a 'national' heritage heralded the government's desire to reorganise the Sports Council, announced in 1994, led to a shift from the aims of 'sport for all' to a more explicit goal of international achievement. From 1 January 1997, the English Sports Council (now rebranded as

Sport England) took responsibility for the development of sport in the community in England. It was only in 1995 that the Government published the first policy statement for sport in the document, 'Sport: Raising the Game'. The document avowed to redress the position of Britain in its 'traditional' sports, most of which were team games. A notable feature of the document were the thirty-eight action points, thirty-four of which were aimed at sport and education. Central to these aims was the premise that each secondary school child would receive two hours of physical education a week.

Sport in schools has become a concern of the 'New' Labour government elected in 1997. The Department for Culture, Media and Sport replaced the DNH, but recognised that many schools did not have the resources to expand their PE provision. Two hours a week of PE is now an 'aspiration', and whilst the 1999 Young People and Sport national survey confirmed that participation amongst 11-16 year olds had risen by 6% since 1994, it also revealed the decline in participation by those aged 7-11, down by 7% from 1994, and a legacy of the policies from the 1980s. Whilst acknowledging the importance of team games recent changes to the National Curriculum for Physical Education, implemented in 2000, have aimed to widen participation by providing opportunities in dance, outdoor activities and a greater access to individual activities related not only to sports participation but also to health and fitness. In 2000, the Labour government published its own policy document: 'A Sporting Future for All', the central feature of which was Specialist Sports Colleges (SSCs), secondary schools which received additional funding to improve the quality of the Physical Education curriculum. The first SSCs had already been designated in 1997 and by 2006 the government aims to have 200 around the country, charged not only with improving sport and physical education in their own school but also in designated 'families of schools', both secondary and primary. School sport co-ordinators, PE teachers whose remit it is to organise more intra- and inter-school competitions, are charged with extending the curriculum, particularly by linking primary and secondary provision. However, recent acknowledgements that some primary school children receive as little as eight hours of PE a year have resulted in announcements by the Government to spend over 150 million in improving primary school facilities.

In Wales, the Sports Council for Wales now advises the Welsh Assembly on sporting matters. Its policies hardly differ from those in England. Central to the work of the Sports Council for Wales is its strategic plan, 'A Strategy for Welsh Sport – Young People First', which was published in 1999. The plan identifies the role of sport within the context of the social and political issues that affect the wider community and focuses programmes on getting more people involved in sport and raising the standards of performance at all levels. The 'decline' of sport in schools has not been measured and it is worth noting that the increased political profile of sport has only recently brought attention to the dearth of investment in community sport since the 1980s. 'A Sporting Future for All' has also explicitly acknowledged sport as a tool of social policy designed to tackle social exclusion and meaning that the rhetoric of 'sport for all' is once again to be tested. It is too early to tell whether current policies will make the rhetoric a welcome reality.

Throughout this period, sport has become increasingly concerned with the principle of equity. The needs of ethnic populations, participants with disabilities and people from lower social class backgrounds have begun to be proactively considered by sports development agencies. For women, the popularisation of active leisure through aerobics and jogging provided a much-needed alternative to competitive sport if wider participation was to be encouraged. The Sex Discrimination Act of 1975, which legislated – albeit incompletely – against inequality of access on the grounds of gender, was a major step toward equity, but in sport the unspoken undercurrent through this period has been that, by playing sport, women are unshackling themselves from their 'natural' gender roles. The Women's Sports Foundation, set up in 1984 as an umbrella organisation for women's sport, has done much to challenge these stereotypes. Indeed, governing bodies of women's sport, for example in rugby union, have ensured that many women's sports are currently amongst the fastest growing (in terms of the number of participants) in England and Wales. In 1991, Wales hosted the inaugural Women's Rugby World Cup and the national league for women's football in England began. Despite proactive work from the Sports Council, the National Curriculum for PE still reinforces traditional gender stereotypes, media coverage of women's sport is only about a tenth of all sports coverage and women's sport is under-funded in such a commercialised arena. However, there remain encouraging signs that women's sport is becoming less marginalised, such as in team sports, track and field athletics and winter sports such as skiing and biathlon.

In Wales, the decline of the traditional industries in the South of the country has been reflected on the field by the comparatively poor performances of the national rugby team. In addition, with fewer grammar schools playing the game and fewer teams in state schools, the historical base of players was being eroded. Defeat to teams such as Romania and Western Samoa coincided with the exodus of many top players to rugby league. Cardiff, Swansea and Wrexham have continued their introspective dominance of Welsh football, but a UEFA ruling in 1993 meant that by playing in the English leagues these clubs forfeited their right to represent Wales in European club competitions. Individual sports have also begun to emerge as areas for participation. Athletes such Colin Jackson, Iwan Thomas and Jamie Baulch provide role models for those interested in sports other than team games. In an ironic twist of fate during recent years, Welsh rugby games were played at Wembley, the English national football stadium, whilst the Millennium Stadium (formerly the Cardiff Arms Park, the citadel of Welsh rugby) was being built. The latter, one of the first for team games with a retractable roof, now hosts major English football events such the FA Cup Final whilst the construction of a new English national stadium for football is expensively and embarrassingly delayed.

Since 1970 sport in England and Wales has become a highly commodified and mediated practice. The growth of television coverage, linked to the evolution of sports sponsorship, has changed the way in which sport is viewed and, more significantly, dramatically increased the money coming into the game. By 1999 the Henley Centre for forecasting estimated that the value of sport to the British economy was over £10 billion, accounting for over 2% of the Gross National Product, whilst nearly 500,000 people were in sport-related employment. Television coverage of sport during the

1970s and 1980s developed dramatically but attendances at mass-sporting events began to dwindle, the primary reason for which was the economic recession of the mid-1970s. However, television coverage was transformed by the emergence of BSkyB, with dedicated sports channels and a seemingly inexhaustible supply of money with which to buy the rights to major sporting events. When the company acquired the rights to football's Premiership in 1992 it cost them £304 million for a five-year deal. By 2001, a three-year deal cost £1.1 billion. Many other sports, notably Rugby Union, Rugby League, golf and cricket, have benefited financially from the proliferation of satellite television coverage.

As Horne et al. (1999: p.217) have noted 'the policy community for sport has been, and remains, largely divided. The three dominant ideologies attached to sport in the twentieth century, amateurism, welfarism and commercialism all currently co-exist and compete for influence ... Hence there is diversity and no single policy model that explains national sports policies'. Sport in England and Wales is a cultural phenomenon and has acquired a social significance. Sports stars such as David Beckham and Ryan Giggs are more recognised than politicians and actors, and idolised by young boys and girls alike. Even at the level of 'grass-roots' provision issues of funding and finance predominate whilst the concern for social justice through sport has become the primary motive for investment in sport outside of the commercial arena. The amateur is little more than a representation of the past, but it is a past rich in cultural heritage and one which requires continued examination in order to make sense of changes that occur in sporting practices.

Participation in sporting activities continues to decline among the adult population of England and Wales, even though young people today have more opportunities than ever before, largely through projects and programmes funded by the National Lottery. However, regardless of whether one examines the past or the present, the most strikingly consistent feature of sport in England and Wales has been its role as a local and national cultural spectacle. Rather than participate, the public would evidently prefer to watch sport from the sidelines, the stands or the armchair – from where the activity is always much easier and mistakes are never made.

Literature

Birley, D. (1993) Land of Sport and Glory: Sport and British Society, 1887-1910, Manchester: Manchester University Press

Birley, D. (1995) Playing the Game: Sport and British Society, 1910-45, Manchester, Manchester University Press

Coghlan, J. with Webb, I. (1990) Sport and British Politics since 1990, London: Falmer Press

Hargreaves, Jennifer (1994) Sporting Females: Critical Issues in the History and Sociology of Women's Sports, London: Routledge

Hargreaves, John (1986) Sport, Power and Culture, Cambridge, Polity Press

Holt, R. & Mason, T. (2000) Sport in Britain 1945-2000, Oxford: Blackwell

Horne, J., Tomlinson, A. & Whannel, G. (1999) Understanding Sport, London, E&FN Spon

Houlihan, B. (1991) The Government and Politics of Sport, London: Routledge

Jones, S. (1987) Sport, Politics and the Working Class, Manchester: Manchester University Press

England and Wales

Mangan, J. A. (1981) Athleticism in the Victorian and Edwardian Public School, Cambridge: Cambridge University Press

Mason, T. (1989) Sport in Britain: A Social History, Cambridge, Cambridge University Press

Polley, M. (1998) A History of Sport and Society since 1945, London: Routledge

Williams, G. (1989) Rugby, in: Mason, T. (ed.) Sport in Britain: A Social History, Cambridge, Cambridge University Press

Scotland

Ian Thomson

The organisation and administration of sport in Scotland conforms broadly to the pattern elsewhere in the United Kingdom, at least until 1945. This chapter, therefore, focuses on sports development after World War II, when it followed distinctly Scottish lines.

Today, there are four major agencies supported by a variety of voluntary and professional bodies. The main agencies are central government through a Minister for Sport; a Sports Council funded by government but operating at arms-length from it; governing bodies of sport; and local government. The power and influence of each agency has varied from time to time since 1950, as has the spirit of partnership. Scotland has maintained a large measure of independence and has resisted attempts to centralise power at UK level.

The Early Years

The Scottish Council of Physical Recreation and the advisory Sports Council for Scotland 1945-1972

The advisory Sports Council for Scotland grew out of the Scottish Council of Physical Recreation (SCPR) which, in turn, began life as the Scottish section of the Central Council of Physical Recreation. The CCPR had made overtures to the Scottish Fitness Council in the 1930's to form a Scottish section but this was rejected. In 1944 May Brown, who was to become the first Secretary of the SCPR, approached Phyllis Colson, the Secretary of the CCPR about forming a Scottish section. (Brown 1979:17). Ms Brown convened a meeting of all national organisations concerned with physical education and recreation including representatives of the Scottish Education Department and the two specialist colleges of physical education. The Principal of Dunfermline College of Physical Education chaired the meeting. The strong bond between the colleges, the physical education profession and the sporting community has been a distinctive element in Scottish sport throughout the past half century.

The meeting endorsed the proposal to form a Scottish section of the CCPR, the submission was accepted and the Scottish Education Department (SED) agreed to grant aid the new body, starting in March 1945. Within a few months Ms Brown had appointed an Assistant Secretary, eight technical representatives and clerical staff, all located in new offices in the centre of Edinburgh. Over the next six years the SCPR acted as a driving force for development across a broad front of physical recreation, physical education and sport. In retrospect its achievements during a period of relative austerity were awesome.

The governing bodies of sport were initially suspicious of the intentions of the new

celebrations to mark the 50th anniversary of the founding of Dunfermline College of which May Brown was a governor. The Queen opened Inverclyde officially in July 1958; accompanied by the Duke of Edinburgh who took a keen interest in the SCPR from his position as President of the CCPR.

It was inevitable that Scotland should seek independence from the CCPR, but this raised important issues which have recurred regularly over the past fifty years, namely the rights of the Home Countries in terms of international sport and the value of one voice for sport in dealings with Central government. In 1951 an informal approach was made, indicating that the tide of national opinion and the growing confidence of the Scottish section was leading to separation and the establishment of a fully autonomous Scottish Council of Physical Recreation. Phyllis Colson, the Secretary of the CCPR wrote to Dr Stewart Mackintosh, chairman of the Scottish section expressing her deep reservations:

> *"Now that the peak of CCPR unity has been reached with the accession of Northern Ireland", she wrote, "the Council is competent to speak with one voice on really big matters affecting physical recreation national policy, to bring to bear the full potential of every part of the United Kingdom and to pursue any decision reached with singleness of purpose. Split into parts (two to begin with and, without doubt, four later on) and you at once dissipate its force, destroy its assured singleness of purpose and open the door for unilateral action – in short, you lessen the strength of the whole and of each of its component parts." (Evans, 1974:138)*

Despite this warning, the SCPR was incorporated as an independent body in June 1953. For the next ten years it maintained as its main aim 'to promote healthy living through physical recreation'. At that time it was not concerned with sports specific development or elite sport. It was an entirely different kind of organisation from the Sports Council which exists to-day.

The SCPR concentrated on leadership training courses in a variety of sports, conducted mainly as residential Summer and Easter schools. From 1948 to 1962 it housed the Scottish Athletics Coaching Scheme but made no attempt to replicate the scheme in other sports. It was heavily involved in the opening up of the countryside for public access to new sports and others which were previously the domain of the landed gentry. Thus it spearheaded the growth of angling, canoeing, mountaineering, pony-trekking, orienteering, sailing and ski-ing, assisting in the establishment of new governing bodies or in the staging of events. Concurrently the Council collaborated with the Scottish Tourist Board in the promotion of Sports Holidays.

One of the Council's major achievements was to retain the Scottish Joint Consultative Committee on Physical Education as a link between physical education and school sport and sport in the community. As in the case of physical recreation the Council created a forum for development without overtly striving for leadership. The Committee staged a major national conference on the future of physical education in Edinburgh in November 1954, and the SCPR undertook the conference administration and publication of a conference report. One of the more radical conference resolutions was that a Degree course in physical education should be introduced. This did not come about for another twenty years. Another sought to persuade central government to utilise revenue from football pools to improve sports facilities in schools. It was defeated heavily. The football pools companies established a Football Grounds Improvement Trust in 1975 which became the Football Trust in 1979. It poured millions of pounds into professional football. To take only one year as an example, in 1987 the Trust allocated £1.3 million to local authorities which led to 71 new pitches, 92 improved pitches, 45 new and 11 improved pavilions. However, school facilities were not improved by Trust funds.

There was little to distinguish the pattern of sports administration in Scotland from England. It was a simple formula of concentrating on the needs of voluntary organisations – leadership training, small grants, and developing a relationship with central government departments of education and promoting a concept of active leisure. The national centres in both countries provided excellent residential facilities for leadership and coach education, as well as venues for national and regional championships and for training camps.

The Wolfenden Report

A group of academics at Birmingham University produced a pamphlet in 1957 entitled *Britain in the World of Sport*. This contained embarrassing evidence that Britain was rapidly falling behind other countries in international sport. A particularly worrying feature was the threat to amateurism posed by countries from Eastern Europe. That year, the CCPR appointed a small independent committee to examine the general position of sport in Britain. Sir John Wolfenden was chairman of a committee which would profoundly affect British Sport.

It was quickly recognised that the Committee was uncovering serious deficiencies in the state of sport. The prospect of a damaging indictment of British sport led the Conservative and Labour Parties to publish policy statements on sport prior to the appearance of the Wolfenden Report. Both recommended a Sports Council of Great Britain, the Conservatives anticipating the future by proposing a Royal Charter to guarantee independence. Both robustly rejected any idea of a Ministry of Sport and they were in accord that sport should come under the umbrella of Education.

Prior to the Wolfenden Report, startling comparisons were made with European countries. For example Britain had 61 public running tracks: Sweden had 800. West Germany had built 75 swimming pools since the war; Britain had built 12. In other words politicians from all shades of opinion recognised that Britain had fallen behind other countries and changes would have to be made in funding and administering sport; but without State control.

The Wolfenden Report *Sport and the Community* (CCPR 1960) was a defining document in the history of British sport in the 20th century. The origins and deliberations of the Committee have been recorded by the Secretary of the Committee. (Evans, 1974:145-168). The central recommendation was that there should be a new body, a Sports Development Council which would distribute £5 million to governing bodies of sport – a huge amount in 1960, plus another £5 million to be sanctioned for capital projects. The Committee presumed that the CCPR and the SCPR would run in tandem with the new Council.

Within months of the publication of the Wolfenden Report, the SCPR held a meeting of representatives of governing bodies of sport. It was agreed unanimously that if Wolfenden was likely to be implemented, a case should be made to government for a separate Sports Council for Scotland and that a sum of money should be allocated by the Treasury for Scotland. Following the debate on Wolfenden in the House of Commons in July 1961, the government agreed that national recreation centres would receive statutory financial support which was good news for the Inverclyde centre. The emphasis shifted from recreational leadership training and physical education to the government's new agenda of raising Britain's image in world sport and investing heavily in national facilities.

Between 1961 and 1965 the fate of Scottish and British sport was increasingly influenced by politicians. The Conservative government which was in power until 1964 took the line that state intervention could only be justified as a support structure for voluntary sector activity. The Wolfenden proposal for a Sports Development Council was rejected. This was defended by Lord Hailsham, Cabinet Minister, Lord President of the Council and Minister for Science who was given responsibility for sport in 1962. He made his views clear in a House of Commons debate in June 1964.

> *"In order to carry out the work ... one must have access to the composite bodies, the CCPR, the NPFA, the SCPR and the British Olympic Association. Either a Sports Development Council is the same as these bodies, in which case it is superfluous, or it is different, in which case it is objectionable".*

He started with limited objectives, namely to make the most efficient use of existing sources of government finance and also to increase the flow of funds to the voluntary sector. Hailsham appointed a small committee of senior civil servants to co-ordinate the various government departments which contributed to health, physical education, recreation and sport. This was essentially a Westminster, UK controlled committee but they invited the SCPR to send two representatives to their meetings which were held during 1963.

As a contribution to government thinking the SCPR took three initiatives. First they submitted policy papers for two of the meetings of Hailsham's co-ordinating committee. The first of these dealt with broad issues of policy for Scotland such as increasing the investment in governing bodies of sport and at the same time strengthening the SCPR as an advisory body to government for Scottish sport. The second policy paper set out an order of priority for national sports facilities, the top of the list being non-residential multi-sport centres around the country.

The second contribution from the SCPR was to ensure that the views they expressed were representative of the 140 members organisations. They organised a national conference in 1963 whose theme was *The Future of Sport in Scotland*. Lady Tweedsmuir the Under-Secretary of State for Scotland emphasised that the Conservative Government were not in favour of a Sports Development Council. She was convinced that the existing set up in Scotland was satisfactory. Following the conference, SCPR representatives met Lord Hailsham and submitted a strategy for Scottish sport. Hailsham's advisor Sir Patrick Renison was taken on a tour of facilities by May Brown and met representatives of local government and governing bodies of sport. He was left in no doubt that there was a need for investment in sports facilities in Scotland.

The third step taken to advance the case for sport was the organisation of five regional conferences attended by local authorities, public bodies and Government representatives to discuss planning of new facilities for sport. Lord Provosts of cities and the most senior civil servants in the Scottish Office attended. The most up-to-date information on sports buildings, surfaces, floodlighting and so on was gathered by SCPR staff and presented to the conferences. This was common language in many European countries but it was entirely new information for civic leaders in Scotland. Finland with almost exactly the same population as Scotland (4.5 million) had fourteen multi-sports centres. Stockholm with a smaller population than Glasgow had six such centres and Germany's "Golden Plan" for sports facilities had provided a sports centre for every community with more than 5,000 inhabitants. By comparison with other small countries in Europe, Scotland was at the very bottom of the ladder. One positive outcome was that the Scottish Office offered 50 per cent funding to Glasgow to build a proto-type multi-sports centre at Bellahouston Park – the first of its kind in the country. It was also the first major government grant for a capital sports project in Scotland which was another indictment of the State's contribution compared to other countries.

Every SCPR conference held between 1960 and 1963 confirmed that despite the Wolfenden Committee conclusion that there should be a Sports Development Council, there was no enthusiasm in Scotland for that idea. The SCPR found a neat compromise. They created a Sports Development Committee within rather than separate from the SCPR and found an ideal chairman in Peter (later Sir Peter) Heatly. He was a legendary figure in Scottish sport with gold medals for diving in Commonwealth Games in Auckland 1950, Vancouver 1954 and Cardiff 1958.

Shortly before the General Election in 1964 the government introduced a raft of measures to help governing bodies and local authorities. The former were now eligible for grants to help meet recurrent costs on administration as well as the running of coaching schemes. Local clubs could apply for capital grants to improve existing facilities or build new ones. The SED issued a circular to local authorities asking them to carry out an immediate review of facilities for sport and recreation in their areas. A survey conducted in 1964 by the SCPR revealed that there was a complete lack of international standard facilities except for football and rugby.

Advisory Sports Councils

A General Election was held in October 1964 and the Labour Party swept into office after thirteen years in opposition. They immediately set about implementing a manifesto commitment to establish a Sports Council. Denis Howell was appointed as a Minister for Sport, a junior position in government but a significant role in sport. Howell's views were very different from those of Hailsham. He was totally committed to the Wolfenden concept of a Sports Development Council. He believed that sport needed political leadership and that this could best be delivered by combining the role of Minister with Chairmanship of the UK Sports Council. In this way sport could have a voice at the heart of government while remaining independent of state control. The new Minister strongly favoured an advisory Council which would not threaten the established authority of the CCPR and the British Olympic Association. This partly accommodated Hailsham's opposition to the idea of yet another sports policy body.

It was also Howell who introduced the idea of regional advisory sports Councils. As an astute, seasoned local councillor from Birmingham he recognised the random, uncoordinated state of local authority provision for sport. He toured the UK persuading local authority associations and governing bodies of sport of the need for a second tier of Sports Councils. (Coghlan, 1990:24). Nine regional councils were established for England plus advisory Sports Councils for Scotland and Wales.

It was clear, early in 1965, that Howell was gaining support within government for his notion of devolved advisory Sports Councils. The SCPR held meetings in Edinburgh and Glasgow (Brown 1979:88) to debate whether Scotland needed or wanted a Sports Council. The meetings were chaired by Dr Stewart Mackintosh, Director of Education for Glasgow, a long-term supporter of the SCPR and a member of the 15-person UK Sports Council appointed by Howell. The upshot of the meetings, both of which were well attended was unanimously in favour of the SCPR continuing in its role of developing sport in partnership with the governing bodies of sport. May Brown later recalled these events

"I was asked to send a letter to the Secretary of State for Scotland putting forward the reasons why the SCPR didn't want a Sports Council and stating that we had the support of the governing bodies of sport" (Brown 1970:88)

In spite of these powerfully argued objections the Sports Council for Scotland was imposed, and Denis Howell travelled to Edinburgh in September 1965 to announce the membership. In his autobiography Howell recalled that the Scottish Office was worried about nationalistic objections and he put pressure on Willie Ross, the Scottish Secretary of State to clarify his position. Ross explained the Scottish hostility to England paternalism but Howell was swayed by the fact that much of international sport is British. He and his team won over the initially hostile audience. Thus a bid for independence was overthrown. Scotland, Wales and the English regions became branches of a centralised system of governance.

Coghlan (1990:24) commented later:

"There are many who believe that this development so changed the face of British sport in fifteen years (1965-80) to make it such that this continues to be the major breakthrough in Britain to date".

Just as the SCPR had broken away from the CCPR it would only be a matter of time before Scotland broke out of a network of advisory Sports Councils powerfully influenced by an England-based parent organisation. Regionalisation would prove to be a half-way house to independence.

The Sports Council for Scotland (SCS) was a very different body from the SCPR. It had been a guiding principle for both the CCPR and the SCPR that members of the Council were appointed as individuals on the basis of their knowledge and experience of sport. The new structure consisted of 29 members of whom a majority represented local authorities. Each of the four local government associations were allocated four places. The SCPR was given eight places which they chose to sub-divide into representatives of outdoor games, indoor games, outdoor activities and women's sports organisations. Four of the remaining places were appointed by the Secretary of State including the Chairman. The other place went to the NPFA. It could fairly be argued that this was a democratic, widely representative body although as a committee of 29 it was not ideal for decision-making.

The Seventies

1970 *Commonwealth Games*

The SCPR secretary agreed to serve as secretary to the new Sports Council for Scotland and the other technical and administrative staff worked for both the SCPR and SCS. This created many anomalies and conflicting priorities but from 1966 to 1970 the two bodies worked in harmony to prepare for the Commonwealth Games. Denis Howell, Minister for Sport was able to persuade Willie Ross, Secretary of State for Scotland to allocate £700,000 for the new Meadowbank Stadium. This was by far the largest sum awarded to sport by the Scottish Office. Edinburgh Council had already met the full cost of the Royal Commonwealth Pool. These facilities were central to the huge success of the 1970 Commonwealth Games. The Scottish Joint Consultative Committee for Physical Education staged an International Conference on Physical Education in Edinburgh to coincide with the Games. It attracted 300 delegates from 31 countries. It was a good time for sport in Scotland.

For twelve months preceding the Games, Scotland and Edinburgh in particular became embroiled in an international controversy which posed a serious threat to the Games. It was the issue of apartheid in South African sport. Less than three months before the Games were due to open 12 of the 18 countries indicated that they might withdraw from the Games. The crisis began with the selection for England of a young coloured cricketer from the Cape, Basil D'Oliveira who, having escaped to England from racial discrimination in his own country, had become a prolific batsman at Test level. He was originally omitted from the England team to tour South Africa in 1969 but later came in as a replacement. The South African Prime Minister stated that the touring team 'as constituted' was not acceptable. The debate about whether the tour should go ahead raged on, culminating in an emergency meeting of the MCC in December 1968 which voted overwhelmingly to cancel the tour. However, South Africa were due to tour England in 1970 and it became clear that there would be massive public protests. Philip Noel-Baker secured an emergency debate in the House of Commons in May 1970 on this issue.

Denis Howell, Minister for Sport and Chairman of the Sports Council convened an emergency meeting of the Council on the morning of the debate. He had received two resolutions, one from the Sports Council for Scotland and the other from the Scottish Commonwealth Games Council urging him to intervene to ensure cancellation of the tour.

Howell made an impassioned speech to the House, speaking on behalf of the Sports Council which had resolved to urge the Cricket Council to cancel the tour; The Sports Council reaffirmed the right of governing bodies to have autonomy in controlling their own affairs and recommended that the Government should not intervene directly. But the Sports Council believed that "the longer-term interests of multi-racial sport in the Commonwealth transcend all other aspects of the issue". The Cricket Council effectively saved the 1970 Games by agreeing firstly to cancel the tour and further, that there would be no more Test tours with South Africa until teams were picked on a non-racial basis.

A month after the Commons debate a General Election was held and the Conservatives won an unexpected victory. Eldon Griffiths took over as Minister for Sport and Chairman of the UK Sports Council. He chaired his first meeting in Edinburgh on the eve of the opening of the Commonwealth Games. At the next meeting a paper was presented outlining the capital investment required for facilities for sport and recreation for 1971-81. He stated that in a period of stringency he as a Minister could not sign the document which as Chairman of the Sports Council he was almost obliged to sign (Coghlan 1990: 63) This dilemma confirmed his view that the Sports Council should be separate from the Ministry.

Executive Sports Councils

In June 1971 the Government announced in the Commons its intention to seek Royal Charters for the establishment of independent Sports Councils for Great Britain, Scotland and Wales. This would sever the connection between the UK Sports Council, and the Sports Council for Scotland and give independence to Scottish sport. The new body would take over from the Scottish Education Department responsibility for disbursing grants to governing bodies of sport. The assets and staff of the SCPR would be transferred to the Scottish Sports Council. The SCPR and the Sports Council for Scotland would be wound up in April 1972 when the new Council came into being. The Government indicated that in all three countries there would be a consultative body, and in Scotland it appeared as the Scottish Standing Conference of Sport, formed in March 1973. The CCPR assumed this role in England.

The Scottish Sports Council (SSC) membership was entirely at the behest of the Secretary of State. The democratic representative nature of the previous Sports Council for Scotland was replaced by the appointment of members in an individual capacity. They were not accountable to any body or organisation and the SSC as an independent body was only accountable for the responsible use of public funds. Its policies for sport were seen as its own business. It was a complete transformation from the SCPR as a voluntary agency working hand in glove with sport and recreation and tourism agencies. It was a long way from a body which connected with local sport by virtue of its membership. But the most profound change which would alter forever its relationship with the sporting community was that the SSC became the paymaster, determining the level of grant aid to each governing body.

Local sports provision

In February 1970 the Sports Council for Scotland published a report, *Planning for Sport in Scotland*, which was heavily influenced by the thinking of Laurie Liddell, Director of Physical Education at Edinburgh University. Liddell would later be appointed as the first chairman of the Scottish Sports Council in 1972 but in the intervening period he pushed forward with eight regional conferences on planning for sport throughout 1971. There was a unanimous recommendation from these conferences that advisory sports councils should be established at regional and district levels. These local councils would help to promote and co-ordinate participation; encourage maximum use of existing facilities, and assist in planning of new facilities.

The planning for sport conferences coincided with publication of the Local Government (Scotland) Bill. The main target was to reduce the 425 local authorities to a more manageable two-tier structure of regions and districts. The Sports Council for Scotland took the opportunity to argue for full inclusion of leisure and recreation in the emerging structures. This would consist of three initiatives. Firstly, each local authority should form a recreation committee and establish a department directly represented on the Chief Executive's management team. That alone would represent a huge advance in terms of recognition of recreation as a main concern of local government. Secondly, within each region a joint consultative committee should be established consisting of officers and members from the region and districts within it. This accurately foresaw the potential conflict between authorities with overlapping responsibilities. Finally, in order to ensure that participants were consulted, advisory sports councils should be formed in every region and district.

These far-sighted recommendations were to receive support from a profoundly influential Select Committee Report of the Westminster Parliament some eighteen months later. From 1972 onwards there has been a tendency for sport to be regarded as one of the social services, and as a positive force in reducing delinquency and youth crime. These claims were re-enforced in the Cobham Report (House of Lords Select Committee, Second Report, 1973). The timing of this report was important. The executive Sports Councils were established in February 1972, three months after the Cobham Committee was appointed and legislation for the re-organisation of local government was passed only a few months after Cobham reported. The proceedings of the Select Committee therefore straddled significant events in British and Scottish sport, and caused the government to consider issues such as the relationship between central and local government in the field of recreation; the shape and scale of local authority recreation services; and the contribution of the voluntary sector to policy planning.

Cobham was emphatic in stating that recreation should be part of the fabric of the social services and the new local authorities should be the main executive agencies, co-ordinating the delivery of recreation services at local level. The Select Committee recommended that every authority should set up a recreation department under its own chief officer. This would provide a requirement for a sharp increase in public sector investment in recreation facilities and services.

In Scotland a working party was appointed to consider the respective responsibilities of the new regional and district authorities. The Paterson Report recommended that the nine regional authorities should be mainly responsible for long term strategic planning and the provision of facilities and services of regional significance. District authorities should provide and manage community sports facilities through leisure and recreation departments. Thus leisure and recreation emerged as a two-tier function which led almost inevitably to overlapping and duplication of effort. Education was a single-tier function which meant that the regional authorities would continue to own and manage school sport facilities and youth and community centres.

The new authorities came into being in May 1975. The Scottish Sports Council was able to report that 76 per cent of local authorities had created separate departments of leisure and recreation during 1975-76, and when composite leisure/education departments were included, the percentage rose to 84. With regard to advisory sports councils, thirteen out of the fifty-three districts had established them and a further twenty-five were in process of being formed.

Starting in May 1973 the four national agencies for tourism, outdoor recreation and sport – the Scottish Tourist Board, the Countryside Commission for Scotland, the Forestry Commission and the SSC – initiated a series of regional planning studies aimed at assisting the regional authorities which were to be elected in 1975 to evolve strategies for these services. It was anticipated that a Strategic Issues Report could be completed before May 1975 and thereafter the authorities themselves would continue the process of gathering data for Situation Reports. A series of regional conferences were held throughout 1974 and 1975. At that time Central Region, which takes in most of the land between Edinburgh and Glasgow included three District Councils, i.e. Clackmannan, Falkirk and Stirling whose population was 350,000.

A number of issues were identified from this, the first comprehensive survey of sports facilities and activities in Central Region. Firstly, although sports facilities in schools were generally adequate, public access in the evenings, at week-ends and during school holidays was either limited or non-existent. Secondly, even in traditional activities such as football, badminton and swimming there was a dearth of good quality facilities. Thirdly, in the case of sports such as basketball and volleyball which were prominent in school physical education, the growth of community sports clubs was constrained by the almost total lack of local sports centres. It was noted that the types of urban recreation activities offered were not relevant to the needs of disadvantaged groups in the community. The prime need was defined as making sport and recreation more relevant to the needs of these groups as a means of reducing social stress. There was also a need to provide for the development of high standards of performance through better coaching.

The new local authorities came into being in 1975 in a dire economic climate. It was not a good time to be advocating a substantial increase in capital spending. Over the next five years there was undeniable evidence of a lack of co-ordination between regional and district authorities. A Committee Inquiry into Local Government reported in 1981 that leisure and recreation exhibited probably *"the greatest diversity of activities, the most confusion among authorities and thus the widest scope for wasteful duplication and competition"*. (Stodart, 1981). The Local Government and Planning Act (Scotland) 1982 consolidated the Stodart Committee's principal recommendation that district and island councils alone should have responsibility for providing leisure services. This led to a rapid increase in the number of district departments of leisure and recreation departments. One serious consequence of the 1982 Act was that it terminated regional involvement in strategic planning, research and co-ordination of sport just at the point when earlier efforts were bearing fruit. The STARPS programme came to an abrupt halt and throughout the 1980's the fifty-three district councils developed leisure services in isolation from each other.

Tensions and conflict

Most commentators agree that the Wolfenden Report triggered changes which transformed British sport. For Scotland the debate was not about British performances compared with other countries. It was more a question of freeing itself from a structure of an administration centred in London. The whole pattern of physical education, urban and countryside recreation and organised competitive sport which emerged under the guidance of the SCPR was quintessentially Scottish. It reflected the culture, topography and relationships which sprung naturally from a Scottish democratic tradition. The composition of the advisory Sports Council for Scotland was a reflection of the enormous contribution made by local authorities.

In retrospect the SCPR should have fought the same battle which the CCPR mounted to retain its independence. If an executive Scottish Sports Council was to be imposed by government decree the SCPR should have become the consultative body which was required in the royal charter to represent the voluntary sector. History has shown that the consultative body which emerged, now known as the Scottish Sports Association, has been powerless. The local authorities which would become statutory providers and funders of recreation services throughout the country were not represented as of right on the Sports Council or the Standing Conference on Sport. There was no collective voice with the authority and resources to resist the bureaucratic tendency of the Council.

Within a few years, the level of frustration with the Standing Conference led to the creation of an Association of Governing Bodies of Sport. Within months of its formation in 1978 it had attracted into membership 30 of the 66 governing bodies. The Duke of Edinburgh agreed to address the first general meeting and delivered a speech which was a campaign for an independent voice for sport and recreation. The rationale for the new Association was a condemnation of the oppositional structure of a Sports Council and a Consultative Conference. Quite simply there was a need for a representative body, not unlike the SCPR, which brought together those who actually delivered sport and recreation. The Association would try to build relationships between governing bodies and the new local authority recreation departments. This might become a forum for genuine partnership and debate about policy issues such as the relationship between education authorities, school sport and governing bodies.

The Association lasted only three years, demonstrating all the weaknesses of a voluntary association. The officers were fully committed to their own governing bodies, there were insufficient funds to appoint staff, the Scottish Office would not recognise the Association, and privately some of the member bodies were worried that their opposition to the Scottish Sports Council could have an adverse effect on their grant aid allocation. The Association collapsed and went out of business in 1980.

The Thatcher Years

Politics and sport came together in the worst possible way during the 1980s. It was not a good decade for sport in Scotland. Seeds of discontent were sewn which led inexorably towards some form of devolution or independence. Mrs Thatcher proved to be a liability to the Conservative Party in Scotland where her Government's policies were deeply unpopular. Generally, sport administrators were non-political but they found themselves at the receiving end of political decisions. The removal of Mrs Thatcher from office in 1990 opened up a new era for sport in Britain, including Scotland. Her successor John Major, was passionately interested in sport.

The first example of Mrs Thatcher's willingness to politicise sport came within months of her election as Prime Minister. She joined forces with America over the Russian invasion of Afghanistan and sought to persuade the British Olympic Association to boycott the 1980 Olympic Games in Moscow. There were full day debates on both House of Parliament but the Association stood firm. Mrs Thatcher did not often experience defeat and this episode did not endear her to sport.

The 1986 Commonwealth Games also provided a great deal of political activity. Edinburgh applied to hold the Games with the memory of the hugely successful 1970 Games in its favour. The 1982 Games in Brisbane had cost £15 million to stage but Edinburgh believed that a budget of around £10 million would be sufficient. After the Games had been awarded, the government announced that there would be no State funding. Despite this blow the City Council decided to proceed in the hope that big businesses would rally to the cause. The campaign to hold the Games had been led by Peter Heatly, then Chairman of the Scottish Sports Council. But when he was elected Chairman of the Commonwealth Games Federation he withdrew from the Organising Committee. Meanwhile the Conservative local authority lost out to Labour in local elections and the new administration took a much different view of proceedings. Thus the climate had changed considerably from the day on which Edinburgh had been awarded the Games.

In the lead-up to the Games, there were various threats of boycotts from African countries in response to rugby tours of South Africa. These were brought to a head when Zola Budd, a young South African born athlete was invited to run at the Daily Crest Games at Meadowbank in July 1995. The City Council was a determined opponent of apartheid and its leader was a former member of the extreme left wing militant tendency. The Council, which owned Meadowbank, erected a banner 'Edinburgh Against Apartheid' in the stadium. Channel Four TV threatened to cancel coverage of the event if the banner was not withdrawn. The Council stood firm and at the last minute the telecast was scrapped. The story attracted nation-wide publicity and did great damage to the possibility of attracting sponsors.

Worse was yet to come. In July 1970 only 16 days before the opening ceremony, the Commonwealth heads of government met to prepare their case against the apartheid movement in South Africa. Mrs Thatcher was the only head of state who held out against sanctions. At that point 58 countries had indicated that they would take part in the Games. A stream of countries withdrew in protest at what was seen as Britain's support for South Africa. The decision to include Zola Budd in the England team did not help matters. Eventually only 26 nations out of the original 58 took part. Mrs Thatcher made a brief appearance at the Games and made no secret of her opposition to sanctions. There were violent demonstrations and heavy-handed treatment of the Press by the police. For the athletes who took part, medals were devalued by the number of withdrawals. For the organisers, it was as if Mrs Thatcher had single-handedly ruined the Games, which ended up in dire financial straits.

Other events over-shadowed the mid-1980s. From about 1983 onwards the Government was drawn into a bitter dispute with the teaching profession both in Scotland and England. Teachers' unions became increasingly militant and the Thatcher government quite intransigent. The Educational Institute of Scotland, representing 80 per cent of Scottish teachers campaigned for an independent pay review. The Government steadfastly resisted. In 1984 a rolling programme of industrial actions began, including suspension of voluntary extra-curricular activities. Within a year school sport was brought to a standstill. In autumn 1987 the Scottish Rugby Union reported that over the period 1983-7 the number of youngsters playing in schools rugby fell from 15,000 to 6,000. The comparable figures for soccer were 45,000 reducing to 4,500. It was estimated that 4 million man-hours per annum of voluntary assistance to school sport were lost.

In response to public concern, the SSC appointed a working party to examine and report on school-aged sport. Its report "Laying the Foundation" was presented in November 1988 and submitted to Michael Forsyth, the Minister for Sport in Scotland. The Report contained 58 recommendations but unfortunately they were not ranked in order of priority and they had not been costed out. Forsyth ignored the Report and appointed another group to concentrate on team sport which be believed had been the main casualty of the teachers' dispute. He not only approved the Report of the Team Sport Inquiry Group but was able to persuade the Treasury to release the sum of £400,000 per annum for three years to establish Team Sport Scotland. This began life in 1991, consisting of a Director and nine co-ordinators of specific sports.

Team Sport was a major success. It was a front-line service dealing face to face with teachers, clubs and governing bodies. In many cases it worked as an arm of the sport, bringing much needed cash to support training and education. A monitoring report published at the end of the first three years (CLR, 1994) reported that about 100,000 youngsters had been introduced to sport and 10,000 teachers, coaches and leaders had benefited from opportunities to undergo training. It was incorporated into the SSC and its future, and expansion was guaranteed.

It was widely anticipated that Labour would win the 1987 General Election. Astonishingly the Conservatives romped home with a majority of 102. In Scotland the Government lost 11 out of its 21 Members of Parliament. This did not discourage Mrs Thatcher from introducing the most unpopular measure of her eleven years in power – the community charge or 'poll-tax' as it came to be known, in April 1988. The riots and public disorder in Scotland was a pale shadow of the huge disruption when the poll tax was introduced in England a few years later. The poll tax virtually guaranteed that the Scottish people would vote at an early stage for independence or devolution. Neil Kinnock put this in words in a visit to Scotland in 1989:

> *"We hold it to be self-evident that in the capital of Scotland there shall be established a democratic, directly-elected assembly to govern with the Scottish people, for the Scottish people, by the Scottish people, in Scotland" (Clements, Farquharson and Wark, 1996;103).*

While this measure was stoking the flames of independence, the Government was introducing another market-led initiative, namely compulsory competitive tendering (CCT). The Local Government Act (1988) imposed the duty on the local authorities to expose defined activities to CCT, and one of these was sport and leisure management.

In practice, none of the large contracts was lost by local authorities but the existence within a local authority of a client group of officers and a contractors group, in place of a unified department of leisure services was ultimately seen as a waste of resources. More importantly it unified the local authorities in their resistance to the Conservative Government. Few tears were shed in Scotland when Mrs Thatcher was forced to resign in November 1990.

The Nineties

Scottish and British interests

The formation of executive Sports Councils for Scotland, Wales and (later) Northern Ireland on purely territorial grounds contrasted with the creation of a UK Council which included but was not restricted to, England. A great deal of conflict would have been avoided if in 1972 a Sports Council for England had been established as an equivalent to the other territorial Councils.

As David Pickup (Director-General of the Sports Council from 1988 to 1993) recalled, any attempt by the UK Sports Council to take the lead in any initiatives outside England was deeply resented by the Scottish and Welsh Sports Councils. (Pickup 1996:59). He regarded them as parochial and unwilling to act in any interest wider than that of their own country. He accused them of 'cloddish parochialism' and referred to them collectively as the 'Celtic fringe'.

By 1990, fifteen years after the creation of executive Councils, no matter how effective the Councils were in their own countries, there was no sign of agreement about policies for elite international sport. There were stirrings of interest in a national lottery, other countries were moving ahead (the Australian Institute of Sport was beginning to make its mark) and as the successor to Margaret Thatcher, John Major showed immediate interest in reforming British sport. The Sports Council submitted a case for a UK Sports Commission (UKSC) with executive powers; a strong coalition of bodies representing the voluntary sector (a British Sports Forum); and a separate executive English Sports Council. Although some progress was made Pickup detected growing hostility from the other Councils to the proposed powers of the UKSC Sports Council, particularly the idea that it should be the sole source of grant-aid for performance and excellence programmes. Scotland also objected strongly to the proposal that the UKSC should assume responsibility for all national sports centres, including Inverclyde and Glenmore Lodge.

There was a long drawn out battle between the Sports Council and the territorial Councils throughout 1992 over these issues. The conflict was brought to an abrupt halt by a new Minister of Sport, Iain Sproat, in July 1993. When he finally introduced a revised structure in July 1994 the powers of the UKSC had been reduced very substantially, and the territorial Councils retained responsibility for elite sport and the management of national sports centres. Indeed only the territorial Councils for England, Scotland, Ireland and Wales would be designated as Lottery distributing bodies. The concept of a powerful UK body for sport had been rejected in favour of nationalism.

The National Lottery
Scotland was not short of ideas for developing sport. A consultative document Sport 2000: A Scottish Strategy was produced in 1988 (SSC July 1988). It was debated at meetings across the country and appeared in final form a year later. The total estimated cost of facilities was £320 million of which nearly £200 million was required for sports centres and swimming pools. Local authorities were asked to meet the bulk of the costs over the eleven years up to 2000. Their contribution would amount to £235 million with the balance being met by the SSC, the voluntary sector and private investors.

The logic of the strategy was unquestioned but local authority budgets were severely constrained. They were faced with the challenge of compulsory competitive tendering for the management of their facilities. And the Conservative government had introduced 'capping' of local authority budgets with penalties for any over-spending. The facilities strategy was doomed unless there was a change of government. The Conservatives were re-elected in 1992 and it was clear that alternative sources of funding were required. The Government had made a manifesto commitment to create a National Lottery if re-elected and John Major who had succeeded Mrs Thatcher as Prime Minister was committed to the concept. The National Lottery Act was passed in 1993.

The opportunity to create a Lottery had arisen twenty years earlier when a Labour Government appointed a Royal Commission on Gambling in 1976. One of the duties of the Commission was to consider how money raised from gambling could be used for good causes. The SSC and the UKSC both provided written evidence about the widespread practice throughout Europe of using tax income from lotteries and football pools to develop sport. Even at that time Britain was one of the last countries in Europe to create a lottery. When the Commission reported in 1978 it supported the creation of a national lottery and it identified sport as one of the good causes which could be funded. There was evidence of substantial public support (Coghlan 1990:107) but the Labour Government rejected the proposal. The Conservative Government, with Mrs Thatcher as leader, consistently opposed the idea of a lottery from 1979 onwards.

The National Lottery Act identified the four terrestrial Sports Councils as distributors, and the SSC programme of awards began in December 1994. Initially, the programme had to conform to government guidelines which initially restricted awards to capital projects. However, in 1996 the Government created new guidelines, concentrated on a) developing sporting talents, particularly of young people, and b) funding major international sporting events. The SSC's share of the total UK Lottery Sport Fund was set at 8.9 per cent, equivalent to about £25 million per annum. The maximum award for capital projects began at two thirds of the cost but in the first two years of operation, lottery grants totalling £75 million contributed to £217 million of new buildings. It was a complete reversal of a long record of low investment in facilities. Revenue programmes covered talented athletes; major events; coaching, and talent identification.

The Talented Athlete Programme provided support for 524 athletes in 1997-98, at a cost of £2.2 million. In addition, at a higher level 30 Scottish athletes were able to receive funding from a UK World Class Performance programme. In the first two years 21 Junior Groups benefited from the Talented Athlete Programme to the tune of £0.67 million. Eighteen major events were supported with an allocation of £1 million and a new Coaching Programme was introduced. It consisted of recruiting National Coaches and secondly assisting coaches to improve their skills. From 1994 to the end of 2000 the National Sports Lottery made a total of over 3,700 awards amounting £134.5 million. (Pringle and Cruttenden 2001: 32).

These are remarkable levels of investment for sport in Scotland but there was a need to ensure that the sporting structures could deliver services to those athletes and coaches who were being targeted. The Australian Institute of Sport provided a starting point for debates about structures for elite sport in Britain. The notion of a large centre was investigated and bids were invited to accommodate a British Academy of Sport. In the end, the Labour Government elected in 1997 chose to throw out this idea and replaced it with a network of regional centres in England, Scotland, Northern Ireland and Wales, plus an administration headquarters in London. The Scottish Institute of Sport began life in November 1998 with a promise of £20 million from the Sports Lottery over four years. The Institute headquarters will be on the campus of the University of Stirling, and six regional institutes have been established throughout the country.

The SSC has received government approval for a strategic plan for distributing Lottery monies over the period 1999-2003 (*Levelling the Playing Field*, SSC 1999). This led to a revised national strategy for Scottish sport *Sport 21: Nothing Left to Chance*, SSC 1998) which has also been adopted by government. The sum earmarked for capital projects has reduced from £23.3 million in 1998-99 to £10.5 million in 2000-01. This will be compensated in part by a substantial injection of £87 million over the period to 2003 from the New Opportunities Fund. This has become the largest of the distributing agencies for the National Lottery, absorbing 33% of the total monies available. In December 2000 the Government announced that £1.5 billion would be distributed by the New Opportunities Fund over a three year period, targeted at areas of deprivation.

The Scottish Parliament

The most momentous event of the 90s or indeed any preceding decade was the creation of a Scottish Parliament. In the 1995 election to the 32 new single-tier local authorities, the Conservatives won only 11 per cent of the vote and failed to win control of a single council. Then, in the 1997 General Election the Labour Party achieved a crushing victory. Within three months the new government under Tony Blair issued a White Paper *'Scotland's Parliament'* (HMSO, 1997). The Scotland Act was passed by the Westminster Parliament in 1998 paving the way for elections to the new Scottish Parliament in May 1999. Labour won 56 of the 129 seats, short of an overall majority, and the Scottish National Party emerged as the official opposition party with 35 seats. Labour and the Liberal Democrats combined to form a coalition administration.

Prior to the Scottish Parliament, there was a Secretary of State and three Ministers, each of whom dealt with a variety of Departments within the Scottish Office. The new structure consists of an Executive, equivalent to the British Cabinet, chaired by a First Minister and consisting of ten Ministers, the Lord Advocate and the Solicitor General. In addition, there are ten Deputy Ministers relating to subject committees and Departments. These subject committees are a unique feature of the Parliament. They not only scrutinise draft legislation but can also initiate Bills. In the first two years the committees have conducted inquiries, interrogated Ministers and modified Bills with a rigour which has brought them great respect. For the first fifteen months there was a Deputy Minister for Culture and Sport, answerable to the Education, Culture and Sport Committee of the Parliament. Following the tragic death of Donald Dewar, the First Minister, his successor Henry McLeish altered the Deputy Minister's title to Sport and Culture indicating his own interest and commitment to sport.

Rhona Brankin, Deputy Minister for Culture and Sport, was a former chair of the Scottish Labour party who tackled her new role with great energy. She set out her agenda on taking office, namely to produce a Cultural Strategy; to increase the number of school sport co-ordinators; to establish a Scottish Football Academy; and to implement the National sports strategy *'Sport 21'*. The Cultural Strategy was indeed produced within twelve months and before demitting office Brankin won a substantial increase in funding for the Arts.

In the run up to the May 1999 elections for the Scottish Parliament, Donald Dewar made a surprise announcement that, if elected, the Labour Party would set aside £1 million for a National football academy. A Football Partnership under the chairmanship of the Deputy Minister was set up within a month of her appointment. It included senior representatives of all the major bodies in football and by January 2000 it was in a position to approve in principle a structure for a national academy. The main elements are:
* A network of high quality training facilities

* A geographical spread throughout Scotland
* A minimum of six centres linked to professional clubs, within three years
* Improved and extended linkages between professional football and the wider community
* Development of young talented Scottish footballers.

The scheme was approved by the leaders of the 32 local councils and sources of funding the capital costs were identified – £5.3 million per centre. It was a fairly daunting task for a female politician with relatively little in-depth knowledge of sport to face the hierarchy of Scottish football. Ms Brankin's political skills stood her in good stead.

Along with the Cultural Strategy and the Football Academy, the Deputy Minister was soon presiding over a comprehensive review of *Sport 21*. This was achieved within nine months using six focus groups, each tackling a section of the strategy. As she became familiar with the issues Ms Brankin's support for *Sport 21* grew. This would be a significant factor in reporting subsequently to the Parliament. The last item on her agenda was school sport co-ordinators. When she was appointed there were 75 of these posts which are jointly funded by education authorities and sportscotland (the marketing name for the Scottish Sports Council). When she demitted office there were 250 co-ordinators and she was on course to have one such post in every one of the 400 secondary schools in Scotland. There is an annual sports lottery allocation of £1.5 million per annum which is guaranteed at least up to 2003.

The Minister for Education, Sam Galbraith, made statements to the Parliament on the Arts and Sport respectively in November 2000. This included an extra £15 million to the Arts over a three year period. Sport also received a boost. This consisted of an additional £2 million per annum to sportscotland (a 20 per cent increase); £3 million for an Active Primary Schools programme; £4 million for the National Football Academy; a £10 million contribution towards the campaign to bring the 2009 Ryder Cup to Scotland and £87 million from the New Opportunities Fund for sport and physical education. This was by far the largest ever increase in funding for Scottish sport. These allocations were in addition to the several millions of pounds which Galbraith had contributed to the costs of the new Hampden stadium for football.

The intervention of Ministers marks a new phase in the relationships of politics and sport in Scotland. Rhona Brankin acted as a voice for sport inside government – something which sportscotland could not do. She shifted power, moved it away from sportscotland towards the Scottish Executive. She did this by assuming her right to chair important committees which might previously have been the preserve of the chairman of sportscotland. She was able to persuade her pugnacious boss Sam Galbraith to allocate additional funds well beyond expectations.

The Scottish Executive and particularly the First Minister, Henry McLeish were exceedingly anxious about the power and influence of non-governmental bodies appointed by government for specific issues, known popularly as 'quangos'. In January 2001, there were 186 quangos responsible for £6.5 billion annually, i.e. one third of the total Scottish Executive budget. There are nearly 4000 members compared to around

1000 local councillors. The Scottish Executive (effectively the Cabinet) agreed to review every quango with a view to assessing if they were necessary or if their tasks could be undertaken by other means. Sportscotland is one of the bodies to be reviewed which could include a re-examination of the role of the voluntary sector and local authorities.

Endpiece

National policies for sport in Scotland over the past half century cannot be viewed in isolation. An objective assessment is that Scotland lagged behind as other countries took full advantage of football pools, lotteries and central government investment to establish nation-wide networks of sports facilities. Within the UK, Scotland was a recalcitrant, nationalistic and essentially negative contributor. There were some positive advances in the early years. The development of the national recreation centres at Inverclyde, Cumbrae and Glenmore brought together governing bodies who otherwise would have been content to pursue their own affairs. The direct access of officers from the advisory and executive Scottish Sports Councils to Ministers at least ensured that politicians were made aware of the issues. But the over-riding impression is that during the 1960s, a period of relative affluence, Scotland suffered from a political consensus that central government should not intervene in sport. The very real advances made during the 1970s can be credited to local authorities, particularly after the reorganisation of local government in 1974. They created new departments of leisure services and invested heavily in them.

One issue above all others dominated sports policy, indeed cultural policy. It was the relationship of the state to the voluntary sector. The state can reasonably claim responsibility for improving the quality of life of all citizens, protecting and improving public health, and providing the means to enhance moral welfare. However, as Cunningham (1980) points out:

> *"While the state may set the outer limits of leisure behaviour and morality through prescriptive legislation and licensing, the development of leisure policy was to be left to the permissive powers of local government, voluntary effort and the commercial sector".*

The state took notice when it appeared that an affluent youth population might pose a threat to public order. Additional funds could be allocated to emergency sports-action teams when poverty, unemployment and alienation led to increasing crime rates in the early 1980s. However, successive governments adamantly refused to accept that culture and sport required a powerful Ministry. The whole tradition of sport in Britain, and in Scotland, was based on amateurism and voluntarism.

The Scottish Office did not develop national policies or invest in national facilities. The Scottish Sports Council's efforts to draw up strategies for urban and countryside recreation in the early 1980s were frustrated, firstly by the withdrawal of the powerful regional tier of local government from leisure and recreation; and secondly by the refusal of central government to provide additional funds to implement sports strategies. There was no Scottish equivalent of Denis Howell to represent the interests of sport nationally and internationally. The absence of an advocate with access to Prime

Ministers meant that for much of the 1980s Scottish sport was in the doldrums. Mrs Thatcher's failure to persuade the British Olympic Association to boycott the Moscow Olympics cast a long shadow on sport. Her personal antagonism to lotteries was not helpful when Scotland was seeking additional funds for implementation of strategies for sport. During her reign additional powers for a Scottish Minister of Sport were unthinkable.

The sum total of a great deal of creative thinking, research and formulation of regional strategies was a growing recognition that Mrs Thatcher's government was firmly opposed to state intervention in this area. During the 1980s when countries throughout Europe were investing massively in sport, attempts to solicit State funding were rejected and the British government remained adamantly opposed to a national lottery. In Scotland, the only major contribution from the Scottish Office over a period of forty years was a grant towards the cost of Meadowbank stadium for the 1970 Commonwealth Games. There was no similar offer of support when the Games were held in Edinburgh in 1986. Planning documents which appeared in the 1960s, the STARPS reports in the early 1980s and the nationally approved Sport 2000 in 1988 all fell by the wayside for lack of investment. There is not a single national sports facility in Scotland which is owned by the state.

The burden of stimulating the development of sport has fallen on the Scottish Sports Council, with a meagre budget, supported by Governing bodies of sport and local authorities. Very few governing bodies could hope to emulate the Scottish Rugby Union who built a national stadium, Murrayfield, without assistance from central government. The 1980s was a stagnant period.

Scottish authorities have struggled to meet their statutory duty to make 'adequate provision' for recreation. There were signs of an impending crisis at the start of a new century. A research report (Campbell 2000) on swimming pools in Scotland estimated that the maintenance and repairs costs of pools would amount to £40 million a year for the next 20 years. Capital expenditure for all local authorities was only £80 million in 1995 and it fell to £40 million in 1999. Revenue expenditure was reduced by 15 per cent over the same period. The advent of the national lottery in 1995 gave hope for the provision of new facilities which local authorities could not afford.

The distributor, the Scottish Sports Council, was not allowed to impose its own vision. It had to wait and respond to applicants who might or might not fit into a national strategy. The capacity to work towards national plans has been limited by the requirement that applicants must contribute at least one third of the cost. However, there has been some progress. Working in partnership with governing bodies of sport and other agencies, the Lottery has funded a national cricket academy and a national hockey centre in Edinburgh; it has part funded a superb national golf centre near St Andrews and a national tennis centre and a swimming academy in Stirling. A national centre for badminton will open in Glasgow in 2001. Overall, it is a story of catching up with other countries.

This somewhat bleak overview is conditioned by the knowledge that in other countries there are national plans and strategies, and that they have operated effectively for at least forty years. Germany's 'Golden Plan' set out in 1962 to equip all communities of all sizes with basic facilities to meet the requirements of children, teenagers and adults. The German Olympic Association, which draw up the plan, secured the support of the federal government, the provinces and local authorities. The total cost, in 1960, was estimated at £569 million spread over fifteen years. The whole plan was achieved in twelve years. At the same time France was adopting an expansion programme costing £102 million over a five-year period, to be borne by central government and local authorities. The state provided £46 million from exchequer funds, and this was at a time when the British government was spurning the Wolfenden demand for state funding of only £5 million per annum for new capital projects.

From 1945 onwards UK governments have recognised the right of Scottish people to have distinctive legal, educational and religious systems and beliefs. However, there has been no such recognition in sport. The idea of Sports Councils operating at-arms-length from government as a buffer between politics and voluntarism has been applied uniformly to the four Home Countries. Funding has been made essentially on the basis of population. The concept of a powerful Ministry with a major budget combining exchequer and lottery funds has been resisted.

A totally new set of possibilities were created after the election of a Labour government in 1997. The first Scottish Parliament since 1707 was elected in 1999. Suddenly there were encouraging signs that the Scottish Executive would give a higher priority to sport. The Parliament has endorsed the national strategy *Sport 21* and a massive amount of lottery monies have been targeted at sport. More people are playing more sports every year. After a prolonged period of under-investment, hopes are high for the future of sport in Scotland.

Literature

Bilsborough, P. and Thomson, I. (1993) 'Sport and Physical Education', in Tranter, N. and McLusky, D. *Central Scotland Land, Wildlife and People*. Edinburgh: Forth Valley Naturalist and Historian.

Brown, M. (1979) *Alive in the 1900's*. Edinburgh: Scottish Sports Council.

Coghlan, J. F. and Webb, I. M. (1996) *Sport and British Politics since 1960*. Edinburgh: Falmer.

Clements, A., Farquharson, K. and Wark, K. (1996) *Restless Nation*. Edinburgh: Mainstream.

Cunningham, H. (1980) *Leisure in the Industrial Revolution*. London: Croom Helm.

Evans, H. J. (1974) *Service to Sport: the Story of the CCPR – 1935 to 1972*. London: Pelham.

Hassan, G. and Warhurst, C. (eds) (2000) *The New Scottish Politics*. Norwich: Stationery Office.

Holt, R. and Mason, T. (2000) *Sport in Britain, 1945-2000*. Oxford: Blackwell.

Holt, R. (1990) *Sport and the British*. Oxford: Oxford University Press.

Houlihan, B. (1991) *The Government and Politics of Sport*. London: Routledge.

Houlihan, B. (1997) *Sport, Policy and Politics*. London: Routledge.

Jarvie, G. and Burnett, J. (eds) (2000) *Sport, Scotland and the Scots*. East Linton: Tuckwell Press.

Jarvie, G. and Thomson, I. (1999) Sport, Nationalism and the Scottish Parliament, *Scottish Affairs*, 27, 82-96.

Jarvie, G. and Burnett, J. (eds) (1994) *Scottish Sport in the Making of the Nation*. Leicester: Leicester University Press.

Kemp, A. (1993) *The Hollow Drum: Scotland since the War*. Edinburgh: Mainstream.

Scotland

McIntosh Commission (1999) *Moving Forward: Report of the Local Government and the Scottish Parliament.* Edinburgh: The Scottish Office.

Pringle, A. and Cruttenden, T. (2001) *Sport and Local Government in the New Scotland.* Edinburgh: COSLA.

Scottish Sports Council (1988) *Laying the Foundations: Report on School-aged Sport in Scotland.* Edinburgh: The Council.

Scottish Sports Council (1989) *Sport 2000: a Strategic Approach to the Development of Sport in Scotland* Edinburgh: The Council.

Scottish Sports Council (1998) *Sport 21: Nothing Left to Chance.* Edinburgh: The Council.

Sportscotland (1999) *Levelling the Playing field; a Strategic Plan for the Distribution of Lottery Monies, 1999-2003.* Edinburgh: sportscotland.

Stodard Report (1981) *Committee of Inquiry into Local Government in Scotland.* Edinburgh: HMSO.

Wolfenden, Sir John (1960) *Sport and the Community: Report of the Wolfenden Committee on Sport.* London: Central Council of Physical Recreation.

Denmark

Else Trangbaek

Multiple elements contributed to the development of physical education, gymnastics and sport in Denmark in the last 200 years. The first is the school, whose *state* influence began at the start of the nineteenth century. The second was *private initiative:* private institutes and folk high schools from about the 1850s. The third is *organisations and voluntary clubs*, established from about the 1860s. Before the 20th century two distinct sports movements emerged, one rural and one centred in the cities, which still influence the sports system in Denmark. Towns industrialized only slowly, and outside the towns a very strong and self-aware social class developed and gave rise to a strong gymnastics movement with roots in rural areas. This contrasted with the sports movement connected to the cities. This division is still visible in the Danish sport system (idrætsystem) today, which has two different organizations with different historical traditions, cultures and ideologies.The aim in the so called popular Danish Gymnastics and Sports Associations (DGI – Danske Gymnastik og Idraetsforeninger) is to strengthen, through sport and other cultural activity, "voluntary association work in order to promote popular enlightenment". The aim of Denmark's Sports Federation (DIF – Danmarks Idraets-Forbund), which is an amalgamation of Danish sports associations, is to work for the "promotion of Danish sport (idræt) and for the popularization of sport in Danish society." In 2000 about 1.6 million people were active members of one of the 14,000 voluntary clubs; most clubs are members of both DIF and DGI. About 40 percent of the active participants are women.

This chapter gives an overview of the development from about 1800 until today. It will be divided into three parts which in some way combines chronology and themes from an institutional and organizational point of view:

I   Physical education in Danish schools in the 19th century – from humanist values to physiological principles
II   Gymnastics at private institutes and folk high schools from the 1850s [i]
III Voluntary organisations, gymnastics and sport from the 1860s [ii]

I. Physical education in the Danish school in the 19th century – from humanist values to physiological principles

The Danish state initiated agricultural and school reforms at the end of the eighteenth and beginning of the nineteenth century, inspired by the ideas of the Age of Enlightenment and conservative utilitarian philosophy. These reforms were crucial for the emergence of a peasant proprietor class as well as for the introduction of gymnastics as an educational measure in Denmark. Gymnastics was on the curriculum by school law from 1814 for country and town schools and the content of the subject was based on German pedagogical gymnastics. With the school law introduced in

1904, Swedish gymnastics with its physiological and rational approach to the body made training of the body the centre of the pedagogical process.

The ideas of the time on education and upbringing

The educational ideals of the scholarly schools were challenged by the ideas of the Enlightenment as liberation of the individual and an incipient interest arose for children and young people as future citizens. The new goal was "True education must make us into human beings and citizens. At the end of the 18th century, schools were established and tests carried out according to the new ideas. Schools were established for middle-class children according to philanthropic ideas which, among other things, had physical education on the school curriculum. The majority of the Danish population lived in the country, and here the reform-friendly brothers, Christian and Ludwig Reventlow, around 1780 organised schools according to the philanthropic pattern on their estates, Christianssæde and Brahetrolleborg. Experienced philanthropists were employed as teachers, and PE was made one of the subjects on the grounds that "Physical exercises increase the strength and agility of the body and are therefore very useful for everyone, although mostly by those who work with their hands" (Larsen, 1913-14).

In May 1789, King Christian VII set up the so-called *grand school commission* for the purpose of drawing up a plan for "improvement of the ordinary school system, as regards Danish schools in the villages and towns ... and measures that can help to educate useful and competent school leaders"(Larsen, 1914). The commission sat for a long time, and the result was affected by the fact that the economic situation changed in the period, partly because Denmark in 1807 gave up its policy of neutrality and became involved in the Napoleonic wars. In 1813, the state went bankrupt, which in many ways meant that conservative currents also dominated the work of the school commission. Against this background, it is interesting that gymnastics was one of the subjects in school, even though "the Chancellery completely cut the proposed teaching in history, geography and nature knowledge" (Larsen, 1914). Of crucial importance for the introduction of gymnastics in schools were Franz Nachtegall's initiatives around the turn of the century.

The father of Danish school gymnastics

Vivat Victorius Fredericus Nachtegall (1777-1847), most often called Franz, began to study theology after his school leaving certificate examination in 1794, but he had to give this up after some years because of his father's death. As a child, Nachtegall had been interested in gymnastics and had also taken lessons in fencing and vaulting. After reading GutsMuths *Gymnastik für die Jugend*, he gained the idea of becoming a gymnastics teacher. Nachtegall began to teach gymnastics and he started the Gymnastics Society in 1798, whose members were students and businessmen aged between 30 and 40. On 1 November 1799, Nachtegall issued a public invitation for the establishment of a private gymnastics institute especially for children. They could be enrolled when they were over 5 years old and were to be taught physical exercises, which consisted of vaulting, jumping, running, climbing, balancing, dancing and swimming. Nachtegall encouraged parents to attend the lessons, and he also invited influential people in society to watch the annual tests, which was to have great significance for his further activities. The Crown Prince, too, was interested in Nachtegall's initiatives and supported him in various ways, perhaps because he considered gymnastics useful for military training. The institute was the first of its kind, whose sole purpose was physical development. Nachtegall saw possibilities in gymnastics as part of general upbringing and education, which "teach the person to be vigilant, to escape from boredom, the most dangerous, most deadly enemy of all joy." However, according to Nachtegall, boredom was not a problem for peasants, "because their life is active", while on the other hand, "boredom is the constant torture of the rich." Precisely this judgement should have been a forewarning of how difficult it would be to implement gymnastics in the country schools, especially for farmers' children. Nachtegall's idea was to bring physical exercises to the children of the common people, which meant that he was referred to as *Citoyen* Nachtegall, the term *citoyen* denoting a person who obliterates class distinctions and makes people equal.

Nachtegall's inspiration was linked to the general pedagogical ideas of the time as well as to the specific possibilities of gymnastics. Thus, at lectures at the University of Copenhagen in 1802, he spoke about methods and history of gymnastics, about the people who had paved the way for the most important revolutions as regards upbringing: "Locke among the British, Rousseau among the Gauls, and Basedow among the Germans", and he welcomed the new era, in that "a person's physical being, no less than his moral and intellectual being, has become an object for the attention of the educator."

The content of gymnastics was influenced by GutsMuths's *Gymnastik für die Jugend*, which had been translated into Danish in 1799 by the pastor at Holmen Church, V. K. Hjort.

The school law of 1814

By Royal Decree of 16 April 1814, gymnastics was introduced in country and town schools. The subject was introduced in primary schools for children, i.e. for both boys and girls, which was in keeping with many of the implemented trials which had underlined the importance of the subject for both sexes. The decree recommended that when weather permitted, gymnastics should be done for *"one hour daily"*, and there were also instructions about how a gymnastics space should look and what equipment should be acquired. In various regulations the difference between country and town was specified, among other things by the fact that, in the country, the extent of teaching could be reduced at harvest time; in Copenhagen schools, it was specified that the subject had special significance for "the working class".

A public notice of 15 June 1828 limited the law to include only boys, a change that was linked with increasing interest in the subject's usefulness in the schooling of future soldiers. In spite of this unfortunate limitation, the public notice was in many ways a boost, as an authorised textbook was published and the training of teachers was increased and improved. Girls did not have obligatory school gymnastics until the school legislation of 1904.

The intention of the government with the 1814 l legislation was to create a school system of fairly uniform standard which was controlled according to more or less the same principles. This meant that school commissions should be established in country parishes with the local pastor and other respected men of the parish as supervisors. Until the middle of the century, gymnastics was institutionalised in the school and,from the point of view of the state, school gymnastics was reasonably successful. Many schools had introduced gymnastics, the subject was on the curriculum of training colleges, it had local supervisors, national subject inspection, and annual reports said that the situation for the subject was not too bad. Thus, Nachtegall mentions that at the end of 1830 gymnastics had been introduced in 2,000 country schools all around the country (Nachtegall, 1930). In spite of this, the humanist world of ideas was in contrast to the economic possibilities of Danish society. In a large section of the population, especially among people in rural areas, there was widespread lack of understanding of the usefulness of physical education for hard-working rural children. Ideas and the structure were in place, but where was the reality?

Doubt about the importance of the subject

In the middle of the century – about 50 years after the introduction of the subject — times had changed. While Europe in the preceding years had been engulfed in revolutions, the Danish king had surrendered his absolute power with the constitution of 1849. This made Denmark a democratic state with a constitutional monarchy. However, the electoral rules were such that the real power still remained in the hands of the few in society, the men of the propertied classes. The upsurge of national feeling in the 1860s and 1870s, combined with the people's struggle for *parliamentary democracy* from the 1880s to 1901, were crucial elements in the formation of the Danish Sports Model.

The absolute monarchy, with the introduction of reforms inspired by ideas of the Enlightenment and the middle-class philosophy of utility, had been crucial for both the rise of a free peasant class and the introduction of gymnastics as an educational measure at the end of the 18th century. But free peasants did not immediately embrace gymnastics as a school subject. Gymnastics suffered from the lack of competent teachers, necessary time, lack of premises and equipment and, in particular, a lack of understanding of the usefulness of the subject. Lack of interest in the subject and its lack of development were most clearly expressed in a proposal, in 1858, for the discontinuation of the subject from a teacher, Kraiberg, and 23 other members of parliament. The proposal was adopted in the lower house of parliament but rejected by the privileged social groups in the upper house. The proposal must be seen as a reflection of dissatisfaction with the state of gymnastics in broad sections of the *population*, who, however, still had no real influence on political decisions.

Those who wanted the subject abolished stated among other things that school subjects could be divided into 1) subjects that were necessary for all pupils, and 2) those that were useful for some pupils. Gymnastics belonged to the second group, as according to the opponents, there was no evidence for its general value, as the subject was only for boys (see Trangbaek, 1987). In addition they believed that "Gymnastics in village schools was there more in memory of Frederik VI's well-known predilection for military matters."

Until the end of the 1850s, the school had been the only milieu where children had experience of being taught gymnastics.

Towards a new era – and new school gymnastics

The ideal underlying the school legislation in 1814 was that the subject of gymnastics should be generally educational. It was thus intended for both boys and girls, but the circumstances in society, both economic and political, contributed to the fact that the goal was extended to include military training too. The indirect link between the subject and the armed forces, as well as the fact that schools were generally controlled by the state, resulted in a certain contempt for the importance of the subject in all-round education. The subject in most schools, and particularly because of teachers' lack of training, became confined to include only simple exercises, such as walking, running and playing outside. There was thus a wide gap between the ideals and the gymnastics done* in real life. But in spite of this, gymnastics was kept on the school curriculum as a useful though not essential contribution to all-round education. This was due in particular to Nachtegall's efforts, as, according to the Danish school historian, Joakim Larsen, "Nachtegall was a practically inclined man with pedagogical sense, a competent teacher and organiser, he understood therefore how to select, supplement and change a given exercise material and also to try out new exercises. But physiological considerations played a subordinate role with him" (Larsen, 1914). Until the 1880s discussions about gymnastics content in the school and the new milieu was not central, except in the private institutes for women. Until then, the problems were continually linked to the lack of training places, premises, equipment and qualified teachers. Gymnastics needed to be renewed, and the matter was taken up through two channels. The hygienic endeavours of the time meant that school gymnastics had to be reformed. And in addition the political situation in the middle of the 1880s brought discussion about the gymnastics system on to the political battleground, which will be explained in the next section. From the middle of the 1880s, discussions about out-of-date school gymnastics increased, and in 1887 the first of two commissions was given the assignment of producing proposals for a solution to how gymnastics could be improved as regards content, the teaching of girls and the training of teachers. The two commissions had sought inspiration in study tours abroad, as well as from a few trials in the new Danish gymnastics milieu, but they forgot – or consciously overlooked – that the milieu had very limited experience with children. In addition to this, it was evidently thought that exercises could be transferred from one social context to another without any negative consequences. The commissions sat for a long time, and the results were not seen until the publication of *Håndbogen 1899* and school legislation in 1904, as well as the establishment of a one-year Gymnastics Teachers Course in 1898, which together represented the visible results of a new era and new ideas. The 1904 legislation changed the basic idea of school gymnastics from the humanist ideas at the beginning of the 19th century to the more physiological and health-oriented ideas at the end of the century, in spite of certain warnings about Swedish gymnastics, as critics found that it "lacked freshness because of pure consideration of physiology" (see Trangbaek, 1987). But the new gymnastics was better suited to what many people wanted as regards health and hygiene, and through institutes, associations and folk high schools, it had achieved acceptance in the population because of its link with opinion-shaping contexts. One problem was that children were perhaps forgotten or crushed in this process of change. In leisure time, gymnastics was a voluntary choice and an important element in the social life of young people, while for children in school it was a subject on the curriculum, where the pupils' experience of coherence and connection with the school and their life was present to only a limited extent. As regards ideas, pleasure was no longer attributed the same vital importance for learning and teaching and the pedagogical rules had changed from proper teaching to correct exercises. The vision of the contribution of gymnastics to general education had ended with its specific role in a hygienic and disciplining project. In this project, there was more room for girls — everything was now under control.

II: Gymnastics at the private institutes and the folk high schools from the 1850s

The private institutes

After the public notice of 15 June 1828 limited physical education to boys only, some initiatives for girls came at first in 1838 with the establishment of the "Experimental School for Instructing Female Youth in Body and Health Exercises" (Proveskole for den Qvindelige Ungdoms Undervisning i Legems- og Sundhedsovelser) at the Royal Military Gymnastics Institute (Det kongelige militaere Institut). This was intended to give school mistresses and other interested people the opportunity to learn how to teach physical education to girls and women. The interest in gymnastics for girls arose from physicians' observations of a lack of proportion in connection with women's physical development. The work done in the trial school was little evident in the private schools, where physical education was gradually introduced, and here the emphasis was on health and hygiene (Possing, 1999).

From 1859 onwards several institutes of gymnastics were established in which gymnastics training was offered within a private framework. The institutes thus became some of the first places where Danish women could meet and practise "organized" physical training. Just as with the work done in the 1830s, the starting point was the detection of various diseases in young girls caused by lack of physical activity. The aim of gymnastics was thus directed towards achieving a generally better state of health, and these institutes could therefore be regarded as pioneers in the new movement towards a higher standard of health and hygiene. One of the central pioneers was the physician A. G. Drachmann (1810 – 1892) who attempted to create a method suitable for girls on the basis of the investigations mentioned above. He worked systematically and examined German and Swedish gymnastics, travelled to France and studied American books on gymnastics. He did not come across any particular system which satisfied his requirements but, on the basis of his knowledge as a physician, he made some demands for his "system" for women. He developed a compound system which in Denmark was called "French Gymnastics". The system emphasized both the aesthetic aspect of the exercises and the desire that the exercises should be carried out at home as well as at school. The exercises did not exceed – at least to any great extent – contemporary norms of femininity, so apparently nobody in the bourgeois family needed to feel insecure. Drachmann – in contrast to many of his colleagues – began with the belief that women's infirmities were caused by inadequate upbringing and by the social and cultural reality of life. In 1878, Paul Petersen (1845-1906), the so-called father of Danish women's gymnastics opened the "Institut for dansk Kvindegymnastik" (Institute for Women's Gymnastics). He started also both a gymnastic and rowing club for women, and a gymnastics club for men. Women from his gymnastic club, "Danish Women's Gymnastics", formed the first women's team at an Olympics. It was in 1906 at the 10 years` celebration of the first Olympic Games in 1906 in Athens, where they gave a display. The Paul Petersen Institute still functions and gives a one-year course for both men and women in gymnastics and sport.

Folk high schools (Folkehojskoler)
The establishment of the Rødding Folk High School in 1844 started a new form of school, inspired by the ideas of popular enlightenment of the poet and cleric, N.F.S. Grundtvig (1783-1882). For the rest of the century, many new folk high schools started, and at many of the schools gymnastics was on the timetable at an early stage. The schools were founded on private initiative and the purpose was to use an "educational-cultural break" of 3-5 months to give farmers' children a chance to be *enlightened*, which could help qualify them as members of a class of self-aware democratic citizens. The young people lived at the school. Young women usually attended the high school for only three months in summer, the young men for five (more rarely six) winter months. The young people were adolescent, on the verge of adulthood (16-20 years old). According to Grundtvig, this age group was best suited to "the inner life". The perception of the body and human beings on which many high schools were based was often characterised by a Christian morality, which in many ways clashed with the urge of young people for fun and movement, and as a pupil from the Askov folk high school wrote later: "at that time, dancing was regarded as very wicked at Askov." Gymnastics was on the timetable from the start to compensate for sedentary life, punctuated by lectures. Gymnastics in the primary school were not very popular with the rural population, but when the same exercises were transferred to a different context, the high school, and had a different purpose, they became popular.

Until about the 1880s the folk high schools taught the well-known exercises from Germany, Denmark and France, but from then the Swedish Lingian type of gymnastics took over and attracted popular support and became associated with a broad cultural movement based on voluntary organisations. In other countries the Swedish gymnastics system especially was used in school gymnastics and by the military. The difference can be explained by an understanding of the structure of the Danish Sports System. The next section goes into greater detail on this. The Danish folk high school taught young people gymnastics that they could teach the public when they went home. In 1920, the first Danish Gymnastics folk high school was established at Ollerup by the famous Danish gymnastics teacher Niels Bukh. Another one, for women only , was opened in 1925 at Snoghøj and managed by two women, Jørgine Abildgaard and Anna Krogh. Both schools were inspired in different ways by the Finnish gymnastics pioneer Elli Bjørksten. The two schools had great importance for continuity in the development of gymnastics in Denmark.

III: Voluntary organisations, gymnastics and sport from the 1860s onwards

The shooting movement – 1860-1900

"What is lost outwardly must be regained inwardly. "
These words became part of the collective consciousness of many Danes in the years after the loss of the southern part of Denmark to Germany in 1864. This defeat brought an increase in national feeling, and the idea of winning South Jutland back became a popular rallying call. The national upsurge had a great influence on gymnastics and organisational life in Denmark. *To be really Danish was henceforth almost the same as to be anti-German.*

In the course of the 19th century, Denmark was reduced to a small country, which at the end of the century had a population of 2.5 million of whom 1.5 million lived in rural areas. Denmark's geographical reduction in many ways awakened a need for a clarification of identity. This clarification had the result that "modern Denmark" was not compelled to take over the structures and norms of other countries, but could largely choose its own way.

On 12 February 1861, the Danish Shooting Associations (De Danske Skytteforeninger, DDS) were founded, on the English example. The objective was to prepare young men through physical activity so that they could take part in the defence of the country. Shooting and drill were the primary activities. Gymnastics arrived later, and the activities were practised in the many shooting associations set up all over the country. In extension of the associations' social objective, the Central Committee was listed in the national budget as early as 1866 and the state granted financial support – a support that the sports clubs and their organisations of that time and later years would have to fight a long battle for. The shooting associations' memberbase was the farming population, who were mainly associated with the liberal party, Venstre, but the organisation was led by city people, particularly military people, who were affiliated to the political right.

After the loss of South Jutland in 1864, the patriotic element in the shooting movement was reinforced, but after France's defeat by Germany in 1871, it became obvious that prospects for the recovery of South Jutland with the help of international alliances were slim. Prussia now headed a German empire. On this basis, the patriotic training of members of the shooting associations became quite unrealistic. Prize shooting and gymnastics became to a greater extent leisure activities. From the mid-1880s, Ling's Swedish gymnastics gained a foothold, and gymnastics attracted its warmest advocates in the high-school movement.

The political situation

The democratic constitution of 1848 did not succeed in breaking the real power of the Danish oligarchy. While industrialisation in the towns progressed only slowly, a strong, self-aware social class developed outside the towns. The farmers were politically organised in the Danish Liberal Political Party, Venstre ("Left"), while the landowners and urban capitalists were organised in the Conservative Party, Højre ("Right"), which retained government power irrespective of the fact that the Party was in a minority in Parliament. In the election of 1884, the "Right" had only 19 deputies, while the "Left" won 83 without being able to overthrow the de facto dictatorship of the right-wing Prime Minister Estrup, who ruled by provisorial decrees. In this political situation the shooting associations were confined by a provisional rifle law, which set up strict restrictions as to who might be a member and where the members could practise. The situation resulted in a raging political struggle between the political "Right" and "Left", with the Danish rural population fighting for democratic rights. Here, the co-operative movement, the folk high school movement and the gymnastics movement became the central stages where people could vent their feelings. When the shooting associations had to live with a prohibition against shooting, gymnastics gained a new, central significance. The old gymnastics system(German/Danish), which "belonged" to the state and thus to the "oppressors" was in this situation replaced by Swedish gymnastics. Swedish gymnastics, which had been known in Denmark before, did not gain real support in Denmark until after a demonstration at the Vallekilde folk high school in 1884. The combination of the political situation, the rural population's struggle for *parliamentary democracy,* the involvement and work of the folk high schools for gymnastics helped to introduce Swedish gymnastics into the voluntary clubs, especially in the countryside, and these formed a crucial element in the formation of the Danish sports model.

The Danish Gymnastics and Sports Associations, DGI, mentioned in the introduction to this section had its roots and identity in gymnastics and the democratic struggle of the last decade of the 19th century, but it went through many changes during the 20th century. The other organisation, DIF, represented modern times and the sports movement of the 20th century.

The period 1900 – 1918

The foundation of the Danish Sports Federation (the organisation uses the Nordic word Idraet instead of 'sport')

The practice of British sport or competitive athletics gained more and more ground in the towns from the 1860s for the rest of the century; sports clubs for rowing, football, gymnastics, cricket, tennis, skating, sailing, rowing, etc., were founded. During this period, athletics spread to new sectors of the population via these clubs. Formerly only the middle and upper classes had the privilege, on their own private initiative, of practising sporting activities, such as riding, horse racing, dancing, sailing, etc., but now sport gradually began to take root among the working class. As in the shooting associations, the leaders and pioneers came from the upper and middle classes. The

Danish historian, Jørn Hansen, has documented in a study that, in the period up to 1880, only three of the 183 pioneers involved in his study had roots in the working class and only eight were women. From 1880, however, a slow development takes place, but this did not change the fact that sport, as part of the process of modernisation and civilisation was set in progress from the top (Hansen, 1995).

The many associations being founded around the country gave rise among some of the pioneers to an increasing desire to create organised conditions for sport. It was against this background that the the Danish Sports Federation (DIF – Dansk Idraets-Forbund) was founded in Copenhagen on 14 February 1896. 18 associations and one special federation immediately registered as members. As early as 1892, attempts had been made to set up an organisation, inviting all Danish sports clubs to join. The result was the formation of the Danish Amateur Union, and it was on the ruins of this organisation that the Danish Sports Federation, DIF, was set up. The discussion of amateur rules was a central part of DIF's work. The amateur concept that gained a key position in its work for many years originated in Britain and was based on the idea that amateur sports should be practised in leisure time for their own sake, without prizes or any other kind of remuneration. The connection between formulation of the rules among the English upper class and middle class and their introduction by the same classes in Denmark in the late 19th century is no coincidence. The middle class in Denmark and much of the rest of Europe was often fascinated by the British lifestyle. DIF's first amateur rules and regulations came into force on 1 January1897 and, with this, amateurism as an overriding principle of DIF's work was introduced. This was how matters would remain for about the next 80 years, until professional football was permitted in 1978.

The relationship between DIF and DDS

From the start, there was no conflict of interest between those who practised the new British sports and the activities of the shooting movement. In actual fact, many of the pioneers who introduced sport to Denmark were in associations under the DDS. The foundation of DIF in 1896 was, therefore, not an attempt to demarcate themselves from the DDS, but more an expression of a wish to create order in their own ranks within the sports movement. In fact, DDS was invited to take part in the meeting that led to the foundation of DIF in 1896, but DDS did not send any representatives. In DIF, it was the activities that were at the centre; people were to compete on equal terms and against others, including from outside the country's borders. Participation in international sports meetings and matches were from the beginning a central objective for DIF. In DIF, the activities were developed and reinforced as an objective in themselves, in contrast to the shooting movement's patriotic objectives. In the beginning, there was a difference in principle, but this was not to have any real significance until the 20th century. DIF and DDS worked excellently side by side, the only stumbling block for DIF being the DDS's close agreements for support from the state. Up until 1929, there was no conflict between sport and popular athletics, but rather a conflict within popular athletics

The Period 1918 – 1945

From one to two popular organisations in 1930

After the introduction of Swedish gymnastics, DDS allowed members to practise gymnastics without shooting, and in time this meant that more and more DDS members exclusively practised gymnastics. It has been estimated that approx.imately 90% of the gymnasts immediately after World War I did not practise shooting. In time, this led to an intensified ideological struggle between riflemen and gymnasts, which first brought a change of name in 1919 to the Danish Shooting and Gymnastics Associations (DDS&G — De Danske Skytte- & Gymnastikforeninger). Because of DDS&G's origins, the shooting associations had a special economic status in the movement. A certain sum of state funds was awarded to the shooting associations in advance, after which the rest was divided among the associations. In time, this met with growing resistance from the gymnasts, who felt that their membership fee was going to ammunition for the riflemen. On top of that came a gradually more obvious difference in behaviour between riflemen and gymnasts. The gymnasts perceived the shooters as people who considered prize shooting and parties more important. Shooting club parties, where heavy drinking went on, were particularly disliked. Instead, in some places, gymnasts began to hold alcohol-free parties. The many divisions led most gymnasts to break away from the DDS&G and take part in the foundation of the Danish Gymnastic Associations (De Danske Gymnastikforeninger, DDG), in 1929. The split in the DDS&G led in 1930 to an incipient modernisation of the old main organisation, which now came to be called DDSG&I. The addition of the word idræt – athletics – in many ways heralded new tendencies within Danish athletics.

Structural changes in DIF

The Danish Sports Federation started with the objective of organising, regulating and managing Danish sports. The instrument of management had in particular consisted of the common amateur rules and regulations, as well as record rules. But after World War I, DIF's control over the Danish special federations finally began to disintegrate. Despite many attempts through the years, common Scandinavian amateur rules were finally abandoned in 1918, and the maintenance of common Danish amateur rules and regulations gave rise to increasing problems. This led to a reorganisation of DIF in 1925, by which the organisation became an umbrella organisation for a number of special federations which were, in principle, autonomous in the organisation of their own areas. This is the role DIF as an organisation still has in relation to the special federations.

The Danish Sports Federation developed a philosophy about *the neutrality of sport* as the basis on which to fulfil the desire to gather "...all the citizens of the country, irrespective of race, faith, social class, political orientation and the like, and on a sports basis to create a sanctuary, and in the association a home for sports.". This neutrality was threatened when the labour movement's sports association, Dansk Arbejder Idræt, and YMCA Sport (KFUM Idræt), with their respective political and religious foundations, applied for membership of DIF. A further problem was that the special federations were not interested in these cross-disciplinary organisations.

YMCA Sport and labour movement sport

In 1878, the Young Men's Christian Association, Kristelig forening for Unge mænd (KFUM) was founded in association with the Copenhagen "inner mission" – an evangelical wing of the Church of Denmark. After KFUM had existed for some years, various Copenhagen associations began to practise gymnastics and football, and the first actual KFUM sports divisions in Denmark saw the light of day in Copenhagen in 1897. However, this interest in sport gave rise to some anxiety in religious circles as there was a fear that young people would forget to observe the Lord's day in the right way. In 1918, the YMCA Sports Federation was founded, because a number of provincial sports divisions wished to unite in order to compete in partnership. Some of the matters that came to make a special mark on the start of the league were about rules for service times, demands and expectations of the members and admission to DIF. In the course of 1923, the management of the YMCA Sports Federation discussed the possibility of applying for membership of DIF. DIF was chosen for several reasons: KFUM sport was primarily an urban phenomenon, the activities were primarily sport-oriented and many KFUM associations were thus associated with one of DIF's special federations. Negotiations began in 1924, but many years of negotiations led to rejection, partially on the basis of concern that this was not entirely a question of pure sport. Negotiations were resumed after the labour movement's sports association, Dansk Arbejder Idræt, founded in 1929, had been accepted into DIF in 1943 and had paved the way for the possibility that federations with certain distinctive characteristics could become members. The negotiations lasted a long time, partially because of the war, but on 17 November 1946, the YMCA's Sports Federation was admitted into DIF, with certain special agreements .

As mentioned above, DAI had been admitted into DIF after many years of to-ing and fro-ing in 1943. Worker sport had grown up in the late 19th century in opposition to middle-class sport, first in Germany and Austria, where it played an important role in sports politics until the Nazis outlawed it in 1933. During the first decades of the 20th century, international workers' sport underwent a bifurcation into a Social Democratic line, organised in the Sozialistische Arbeiter Sport-Internationale (SASI) and a more revolutionary, Communist-orientated line, Rote Sport Internationale (RSI), respectively. In Denmark, the political fronts were sharply delineated only for short periods. Denmark's industrialisation progressed slowly, characterised as it was by small companies and a large artisan class. This meant, compared with many other countries, a more homogeneous and extensive labour movement which quickly divided into professional and political branches. The professional struggle focused particularly on improving the material living conditions of the working class, while the political by means of Social Democracy worked on achieving government in order to secure the workers' economic and political equality. The objective was to a great degree the same, but the focus was different. In Denmark, the first worker sports clubs appeared in the 1870s and 1880s. These clubs can be characterised by the fact that they attracted particularly craftsmen, they a had relatively short life span and they were distinguished by a culture involving many activities of a non-sporting nature. During the 1890s, there was a change in this pattern. Focus was set on sport and many new associations arose, most of them including the word *arbejder* (worker) in their names, for example: *Arbejdernes* Bicycle Club (1894). Many of the clubs joined DIF and participated in the organisation's competitions. Some of the clubs were even among the leading clubs within DIF. Only on an extremely limited scale were they oriented towards political activities. In KFUM Idræt, demands had been made of members regarding membership of KFUM, compliance with rules regarding service times, etc. In a similar way, professional and political demands were made on the members of DAI, although only for short periods, but the result was, in most places, that the clubs were open to all. The Social Democratic Party, which made up the bulk of the labour movement's base of support, initially showed only little interest in worker sport. The international development of worker sport played a part in an incipient Social Democratic involvement in sport. At the end of the 1920s, a split in international worker sports arose between the Social Democratic SASI and the Communist RSI. This led the German Social Democrats to recommend that the Danish Social Democrats take control of Danish worker sport in order to avoid possible Communist dominance.

On 7th May 1929, an article was published in the Social Democratic Party's daily, "Social-Demokraten", under the headline: *To Denmark's Workers and Athletes*. The article was a declaration of support of sorts, and signatories included the Social Democratic Prime Minister, Thorvald Stauning (1873-1942), in favour of the establishment of a Worker Sports Union, which took place shortly afterwards, on 19th May. The Social Democrats were opposed to DIF because of its middle-class leadership, but there was still support for the worker clubs being members of both DIF and DAI, as it was thought that the worker sports clubs' numerical strength would allow workers' interests to secure a democratic leadership of DIF and contribute to making DIF healthy from within. The situation in 1929 was indeed difficult, as almost all workers who played sports in associations were organised under DIF. Thus it was estimated that 70,000 workers were organised in DIF, which amounted to approx- imately three fifths of the members of DIF. A disruption of DIF would thus create big problems for both DIF and DAI, and this was a conflict the Social Democrats did not want. Thus, at the time of the foundation of DAI, there was no requirement that the associations should choose sides between DAI or DIF. The relationship between DIF and DAI led to an ideological balancing act in subsequent years, and this resulted in a showdown in 1930, which led to a demand to the associations to choose sides – for or against DAI/DIF. Out of the 14 associations that had dual membership, 12 chose to remain in DIF. The problem for DAI was that sport in DAI was not significantly different from DIF sport, but the conflict was an organisational defeat for DAI. DAI now had a severely reduced membership and an inadequate organisational apparatus, incapable of looking after all the practical problems associated with sports work: events, tournaments, championships, training, etc. On top of that came falling recruitment as a result of constant unemployment right through the the 1930s. Secondly, these was a lack of economic support from the Social Democrats, and finally, the collapse of the international partnership in 1933, when the Nazis crushed the German worker sports federation. The Social Democrats partially excluded DAI. As chairman of a ruling party, Stauning was busy expanding his electorate and reforming the Party from an actual labour party to a people's party, as illustrated in the work programme of 1934: "Denmark for the people". The practical problems of everyday life in DAI gradually contributed to an altered awareness of the federation's political function and possibilities.

The isolation of the organisation led to a greater degree of political demonstrations, of which DAI's attitude to the boycott of the Olympic Games in Berlin in 1936 was the most striking. However, as early as 1935, DIF had made an amendment to the law, which created an opportunity for associations and special federations to co-operate with the DDSG&I and DDG in association with national meetings. The incipient de-ideologisation of DAI was the reason that overtures were made between DAI and DIF in 1936. The result was a sports agreement in 1937, by which DAI was given the same facilities as the DDSG&I and DDG. A consequence of the agreement was that DAI to a great extent gave up its independence and submitted to the authority of DIF in key areas. In the new laws that were passed at the DAI congress on 14 February 1937, passages that made direct reference to DAI's association with the working class were deleted. Neutrality had won, and in the following years the partnership functioned smoothly. Negotiations about DAI's admission to DIF were accelerated by the German invasion of Denmark on 9 April 1940, with respect to the "serious factors" that placed an obligation to co-operate in sport. In the years 1940 and 1942, there were a number of negotiations about guidelines for partnership. The result was that DAI was given membership of DIF on 6 May 1943, as a joint organisation in the same way as a special federation, although with certain provisos, particularly in relation to members' participation in international competitions. This could only take place through membership of DIF's special federations.

Admission to the sports community had required KFUM Idræt and DAI to be neutral. But DIF as a central organisation was now brought into a new situation, as the special federations had been supplemented by two strong cross-disciplinary federations. The desire for neutrality had created a new DIF. At the end of 1945, there were a total of 25 special federations in DIF.

The period 1945 – 1970

On 9th April 1940, German troops rolled in over the Danish border in South Jutland, and German ships entered Copenhagen Harbour – Denmark was occupied. DIF initially wished to cease all sporting co-operation with Germany. During the first six months of the occupation, however, the Danish government persuaded the Federation to change its attitude, and, from the autumn of 1940, DIF agreed with the government's official policy of co-operation with Germany. As a side benefit of this, the international sporting co-operation with the Scandinavian countries – especially Sweden – got moving again. The war and the occupation played a part in building bridges across the divisions in the Danish population. All of the sports organisations saw an increase in membership during the war years. For example, DIF's membership doubled in the course of the five years of the war. This occurred despite a shortage of materials, travel difficulties and various restrictions on athletes. Finally, as the war came to a head, sport was struck by the persecution of Jews, military officers and police, curfews and "Schalburgtage" – German sabotage attacks on sports facilities. When the chairman of DIF was to report in 1945, he asked whether these many "new proselytes" had arrived out of an acknowledgement that they wanted to, or because "the immediate conditions and restrictions in other areas" had driven people to the sports grounds. He concluded that the line that sport had taken in the war years with the "Sport for All" policy had been followed and "had borne fruit". The restrictions of the war caused a certain reorganisation of sport, which in the long term would be seen to appeal to broader social groups. The explanation may be that, despite the problems of the war, sport continued to offer leisure activity to the population at a time that was otherwise fairly dull. In addition, many associations reinforced their alternative activities, such as social events and parties.

The public sector and sport

Sport was growing, and support was needed to develop it. The state funded the work of the central organisations on a small scale. However, DIF represented sports significantly less than the popular organisations. On a local level, there was no law obliging local authorities to support sport. Nevertheless, local authorities funded sport by laying out and maintaining facilities, and by providing building sites and premises.

As early as 1910, DIF had requested the inland revenue department to reject applications for lottery grants from federations under DIF, because it would damage Danish sport if competitions gained "a pecuniary element". In 1934, however, football pools were permitted in Sweden, and this gave the Swedish state the equivalent of 1.2 million Danish kroner for sporting purposes in the first year. This inspired Denmark's Olympic Committee (DOK), founded in 1905, to apply to the state in 1936 for permission to set up football pools. But the Danish Sports Federation (Dansk Idræts Forbund) was still opposed to it and the application was also rejected by the Minister of Finance. However, only three years later, the board of DIF applied to the Ministry of Finance for permission to organise football pools. The application was never answered and the question was not taken up again until after the war, when the sports organisations again applied for an increase in government grants. In 1946, DIF sent a resolution to the government and parliament, asking that pools be introduced, just as in the other Scandinavian countries. Pools had also been permitted the same year in Norway. After long negotiations and a very emotionally charged debate in parliament and the media, and strong organisational pressure from DIF, the Act was passed, on 1 June 1948.

Football pools were launched on 8 May 1949. The Act was to a great extent inspired by the pools acts in Sweden and Norway respectively, as well as the regulations for state gambling. However, it was not permitted for young people under 18 years of age to take part in the pools. The surplus was divided between "sporting purposes" and "cultural, charitable or other non-profit ends". The money for sports went directly to the organisations as a lump sum, without a requirement to monitor the use of the money. In this, the Pools Act in Denmark came to differ from that in either Sweden and Norway, where the whole surplus was allocated by the state.

The growth in sports during the 1960s led to an increased need for funding sport in order to be able to ensure a qualified development. The central organisations had with the Pools Act achieved their means, while sports in the locals sports clubs still had to fend for themselves through members' subscriptions, revenues from balls, parties and the like. After years of negotiations came the desired result when, in 1968, the Recreation Act was passed. This was in many ways a culmination of welfare thinking, as now even people's leisure activities could be partially paid for by the public sector. Through this law and individual municipal schemes, the sports associations could gain support for teaching, training and activities. The Act was replaced in 1990 by the General Education Act, which supports the work of voluntary associations through subsidies for premises, membership support, etc.

Another sports organisation – the Danish Association of Company Sport

Company sports have existed just as long as the traditional association-organised sports, but the national organisation did not arise until growing public support for sport created a need for an organisation to represent company sports to public authorities and the other sports.

Company sport's biggest problem was that it did not get a share of the government grants for sport, nor did it have the same access to sports centres and pitches as other sports clubs. As a result, company sports wanted to become members of one of the central organisations. As early as 1942, the two Copenhagen company sports associations became members of DDSG&I. But with the formation of the Danish Association of Company Sport (DFIF — Dansk Firmaidræts Forbund) in 1946, the federation applied for membership of DIF. DIF was favourably inclined, but as in previous cases where interdisciplinary federations sought membership, the special federations, and in this case especially the Danish Football Association, were opposed. As a result, DFIF became an independent organisation on a par with other central organisations. For the first five years, DFIF had to take care of itself without public subsidies, and the federation was not given an equal footing with other sports organisations until the revision of the Pools Act in 1976. Nevertheless, company sports have been one of the strongest-growing areas of organised sport.

The popular organisations

As sport spread, an ideological armament in the popular organisations became necessary in order to be able to distinguish themselves from sport under DIF. Important here was the emphasis that the practice of sport should not be an end in itself. Otherwise, the concept "popular" could not be associated with the movement. As activities in the various central organisations have come to resemble each other to an increasing degree, it has become important to be able to differentiate in other ways. The division in the second half of the 20th century became no longer an ideological division between gymnasts and riflemen, but an ideological division between popular activities and sport. By emphasising their popular roots, DDSG&I and DDG had come to resemble one another, just as, in many ways, they had the same foundation in the Grundvigian movement, the Danish Youth Associations (DDU), founded in 1905. Membership of the youth associations had fallen sharply since the war, and in many places the local youth association had been united with the gymnastics association. This also meant that many leaders of popular sport thought it appropriate to consider a merger, as members were to a great extent the same. At the same time, it was considered necessary because, in the opinion of several people, the vision of "the whole person" applied to all three organisations. One of the problems for DDSG&I was, however , that they found that the youth associations were in their eyes too Christianity-oriented. This was a consideration reminiscent of DIF's misgivings at the time KFUM Idræt gained membership. After many negotiations, DDG and DDU finally merged, and the formation of the Danish Gymnastics and Youth Associations (DDGU) took place on 18 July 1964, and DDSG&I continued as an independent organisation.

The period 1970 – 1990

In the late 1960s, Danes had gained social insurance through a modern welfare policy. The strong growth and the mental changes associated with this contributed to the creation of a socially-conscious critical and political youth movement, which established itself particularly within higher study programmes and in many ways became opinion-forming. Besides these movements, there simultaneously arose so-called grass-roots movements, such as "No Nukes"and the "People's Movement against the EEC" although, despite the great efforts of the latter, Denmark became a member of the EEC by a slim majority in 1972.

The growth in public participation in sport continued to rise as an increase in sports facilities with free access and the increasing state and municipal funds provided good opportunities for sports. The many new members, including new groups of young people, children, women and the elderly, did not always feel attracted by the traditional sports clubs. They soon created their own kinds of organisations, through the Trim Movement, street activities such as street basketball, skateboarding, roller skating, private gyms, etc.

Where conditions for elite sport and Sport for All had not formerly been significantly different, clear differences in expectations and requirements developed during the 1970s. For example, the number of elite coaches doubled, new demands were made on methods of qualification and training, which meant increased demands on the economy and, as a result, elite sport began to look for new means of finance and collaborators. The problems were put to a debate and after several years' committee work and analyses of Danish elite sport and various international elite sports models, the *Act on the Promotion of Elite Sport* came into force in January 1985. At the same time, a non-profit institution, *Team Denmark*, was established to take care of the task. Through the law on elite sports, the state and the private sector began to push for professionalisation and commercialisation of Danish sports, which began especially in 1978 with the introduction of professional football.

Team Denmark – a model for elite sport

The Elite Sports Act was ratified in Parliament, and it became Team Denmark's assignment to look after the overall planning of elite sports, to improve utilisation and design of facilities in collaboration with municipalities and county authorities, to promote training and instruction opportunities for elite athletes over the age of 15 years, to promote the results of sports research to instructors, coaches and active athletes, to reinforce consultation and service of sports medicine, to establish support provisions for educational, union/employer and social service for elite athletes, including the provision of necessary consultancy services for these, to provide individual economic support for elite athletes and to look after marketing and sales of rights and benefits in association with elite athletics.

The haziness there had formerly been about society's attitude to elite sports was eliminated with the new law, and this was the starting signal for Danish athletes to assert themselves in international sport. The Act stressed that investment in sport should take place in a socially defensible way, by which it should be understood that active athletes should either be in education and/or in employment, in order to enable them to continue a sensible way of life after the end of their sports careers.

The financing of Team Denmark has to take place through interaction between the state, sport and the business community. This constellation has turned out to be viable and has contributed greatly to the fact that Danish elite athletes have lasted the distance under intensified international competition. The Act and the work of the institution in 2000 have been subject to an evaluation that gave rise to only a few adjustments.

The fusion of the 1990s – and the organisational structure of sport in the 21st century

In DIF, in the period from the organisation's beginning up to about 1990, there was talk about integration of a number of new special federations. For some federations, this happened shortly after their establishment, and for others, such as the Danish Cycling Union, not until 61 years later, partially because of its relationship with tote gambling. These integrations were usually fairly painless, though not for Danish Worker Sport and the YMCA Sports Federation, which led to a long debate about ideology, in which DIF gave a more explicit formulation of the meaning of an ideologically, politically and religiously neutral organisation. Precisely the recognition of sports for their own sake, with activities in the centre, made it relatively simple to take in new members, and thus to capture the multiple opportunities of sport. Thus, at the start of the 1990s, DIF was the central organisation for 54 special federations, each with its own professional sporting identity – but with the ideals of sport and a belief in the intrinsic value of sport as the common estate.

The growth in sports and the desire of all of the organisations to keep up with developments meant that they began to resemble each other more and more. The activities, tournaments, training , etc., could be difficult to separate for the member associations, which were most often members of at least two of the central organisations and often of three. Thus, it was natural that merger ideas were again taken up, as by the DIF chairman, Kai Holm, at the annual meeting of the organisation in 1990. He argued that mergers and increased partnership would be appropriate and to the benefit of associations and active members. He gave some examples of how this could take place, for example, a union of DDGU and DDSG&I and/or a union of the riflemen in DDSG&I and DIF. He considered it unfortunate that a distinction was made in Denmark, in contrast to most other countries in the world, between DIF and the National Olympic Committee (DOK). The discussions dealt with how many sports organisations there should be and who should merge with whom. The result was that five organisations: DDSG&I, DDGU, DIF, DOK and DFIF, became three (two large and one smaller) and besides these also Team Denmark. In November 1992, DDSG&I and DDGU became the Danish Gymnastics and Sports Associations (DGI) and, in February 1993, DIF and DOK became the National Olympic Committee and Sports Confederation of Denmark (Danmarks Idræts Forbund, DIF).

DIF's objectives are still based on the idea that the activities are a means to enlightenment and recognition.

This is a tradition that places it in a conceptual framework of *national* cultural and educational politics that was originally associated with rural areas. On the other side is Denmark's Sports Federation, which looks after both elite sport and Sport for All, associated with a philosophy of activities as a goal in themselves, which places them in an *international* conceptual framework of leisure- and welfare politics that was originally associated with developments in the towns.

Sport in Norway and Sweden, for example, was almost from the start united in a national federation, and discussion about organisations in Denmark in recent years has also dealt with the advantages and disadvantages of a united Danish organisation for sport.

Literature

Trangbaek, Else et al. *Dansk Idraetsliv* (Danish Sporting Life), Gyldendal 1995.

Trangbaek, Else (1989) *Mellem leg og diciplin, Gymnastikken i Danmark i 1800 tallet (Between play and discipline. Gymnastics in Denmark in the 19th century)*. Copenhagen: Auning.

Hansen, Jorn (1997) "Politics and Gymnastics in the Frontier Area post-1848", in *The International Journal of History of Sport*, vol. 14, no. 3, December, pp 25-46.

Eichberg, Henning (1993) "Popular Gymnastics in Denmark: the trialectics of body, culture and nationalism", in *History of European Ideas*, vol. 16, nos. 4-6.

Ibsen, Bjarne (1999) "Structure and Development of Sports Organisations in Denmark", in Heineman, Klaus (ed), *Sport Clubs in Various European Countries*, pp. 241-268.

Jorgensen, Per (1999) "From gymnastics to supermarket. Physical Education in Danish Schools in the 20th Century", in Kruger, A. and Trangbaek, Else, *History of Physical Education and Sport from European Perspectives*, Copenhagen, pp. 27-45.

Trangbaek, Else (1993-94) "Women, body and sport in Denmark at the end of the 19th century", in *Stadion, Internationale Zeitschrift fur Geschichte des Sports*, Academia Verlag, pp. 239-258.

Trangbaek, Else (1996) "Discipline and emancipation through sport. The Pioneers of Women's Sport in Denmark", in *Scandinavian Journal of History*, no. 21, pp. 121-134.

Trangbaek, Else (1996) "Danish gymnastics: what's so Danish about the Danes?" in *The International Journal of the History of Sport*, vol. 13, no. 2, pp. 203-214.

Trangbaek, Else (1997) "Gender in Modern Society: Femininity, Gymnastics and Sport", in *The International Journal of the History of Sport*, vol. 14, no. 3, pp. 136-156.

[i]The first two sections are based on primary sources and literature

[ii]This section is based on a combination of primary sources and literature, but the main references are the two- volume work *Dansk Idrætsliv,(Danish Sportlife)* Gyldendal 1995 – written by Jørn Hansen, Niels Kayser Nielsen, Per Jørgensen, Bjarne Ibsen and Else Trangbæk

Germany

Arnd Krüger

With the exception of the Nazi years, Germany has always been a union of states or a federal state with autonomy in the cultural sphere (such as sport), vested in the single states. Today, after the unification of West Germany (the Federal Republic, FRG) and East Germany (the German Democratic Republic, GDR), it is a Federal Republic with sixteen states. But in the early nineteenth century there were as many as three hundred states in a loose, more or less theoretical Empire that also included present-day Austria, the Czech Republic and Slovakia, Luxemburg, some of northern Italy, northern Croatia and western Poland. The right to educate teachers (and coaches) is a state right. The central government encourages a co-ordination of some sort, but it cannot enforce it. The central government is, however, responsible for national representation even in the cultural sphere (Krüger 1987).

It can be claimed that the current German sport system had its origin in Germany's attempt to prepare for the Olympic Games of 1916 which were supposed to have taken place in Berlin (with the Winter Games in the Black Forest). During a major debate in the national parliament in early 1914 it was agreed that the national government and not the single states were responsible for elite sports, that the single states were, however, in charge of the basis of sport in the clubs. Parliament not only provided money to stage the Games, as had been customary in previous Olympics, but it also sanctioned the state authorities to select the best athletes and prepare them for the Games, as well as paying for national coaches and the administration of elite sports. This division of responsibilities has been the case ever since (Krüger 1991a; 1995).

1. The Foundations

When these decisions were taken by the imperial parliament, the German system of physical education and sport, based on sports clubs and societies, was already one hundred years old and the strongest in Europe in terms of membership. Although riding, shooting, and fencing have an even longer tradition and still celebrate their traditions on a regular basis, particularly with city shooting *Fests*, the larger part of the movement for physical exercise was started as a reaction to the Napoleonic occupation of most of Germany (1792-1815). Friedrich Ludwig Jahn (1778 – 1852), later termed the *Turner* father, brought together high school (*Gymnasium*) and university students to train and raise a guerrilla army against Napoleon and his allies in the name of German nationalism.

Guerrilla warfare had just been "invented" against Napoleon by the Spanish, and Jahn tried to copy this. He therefore used physical exercise – which the educator GutsMuths (1759 – 1839) had recently written about and which Jahn had personally experienced at university – to enable youth to head for the woods and fight Napoleon.

The exercises, therefore, were not geared towards competition, but to personal improvement, skills useful for the guerrilla fighter, like climbing, fencing, zig-zag-running between trees (not sprinting), swimming, horseback riding. These special gymnastics Jahn called *"Turnen"*, the modern- day version of preparing for a *"tournament"*; young people were following the tradition of medieval knights ready to fight for king and fatherland.

Turner clubs were founded in all major cities and university towns. The universities played a particular role as intramural exercises in riding, fencing, vaulting, and dancing had been practiced in the universities since the Middle Ages. Jahn's volunteers were a little late to play a major role in the wars against Napoleon, but they readily took up their civic duty and 'human rights'. At the end of the Napoleonic occupation, the Vienna Congress prohibited the *Turner* clubs (1819 – 42), as the *Turners* had fought not only against Napoleon, but also for German unification, and some even for democracy. Unification would have meant that of the three hundred or so German ruling princes (and some princesses) all but one would have lost their role as heads of state. Jahn was jailed for seven years and then banned from living in or near a town with a university or high school. Of this first wave of clubs, only two survived, one in Mainz and one in Hamburg – insofar as the Free (and liberal) Hanseatic City ignored the decisions of the Vienna Congress just as much as the Archbishop and the liberal citizens of Mainz.

The *Turners* also played a leading role in the German Revolution of 1848/49 as the call for unity and democracy was still dominant. Again, the reactionary forces won, and many German *Turners* emigrated to North and South America (the *Forty-Niners*). The only right that the German citizens gained in that Revolution was the right of free association. Any group of at least seven adults had the right to form a non-profit association (club). These clubs, at first *Turners*, later on all other sports and any other physical activity, have been the basis of the sports movement ever since. Today, the German sports federation has 27 million members organised in about 85,000 clubs, which come together in county associations (again on the basis of an independent non-profit "club"), which form the German sports federation and the individual sports governing bodies; all of them are independent membership organisations according to the rules established in 1848.

After the Revolution the "right to free association" was achieved, but at first it was tightly controlled. The German *Turner* federations of 1848 therefore did not last long, many of the *Turner* Clubs disbanded as they were more interested in the aims of the Revolution than in the gymnastic content of *Turner clubs*. A "political" association was not permitted to have 'youthful' members, i.e. the association had no chance to recruit young new members. A German National *Turner* Federation (DT) was therefore only founded in 1860 when the Turners accepted that an "apolitical" organisation – doing gymnastics only – which did not involve itself in any politics, other than those that were supportive of the government, would have a chance to live and grow. The paradigm that sport and politics do not mix was learned by the *Turner* clubs the hard way, as they were disbanded twice, lost their property twice, lost their chance to recruit young members (under the age of 20) on those occasions when they acted in 'a political manner'. Right up to today, the *Turners* and all sports organisations have insisted, with the exceptions of the Nazi and the GDR years, that their activities have always been "apolitical".

Socialist organisations were, therefore, prohibited to recruit members under the age of 20. Eventually all socialist organisations were banned (1878 – 1890). When the ban was lifted, socialist members left the *Turner* clubs and formed their own worker sports federation. As worker sport was extensive in Germany and well organised, it soon gained considerable importance in the international worker sports federation (Krüger & Riordan 1996).

The other nineteenth century traditions that can still be seen today stem from the *Barrenstreit* legislation (1861-62). Swedish gymnastics were said to be rational, scientific and conducive of good health, and had the potential for military preparation of the gymnast who was learning discipline and fitness. While all over Europe Swedish gymnastics were gaining ground, the Prussian Chamber of Deputies had to decide whether German *Turnen* or Swedish gymnastics should be taught in the Prussian Military Academy. As the graduates of the Academy not only influenced the fitness system of the Prussian army, but through the armed forces all of North German physical education, the Members of Parliament, after hearing many learned opinions, decided that the German system was superior – despite the medical opinion of the rest of Europe. Health, as a major motive for physical education and sport was, therefore, cast out of the German system and only gradually came back in, over a hundred years later in the 1980s. The main aim of *Turnen* was national education and military readiness.

Although a German Empire had been the result of the war against France of 1870/71, the Empire still had as many as thirty-five states, so many things in the cultural sphere were not co-ordinated. The Prussian-dominated Reich was smaller than the cultural entity that had previously been defined as "Germany". This was particularly a problem for Austria, having an Emperor herself, as most of the *Turner* and sports organisation that had formed their federation prior to the declaration of the Empire had members in Austria (which legally included Czechoslovakia) as well. When world sports organisations started to be formed in the last years of the nineteenth century, "Germany" was constantly a problem, as officials insisted that the boundaries of a sports federation ought to be identical to the boundary of a state, while for many federations it was the traditional cultural entity.

Sports (football, athletics, horse racing, etc.) came from Great Britain in the last third of the nineteenth century and were played at first in those parts of Germany that had most contacts with Britain, i.e. the North and West. It also was at first restricted to the classes that enjoyed most contact, i.e. the nobility and merchants. When Pierre de Coubertin tried to revive the Olympic Games, the DT objected in strong terms to German participation because Coubertin was French (the *Turners* hated the French as enemies of the Napoleonic war) and the German Turner Federation (DT) had not explicitly been invited, despite being by far the largest voluntary organisation for physical exercise in the world (with more than one million members). It also objected because it resented individual competition favouring individual attention – in *Turner*

Fests everybody who did better than a certain predetermined result was declared a winner, i.e. sometimes more than fifty percent were proclaimed winners. The young sports organisation, however, formed a National Olympic Committee at the last minute, the imperial household supported the sending of the team financially, and Germany was thus represented quite well from the 1896 Olympics onward in Olympic matters.

Turnen, according to Jahn and later Spiess, were the major physical activity in the school system. In the Great War this system underwent its hardest test as the essence of *Turnen* was readiness for warfare. In the middle of the War, the Imperial War Ministry changed policy. Having favoured *Turnen* above all other exercises, it now recommended sport. It is questionable whether this was the result of the actual superior fitness of the British military, prepared on sporting grounds; it is more likely that it was British military propaganda making use of the symbolism of football that worked on the Germans. This was the beginning of the downward trend of *Turnen* in Germany: never again were they as strong in relative terms as prior to the Great War (having five times more members than all sports combined). But they have remained one of the largest – today second largest behind football – German federations up to the present time.

Another decision immediately prior to the Great War has had an impact up to today: the IOC decided at its Paris session that in the medal table of the Olympic Games – then still officially published by the IOC – a woman's medal should carry the same weight as a man's. The vote was opposed by Coubertin and the French, by the United States, Japan and Turkey (Krüger 1997). In preparations for the 1914 Games, and especially after the War, Germany made every effort to win women's medals. This meant that women were fully and equally integrated into sport. Women had men as coaches and were treated like 'junior men'. Male coaches ignored the medical opinion that women should not engage in competitive sport, just as they had ignored medical opinion about sport being bad for a male athlete's heart (Fenner 1999).

2. The Weimar Years (1918 – 33)

At the end of the Great War the German Emperor abdicated and Germany had its first democracy. In line with the Peace Treaty of Versailles, Germany's armed forces were drastically reduced in strength, Germany lost territory and its colonies, and the country was banned from such international organisations as the League of Nations. In all areas of life there everybody was searching for a new order. There were countless sports organisations which claimed to speak for all Germany, staged "national" championships, and published their own national sports papers. But, according to international rules, only one could be the sports governing body and a member of the international sports federation. There was the same diversity in international sports, 'bourgeois' sports (which called themselves "apolitical"), social democratic sports, communist, Protestant, Catholic, two different Jewish international sports organisations, etc. Many international sports federations excluded Germany until 1925, when it was also admitted into the League of Nations. Only in 1928 was Germany able to participate again in the Olympic Games.

In worker sports, Germany played an important role right from the start as the social democratic as well as the communist international organisations had important German leading officials. When Germany was readmitted to the Olympic Games, it was soon taking a leading role in Europe, coming second to the United States at the 1928 Amsterdam Olympic Games. After the Great War, sports expanded considerably. The bourgeois sports organisations succeeded in uniting (although the *Turners* sometimes abstained) and used their lobbying power to pressure the government into investing heavily in sport. The cities were willing to build huge sports complexes with the muscle power of their unemployed. A Sports Academy was built in Berlin with government approval. A sports space Bill was proposed and, although it was never enacted, it provided a basis for the continued increase in the amount of sports space (football grounds, gym halls, public swimming pools, etc). The Bill called for equal living conditions, defining how much sports space per capita should be available in all of Germany. On the whole, Germany was looking more to the United States for guidance in sport than to any other country. The American way of preparing sports coaches was seen as a model, and American sporting manuals were translated (1991a).

The German-American connection can also be seen in a different field of physical culture: German modern dance was at the centre of modernity (Toepfer 1997). The American Duncan sisters were active in Germany and the openness of German culture influenced the world. German 'openness' went so far that the nudist movement was much more widely accepted than in other countries – often combined with dance and/or sport (Krüger 1991b).

3. The Nazis Years (1933 – 45)

When the Nazis came to power in January 1933, they had no plans for sport, nor a Nazi sports federation. In those areas in which the Nazis did not know what to do, they looked to Fascist Italy where the fascists had been in power since 1925. The Italian model gave elite sport a prominent place in Nazi policies, ensuring a positive image for the Aryan ideal and physical fitness for the war to come, demonstrating the racial superiority of the German people, and achieving a 'culture of consent'. To possess power was one thing, to maintain it one had to win the hearts of the people, and success in sport was one way to do that (Krüger 1998b).

The Nazis "co-ordinated" the sport movement. Each sport was to have only one federation with a *Führer* (leader) who was a Nazi and who had to ensure that this sports federation was run along Party lines. The area of responsibility of the regional federation was to be identical with the political boundaries of the individual states (after 1938, they were called Nazi Party districts – which meant little difference in most cases). Thus, a sport official was responsible for exactly the same area as a government official.

This was new, as traditionally the boundaries of the regional sports associations had grown out of historical necessity. The sports clubs in the centrally located city of Göttingen, for example, belonged to many regional sports associations – in football and athletics to the *West German Ball Playing Association* (seat Duisburg, 300km west, based on the strengths of football), in rowing and canoeing to the *Leine-Weser Gau* (seat

Bremen, 300km north, following the flow of the rivers), in skiing the *Harz-Gau* (seat Braunlage, 60km east, following the mountain ridge), in *Turnen* to the 7th *Turnkreis* (seat Kassel, 40km south, following the lines of road and rail communication). In line with Nazi rules, Göttingen was now in the *Prussian Provincial Sports Association of Hanover* for all sports with its seat in Hanover, the provincial capital, 120 km to the north.

Combining forces meant many organisations being dissolved. The Nazis began to deal with the communists and social democrats directly after coming to power in 1933. All their clubs and associations were prohibited. Individual members could, however, join the "regular" co-ordinated sports clubs. On the whole, most athletes did join, while officials did not. To prevent clandestine socialist organisations inside the sports clubs, the old bourgeois clubs were not permitted to accept more than twenty percent of the socialists as new members. The ideas of worker sport were thus fully integrated in the new clubs, which had its effect after the War.

The Nazi ideology that employers and employees were all working for the same cause became apparent in the founding of the *German Labour Front* (DAF), an organisation which included the former trade unions and the employers' organisations. DAF set up the *Kraft durch Freude* ("Strength through Joy") movement which also took over factory-sponsored sports. Although this seemed to be under tight Nazi control, it was often a place where former worker sports coaches were able to find a new job. It also became the basis for mass tourism in Germany.

Nazism as an ideology assumed that the Aryan race, i.e. the racially pure Germanic people of Germany and Scandinavia, were superior to everybody else, that racial mixture was bad, that German blood should be improved by eugenic means. Positive eugenics meant that people with pure Aryan genes were encouraged to procreate more, while negative eugenics meant that people with what was defined as "inferior" genes were exiled, sterilised or murdered. While eugenics was a theory much used all over the world, the forced practice of it was almost unique to Germany. Much depended upon the different definitions of Darwinism: while in Britain and the United States the survival of the fittest meant of the fittest individual, in Germany it was defined as the fittest race (Krüger 1998a). The state therefore took action to brand weakness a crime, and non-Aryans were to be persecuted. Jews were excluded from the "co-ordinated" clubs; at first this meant an increase in Jewish membership of the Jewish sports clubs. After 1936, owing to emigration and considerable pressure on the Jewish clubs, their numbers decreased, and after 1938 they were closed down. From 1942 onwards Jews were systematically killed – six million in all (Krüger 1999a). It was difficult enough to define what constituted being "Jewish". Gypsies (*Rom*) and *Sinti* were far more difficult to define. Many Gypsies prominent in sport managed to survive – others ended up in concentration camps and were later killed like the Jews.

Protestant and Catholic clubs and federations were dissolved in 1935. Their clubs could continue if they accepted a Nazi as Fuhrer, if not, they also had to disband and their members could individually join official clubs. As of 1936, all youth sections of the sports clubs had to be part of the Hitler Youth, the Nazi Party youth organisation. The national Sports *Führer* was a government and Party official. This finally meant that the long-held notion that sport and politics should not mix was fully abandoned. It also meant that the bourgeois sports federation had gained twenty percent in membership, in all sports there was now only a single German championship and almost all people interested in sports were involved.

The Olympic Games of 1936 had been awarded to Berlin back in 1931. When the Nazis came to power many international sporting groups questioned the wisdom of having the Games under Nazi rule, as the Nazis had proclaimed sport as a means to prepare for war, while the Olympic Games had always assumed a more peaceful role. The Olympics stood for human rights, while the Nazis had utterly ignored human rights early on in their rule. In June 1933, however, the International Olympic Committee (IOC) ruled that the Games should remain in Germany provided IOC members retained the overall say in running the Games and that German Jews had a chance to qualify for the German team.

The Nazi regime invested an enormous amount of money in the Games and gave the Olympics new importance. The Olympics Games of 1932 in Los Angeles had been the first with more than a million spectators, Berlin had 3.7 million. At the Olympic Winter Games in Lake Placid in 1932 there had been fewer spectators than at the Opening Ceremony in the Winter Games at Garmisch-Partenkirchen in 1936 alone. More than 300 million listeners followed the Berlin Olympics on radio throughout the world.

1936 turned out to be a gigantic propaganda success for the Olympics. The question is whether it also served as propaganda for the Nazis. Inside Germany this cannot be denied, as it showed that international organisations could be hoodwinked into believing German peace calls. The IOC was so enthusiastic about the German Games that it gave the Olympic Winter Games of 1940 again to Garmisch-Partenkirchen, as late as in 1939 – after Germany had already invaded Czechoslovakia as a prelude to the Second World War.

The 1920s and 1930s were also a time of the first German *Fräuleinwunder*. German women in sports such as athletics were by far the most successful in the world. At the Women's World Athletics Championships in 1930 (Germany came first with 57 points, Poland second with 26 points, Great Britain third with 19 points), in 1934 (Germany came first with 95 points, Poland second with 33 points, Great Britain third with 31 points) and at the Berlin Olympics, German women dominated events. This was partly thanks to the fact that Germany had started earlier than most other nations with women's sport and that women had not had to fight to build up their own infrastructure; they were fully integrated members – prior to 1933 and in the Nazi period as well. Although the Nazis were reluctant to allow women to compete, as they regarded women's place as being in the kitchen and as mothers of strong future soldiers, the Propaganda Minister Goebbels enjoyed counting medals, as previous ministers had done (Czech 1994; Fenner 1999).

During the Second World War, Germany was active in promoting European sports federations and European championships. There were two strategies: as the majority of countries on the European continent were under the domination of Germany and its allies, European sports federations were directly founded by the pro-Nazi powers.

Britain was always invited and always declined. Then a board was elected which represented only the pro-German Axis powers. If the international federation was under German domination to begin with, then the international federation directly founded a European pro-Nazi section. There were consequently many European championships even as late as 1943.

Sport continued in Germany all through the War. It was one of the few areas of "normality" in which friends could meet. As late as the summer of 1944 professional international cycle races and boxing matches were being held. German championships in almost all sports were also still contested in 1944. Football regulations and other eligibility rules were changed so that players could switch clubs at very short notice, to ensure that they could play when stationed away from home. Club life was maintained, particularly by women and elderly men and those who had been wounded or were in jobs considered indispensable for the war effort (Krüger 1993).

Germany uprooted forty million people in the war. Many foreign workers in Germany lived and slaved under cruel conditions. If they had a chance to engage in sport at all, they hardly mixed with the German clubs.

As a result of total defeat in the War, Germany's cities in the North and West were destroyed. On the other hand, many towns and cities had not been touched at all. Living conditions towards the end of the war varied tremendously, depending upon the degree of local destruction, the distance to the front and allied airfields, the amount of local industry, and the degree of involvement in the local Nazi Party. People strongly identified with the churches were most resistant to Nazism, while much of the political opposition had either gone into exile or had been killed. Collaboration or degree of guilt were hard to identify.

4. Occupied Germany (1945-1949)

The War never managed to kill off sport. There was already rowing on the Rhine and football in the Ruhr before Berlin had signed its unconditional surrender. Sports clubs continued business as usual, provided that the facilities were still useable after bombing raids. The city offices reminded their sports clubs in February 1945 that they should not forget to collect their expenses for coaches and their travel to championships in 1944.

After the War, occupied Germany was split into four zones of occupation, British North-West, Soviet East, American Centre and South, French South-West. The capital city of Berlin was itself divided into the same four sectors surrounded by the Soviet zone of occupation, but for prestige reasons all the powers wanted to have a part of the German capital. At first the four powers agreed on unified arrangements in regard to sport for occupied Germany, i.e. Military Ordinance Number 23 ruled that all sports clubs had to be dissolved by 31 December 1945. New ones could be initiated thereafter.

The way this was executed was quite different from Zone to Zone, however. In the British Zone, it meant that in most cases the sports clubs dissolved themselves on paper only and the very same clubs (dropping the foundation date) founded themselves anew on 2 January 1946 (January 1 being a holiday). Although there were some local variations, as the local occupation officers had the authority to decide, sport was considered by the British as a means for democratic re-education and was therefore encouraged at club level.

In the Soviet Zone the clubs remained closed. Since the sports clubs had become sub-sections of the Nazi Party in 1938, by definition these were Nazi organisations. The Soviet forces were afraid that these could develop into undercover Nazi organisations. This was also influenced by the leaders of German worker sport who had emigrated to the USSR and had now come back to re-organise sports under the dominance of the old worker sports movement. They, therefore, organised sport along the lines of the trade unions and the *Freie Deutsche Jugend* (FDJ), the Communist Party Youth. This had the same results as the inclusion of sporting young people into the Hitler Youth in 1936: you could only participate in competitive sport if you were either in a trade union or in the Party Youth. It therefore eliminated "capitalists" and religious groups from the sports movement (Buss & Becker 2001).

In the West, as the three western zones were soon to be called, nothing much changed. The leaders of the new sports movement were soon the old ones (Nazi or not) if they had survived the war. They retained from the Nazi era the way the sports federations had been regionally co-ordinated. During occupation this turned out to be most expedient inasmuch as the sports leader would address an occupation officer responsible for the same area.

In the summer of 1945 there was little organised sport, but some events took place, such as a triangular track meet between military and ex-military athletes from Germany, Britain and the United States in Andernach, Rhineland. In 1946, in spite of military rules that prohibited sports organisations and tournaments above county (state/district) level, there was a series of German championships in sports like athletics. Football had its first national champions again in 1948. Sport drew enormous crowds. Professional sports boomed. As there was little of substance to buy and after the stress of the war people were looking for simple joys with friends, so they spent a huge amount of money on entertainment – including sport.

The sports organisations grew first at the level of the Zones; in most sports the Western Zones co-operated with each other. It was hard to include the Eastern Zone as there sport was based on different organisational principles. The Western organisations, bearing in mind the war experience, had tried to keep sport and politics apart. In the East it was the opposite. Again all sports leaders insisted that what they were doing was in the best interests of the state.

5. Federal Republic of (West) Germany (1949-1990)

After a lengthy struggle for the reconstitution of West German sport, the German Sports Federation (DSB) was founded in December 1950. It was a compromise between the interests of elite sports represented by the sports governing bodies, and the leisure time sports represented by the state sports federations. It can also be seen as a compromise between those sports leaders who wanted continuity with their previous (Nazi) sport and those who came from worker or religious sports groups who wanted their view of sport to gain more influence. It was by a very slim majority of one vote in parliament that Germany voted for a conservative government, and the same slim majority existed in sport.

A club had to register all its members twice, once through the county (state/district) federation, and again by sport through the respective sports governing bodies. In addition there were several nationally "attached" organisations, like the sports medical professions and federations for specific membership, like Catholic sports, police sports, the naturalist movement, etc. A compromise could be achieved since the National Olympic Committee (NOC) had become a fully independent organisation which was responsible only for German representation at the 1948 London Olympics. That meant that it only had a function for several weeks once every four years, but it had a great deal of prestige. The old sports leaders maintained their influence in the NOC.

Many people who had been active in Nazi sport and had held prominent positions retained or regained their position in the post-war FRG. Karl Ritter von Halt, Hitler's last *Reichssportführer* (1943-45), retained his position as IOC member, became honorary President of athletics and President of the new NOC. Carl Diem, chief representative of international Nazi sport, became Honorary Secretary of the NOC and head adviser to the German government for sport (inside the Ministry of the Interior). On the other hand, a new President of the newly founded DSB was voted into office: Willi Daume. As his professional head administrator (and main ghost writer) he hired, however, Guido von Mengden who had held the same position from 1933 to 1945. The continuity went so far that von Mengden, who had worked extensively in Nazi propaganda for the 1936 Olympics, retained this position on behalf of the German government for the Munich Olympics of 1972, after having already retired from the DSB.

An Olympic Society was founded to spread the Olympic idea. It resurrected the old sports space law and encouraged the construction of sports stadia, in what was called the *Golden Plan*. In view of the destruction of many sport facilities during the war in some areas, it seemed sensible to have equal living and recreational conditions in areas badly and hardly affected by war. The cities received guidelines on how much recreational space was reasonable; eventually it was agreed that there should be two square metres per person.

The DSB had little power at first as it had only small funds available to it. Its main function was that of co-ordination, encouragement and campaigns. Particularly its section "Sport for All" was successful in initiating a series of campaigns to help the clubs increase membership. It initiated the *Trim* movement which was a gigantic success. Table 1 shows the membership in sports clubs within the West German DSB and the DTSB of the GDR. It should be noted, however, that the data represent membership and not members, i.e. if somebody belonged to more than one club, that person was counted more than once. Nobody had a complete list of all members of the sports clubs. Membership figures were reported for insurance purposes and to determine the voting power of the body (See Table 1).

The importance of the sports governing bodies changed somewhat over the years. It is interesting to note that different sports applied different policies concerning their non-competitive membership. While most sports federations asked for the same

Year	Members DSB (millions)	Members DTSB (millions)
1950	3,2	-
1955	3,8	-
1960	5,3	1,4
1965	6,8	1,8
1970	10,1	2,2
1975	13,4	2,6
1980	16,9	3,1
1985	19,3	3,6
1988	20,5	3,7
1990	23,8	-
1995	25,9	-

Table 1. Membership of the DSB and the DTSB

membership dues from all clubs, the *Turners* had very low membership fees so as to maintain a leading role as one of the largest German "sports". Many clubs, therefore, register their non-competitive members as *Turners* for financial – and not ideological – reasons; the reported figures therefore have some flaws.

The DSB succeeded in bringing under one roof everyone having something to do with sports in a very wide sense. Chess and naturalism are regarded as sports. While in chess it is the competitive aspect that plays an important role, in naturalism it is tradition: the nudists joined the co-ordinated Nazi sports movement in 1933 to avoid dissolution as a 'lewd' activity and therefore enjoyed relative freedom in a country where clubs had to be organised in some federation – and retained their 'sports' status after 1945 (Krüger 1991b).

The FRG attempted to participate in the Olympic Games of 1948, but the IOC did not permit this, just as the IOC had refused German participation in the 1920 Games after the Great War. In 1952 the question arose of how many German teams should take part. The *Saarland*, a German industrial province next to the French Lorraine basin, had become an independent political entity under French domination and entered the Olympics with its own team. The Saar was re-integrated into Germany on 1 January 1957 after a referendum in 1955. The FRG asked the IOC if it could participate in the Games as Germany, including the GDR. The GDR asked for two German teams, i.e. a separate representation for the GDR.

In 1952 the GDR was left out as the IOC took the side of its West German members. Avery Brundage, the IOC President, came up with a very American solution that had no German tradition, but was accepted because of its fairness: there should be All-Germany trials for the teams, and the winners would be included in the German team, just as happened in the USA. Whichever side had the majority of team members would have the right to nominate the spokesperson for the team. This was a pro-West decision, with West Germany having three times as many people as the East.

	FRG					GDR			
Year	Gold	Silver	Bronze	Position		Gold	Silver	Bronze	Position
1952	0	7	17	8		-	-	-	-
1956	5	9	6	8		1	4	2	14
1960	10	10	6	4		3	9	7	7
1964	7	14	15	4		3	11	5	8
1968	5	11	10	8		9	9	7	5
1972	13	11	16	4		20	23	23	3
1976	10	12	17	4		40	25	25	2
1980	-	-	-	-		47	37	42	2
1984	17	19	23	3		-	-	-	-
1988	11	14	15	5		37	35	30	2
1992	33	21	28	3		-	-	-	-
1996	20	18	27	3		-	-	-	-
2000	14	17	26	5		-	-	-	-

Table 2: Success in the Summer Olympics after 1948: FRG and GDR

Eventually. However, it was the basis for the success of the GDR and of their system as they worked systematically to gain more places in the team. The results of the FRG and of the GDR in the Summer Olympic Games can be seen in Table 2.

The first major success of Germany after the War came with winning the Football World Cup in Switzerland in 1954. What is more, these were mostly the same people who had fought in the war. Sepp Herberger, the national manager, had been team manager during the Nazi period. In the FRG the football victory was taken as a symbol that Germany was back (*Wir sind wieder wer!*). West German football was only semi-professional at the time and it had won against professionals from Western Europe and the "state-amateurs" from the communist bloc. As of 1963 football became professional in Germany too, when the *Bundesliga* was introduced. This helped Germany to make it to the final of the Football World Cup in 1966, losing only by a disputed goal to England.

The FRG received the right to stage the 1972 Summer Olympic Games in Munich. As the FRG had not done too well in the 1964 Olympics, several steps were taken to improve the standing of elite sports: a sports aid foundation was created to support financially the best athletes and those that were likely to become the best in future. East European standards were applied and the athletes were placed into the categories of 'Cadre' A (top 8 at the last Olympic Games or World Championships), B (additional number of top athletes needed to have twice the number that may be entered in the Olympic Games), and C (two times A+B). A-Cadres were able to live from Foundation money in spite of the claim that they were all amateurs. The Soviet bloc was also copied in another field: as of 1970 (1971 for draftees) the German military had special units for elite sport in which athletes did three months basic training followed by training in their respective sport.

A central agency was set up within the DSB to co-ordinate elite sport. This "Federal Committee for the Advancement of Elite Sport" (BAL) was an element inside the FRG that was alien to tradition, as it required a degree of centralisation that was not there in a federal system. Yet with the help of government money (the Ministry of the Interior had remained in charge since 1914), it succeeded in applying East European training theory to elite sports. The former Secretary General of Polish Sport, Tomasz Lempart, was hired to ensure the highest standards of East European knowledge. With the Berlin Wall separating the two Germanys since 1961, it was next to impossible to lure somebody from the GDR to the FRG, as it was exceedingly dangerous to cross the divide. BAL organised coach education, a journal for coaches, a coaching academy, scientific training, and the application of research to the actual training process. It was therefore able to halt the decline in West German performance internationally.

The 'cultural revolution' of 1968/69 had its effect on sport too. The European Athletics Championships in Athens in 1969 were boycotted by the West German team. The East German world record holder Jürgen May had been paid by Puma (all the GDR was an *Adidas* country) to run in their shoes at the 1966 European championships. He was banned by the GDR as a "professional" but fled to the West. Although the ban was lifted, he was not permitted to compete for the FRG for three years after changing citizenship. This was poorly explained to the West German team who had learned on their way to Athens that their team-mate might not be able to compete. The team therefore took a vote without consulting the management and decided not to compete if Jürgen May was banned. Although the International Federation explained the situation, the team took a second vote and boycotted the competition. This resulted in the President of the Athletics Federation not standing for re-election (he had lied to the team and called them a bunch of *Chaoten*). Henceforth a male and a female athlete, as spokespersons of the team (and as a consequence, in all other sports), were represented on the national board (Krüger 1999e).

The Munich Olympic Games started on an extremely friendly note. But Willi Daume, Chairman of the Organising Committee, fell victim to his own ideology and carelessness. Assuming that there was something like an Olympic truce as in antiquity, he disregarded all advice on tighter security at Olympic sites, including the Olympic Village. It was more difficult to enter the female section of the Olympic Village from the men's side than to enter the men's section from the outside. A Palestinian terror group thus climbed over the fence unnoticed at night and attacked the Israeli apartment in the men's section of the Olympic Village.

As the Israelis had expected such an attack (the Israeli press had been full of articles prior to the attack about the lax security in Munich), only those in the team on active military duty or in the secret service remained in the apartment, while most of the athletes were with friends spread all over the city of Munich – no more than one person with a friend to make an attack unlikely. Two Israelis were shot in the attack. Nine were kept hostage. In a shootout with incompetent Bavarian police, all the Israeli hostages and two Palestinians were killed. The favourable impression which the Olympic Games were intended to have was thus spoiled, but it did demonstrate that Germany was not a police state any more as it had been in the Nazi era. It also spoiled the chances of Willi Daume, one-time Vice-President of the IOC, to become President of that body.

The Munich Olympics was a time of the second German *Fräuleinwunder,* with German women winning more medals than the men in major sports like athletics. What is more, this second generation of *Fräuleinwunder* – despite still being trained by male coaches – made their way into all sorts of leadership positions: Liesel Westermann, discus champion, became sports spokesperson for the German Liberal Party, and a member of a state parliament, Ingrid Mickler-Becker, long jump and pentathlon champion, became a conservative MP and a junior minister in a state government, Heide Rosenthal, pentathlon and long jump champion, became Vice-President of the Athletics Federation and a successful businesswoman.

The IOC also started to tighten drug control from 1972. Dr. Manfred Donike, head of West German drug control, started to develop many of the techniques that are now used internationally. The Federal Government invested heavily in drug control and Germany was subsequently also one of the first countries to ensure out-of-competition testing on a regular basis, from 1990. This did not stop the use of performance enhancing drugs. Since some of the most popular sports, like professional tennis, football and motor racing, have their own far more lenient doping codes, there is no German anti-drug law specifically for sport. Over the years this has resulted in an endless discussion about drug-taking as an unethical practice, on the one hand, and the individual human right to do what one pleases with one's body, on the other. The Federal Government, irrespective of political orientation, has supported all national and international anti-drug regulations and initiatives.

In 1974, the FRG organised the Football World Cup and became champions. This was the glorious period of German football as the team around Franz Beckenbauer also won the European title in 1972 and came second in Europe in 1974 behind Czechoslovakia.

Even if the results of elite sport were not always as good, the FRG was often called upon to stage international tournaments as it had excellent facilities, expert management, and plenty of Federal money for sport as a means of national representation. When it came to the 1980 Moscow Olympics, however, the DSB and the National Olympic Committee well understood the golden *Zügel* (harness) on which it was hanging. The US government called for a boycott of the Moscow Olympics after the Soviet invasion of Afghanistan. Instead of supporting the Afghan people with arms against their invaders (which the US did later on), President Carter called for a token reaction: boycott of the Moscow Olympics. Sixty-three teams eventually boycotted the Games or abstained from going, 16 of the 81 teams entering the stadium at the opening showed their protest in some other form. The boycott was mainly carried out by Muslim countries like Afghanistan or staunch American allies like the FRG. The sports movement did nothave the strength of will to resist government pressure. Sport was receiving too much public funding to give that up for something as "trivial" as the rights of athletes to take part in "their" Olympics. All the athletes voted to go, but a 59:40 majority on the NOC voted against going. A compromise, like going and protesting, as Britain did, was not even discussed. In Germany compromise was considered a weakness.

When amateurism at the Olympics was brought to an end by the IOC Congress in Baden-Baden in 1981, athletes in the FRG did not profit as much at first as those in other countries, as sham-amateurism had been present in most sports anyway. After the cultural revolution of 1968/69, the implicit discrepancies of sport were publicly discussed, with sham-amateurism being one such issue.

The pressure on young children to do well, particularly in sports like gymnastics, figure skating and swimming, was publicly castigated as child labour. The totalitarian if not fascist-type character of elite sport was a third issue that raised doubts about the feasibility of elite sports (Ofstad 1989; Tännsjö & Tamburrini 2000). Yet, being neighbours to the GDR system helped to overcome most of these arguments: there was a mutual consensus in the population that the FRG should do as well as the GDR – if not better. The GDR claim that its sport system demonstrated that socialism was superior to capitalism in managing human resources was a constant thorn in the flesh of the FRG. This ensured a constant flow of government money into elite sport.

6. German Democratic Republic (1949-1990)

The GDR had started with worse conditions than had the FRG. While the FRG received Marshal Plan Aid, the Soviet occupation forces dismantled many useful things, like train lines and factories and transported them to the Soviet Union as reparations for the devastation the German Army had caused. While the FRG continued to use the expertise of Nazi sport leaders, teachers and coaches, the GDR tried to replace all Nazis. This meant, on the one hand, that young people had a chance to succeed, and, on the other, that it took some time before the gap between young and old was closed. In 1950 GDR sports took off. The sports movement, the German Federation of *Turnen* and Sports (DTSB) was formed, co-operating closely with the Communist Party and the Government. It was structured as in the Nazi era – only with many opposite political ideas. A German College for Physical Culture (DHfK) was built on the Soviet model in Leipzig, Soviet scientists and coaches brought their expert knowledge and athletes were concentrated in training centres sponsored by state-owned companies. GDR sportspeople could therefore start much earlier as state amateurs in most sports than in the FRG. Research into elite sport was concentrated in a small number of centres and research issues were co-ordinated.

The grip of the Communist Party steadily grew tighter. In 1952, the five regional states which had constituted the GDR were abolished and replaced by fourteen administrative districts and a central government. The population was pressured into more productivity, while at the same time leaving the GDR was made more difficult – yet still possible. In 1953, public protests occurred in several cities, but the protests were crushed within a few days by Soviet tanks. As nobody from the West intervened, it became obvious to the population of the GDR that they had been abandoned by the West. The liberation rhetoric of the FRG was nothing but hot air. East and West each had its own territory and had to make the best of it. In most of the GDR, the reception of FRG radio and television was possible, which ensured that in many ways the GDR public was under a strong Western influence.

From 1960 a dragnet for talent selection was used all over the GDR to seek young talent in the schools, to make sure that nobody was left out. With the building of the Berlin Wall in 1961, the authorities made sure that talent could be preserved and would not disappear into the FRG. Competition with the FRG for places in the joint Olympic team had its logical result: while at first sports considered 'bourgeois', like tennis, golf, riding etc., it was now a question of 'medal intensity'. In a sport like ice hockey you need eighteen players for one medal, while for the same ice space speed skaters could win twelve times as many medals. Particularly gymnastics, athletics and swimming were thus favoured, as they provided the best chance to win plenty of medals. Today, the same questions are still being discussed in the united Germany.

GDR sport is best remembered today for the quality of talent selection, the coaches, and the doping system. In terms of talent selection the first talent was scouted for in kindergartens which had mandatory physical exercise classes. Gymnasts were selected before primary school. In primary school, every year talent tests were made according to the principles applied for particular sports or groups of sports. This had cruel, but logical consequences for the school curriculum, e.g., if your hands and feet were not big enough to have a talent for swimming, why teach that child swimming? Pool time was limited and reserved for "talent". With small hands and feet you could only learn to swim with your parents in a lake in the summer.

Once you were identified as a "talent" you were placed in a group that received three to four times training sessions a week (six to eight hours). If you developed well in such an intensive children's group, you had the chance to go to a children's and youth sports school (KJS). After 1961, one other requirement for being accepted into such a privileged school was that you had to have few if any contacts with relatives in the FRG, to make sure that the training knowledge remained "secret". Parents loved the KJS and so did the children. It provided expert coaching and teaching in privileged groups much smaller than in the regular school system. While most students only attended school for ten years, the chances of an academic career were much better if you attended such a privileged KJS where your teachers received extra pay for every pupil that passed the final examination. Children therefore trained hard seven days a week from the age of 14 in most sports, and still finished school with high marks.

In winter sports the holidays were reversed — long holidays in winter and short ones in summer. The school curriculum was adapted to training and competition needs. If you did not keep up academically, you received expert tutoring. If you did not keep up with the training and performance schedule, you were relegated to the regular school system, but were often retained by the local sports organisation as a potential voluntary club coach. If you were successful, you were advised about the kind of jobs most suitable and best compatible with the sports career. While in general the GDR public was treated quite roughly, top athletes were pampered (Teichler & Reinartz 1999).

At first sport was used to show the flag and display an international presence. The then Communist Party Chairman Walter Ulbricht talked about his "diplomats in track suits". Competition with the FRG was the main event of the year. Apart from national team rivalry, there were many club competitions up to 1961, when the Wall went up and made future competition impossible. Most of the Olympic trials of 1964 were therefore held in Sweden and Czechoslovakia, as the GDR did not want them in West Germany at all. The 1968 team was the first in which there were no internal German selection competitions – after all, the GDR had had the privilege of providing the team spokesman in 1964, and that was not the way the FRG wanted to be represented.

The education of coaches was also put in the hands of the DHfK. While in the FRG the DSB prepared coaches itself, being sceptical about an educational system that discouraged early specialisation and elite sports, the GDR system was well co-ordinated. A coach received a university education in coaching. A central research institute provided the expert research and its application for the needs of respective athletes. An open and a "secret" periodical was published to ensure that all scientific knowledge on elite training was sufficiently widespread, but would not leak out either to the West or to the East.

Secrecy was also secured by the GDR having an all-embracing system of spying on its own population. The *Stasi* convinced many that it was better to co-operate than to resist. In some areas every tenth person was a secret collaborator of the *Stasi*. Most of the detailed knowledge about drug-taking in the GDR does not come from the formal sports sources (as they destroyed most of it in late 1989), but from *Stasi* files. Of course, the *Stasi* also shredded many important files – but while doping was important for sport, it was not for the *Stasi*, which was involved in far more criminal activities (Teichler & Reinartz 1999).

Research included the use of all manner of "supporting measures". This included not only legal supplements, electro-myostimulation and the like, but also illegal doping. This was particularly the case with anabolic steroids which help to increase muscular strength and the speed of recuperation from training workouts. Too many steroids are dangerous for the body, particularly the liver. The system was so efficient that a liver test was eventually included in the talent selection process: if you wanted to become a top-class athlete in any power, strength, speed or endurance sport you were supposed to take steroids. If your weak liver would not stand it, you were dropped from the system before entering a KJS. After German unification doctors and coaches were put on trial for the doping of minors; in the case of adults it was impossible to sue as injury incurred by mutual consent is not a misdemeanour. Suicide is not a crime. In the 1976 Olympic Games the tiny (fewer than 17m people) GDR did even better than the USA. It was the first Olympic Games with thorough drug control, but GDR athletes were better at beating the system since their medical system fully supported them with 'masking' agents.

To assess the true position of the GDR, it is better to examine the 1972 Olympics. Here the use of steroids and other substances that were later banned (with the exception of amphetamines) was still legal. So there was a reasonable level playing field. The GDR came third behind the USSR and the United States, but ahead of the FRG and the rest of the world.

After 1981 the GDR lost some of its advantage in international sports. The state amateur lost out to the Western professional. The head start made by the GDR in drugs was gradually reduced. After all, medical substances were hardly ever invented in the GDR – they were just applied there more thoroughly. The next generation of training aids was no longer affordable by the GDR. The GDR boycotted the Los Angeles Olympics in 1984, following the example of the USSR.

On the whole, the GDR sport system was extremely expensive as a vast number of people were put at the disposal of elite sport. After 1984, the GDR government started to realise the financial burden of the huge (unproductive) secret service, the many border guards, the privileged working conditions of many – including in the sports system. The economy was gradually crumbling as it could not maintain the burden of keeping up with international standards.

The labour unrest in Poland (*Solidarity*), *Perestroika* and *Glasnost* in the USSR and similar developments in the rest of the Eastern Bloc resulted in the tearing down of the Wall in 1989 and German unification one year later. In 1989 the two German sports federations, DSB and DTSB, negotiated the terms of sport after unification. Eventually, these negotiations were given up as it was clear that the GDR would not join the FRG as a monolithic state, but that the GDR would subdivide itself into its traditional five regions which would enter the FRG individually. So the DTSB would not be a negotiating partner; rather it would become the central sports agency for the entire country.

7. Federal Republic of Germany (1990 – 2002)

The Treaty of Unification between the two Germanys mentioned sport only in one paragraph. The FRG was keen to maintain the erstwhile GDR Central Research Unit for elite sport (FKS) and guaranteed its continuation, but he DTSB, the DHfK, the KJS, everything that had made GDR sport a world power was dismantled. The DHfK was converted into the Faculty of Sports Science of the University of Leipzig, and the contracts of about two thirds of the staff were terminated. The new FRG now has 67 departments or faculties of physical education or sports science and one Sports University in Cologne. The FKS has also since been dismantled with two thirds of staff contracts being terminated. A period did exist, up to 1992, when there was still a liberal exchange of ideas and joint conferences on drug use which were federally funded. The main question to be resolved was how to merge the two systems of drug use, that were not compatible.

The GDR had had a centrally-planned and co-ordinated system that used steroids as a regular training aid, on the whole starting with athletes three years younger than in the FRG. Steroids in the FRG were the responsibility of the individual training group and were generally not applied to minors. This made it difficult for the coaches to select talent for the national junior "C-Cadre". Do you select the best athletes who had already been on steroids for three years or those who had no experience of steroids? Who would be the best athletes in four years time, at the next Olympics? As these questions could not be agreed upon, a double Cadre system, one from the East and one from the West, was maintained (with twice the number of coaches) from 1990 to 1992.

After 1992, the number of coaches was reduced to "normal", i.e. in the former GDR, nine out of ten coaches were fired and either went to teach in school, went to coach abroad, or competed for jobs inside Germany. Severe infighting for well-paid coaching jobs started in which it was customary to call the job applicant a *"Fachdoper"* (expert in doping), to gain an advantage in employment.

On the whole, the sports system of the old FRG was perpetuated in the new Germany. While the GDR had a number of laws regulating sports, there has been no federal sports law either in the old FRG or in the new Germany. Only three of the "old" eleven states of the FRG and all of the five "new" ones from the GDR have regulated sports with the help of state sports laws. Now that the advantages of the old GDR system are mainly gone, the new system is still in the forefront of world sport, but back to where the old FRG was. There is, however, one main difference: now that the immediate competitor next door has gone, there is far less government money being put into elite sport. The rivalry between the political systems had attracted much of the funding: no rivalry – no funds. Thus, school physical education has been gradually declining in the past ten years from close to three hours weekly to little more than two hours per week. Previously, the use of public sports facilities by local non-profit clubs was free. Then service charges were asked for cleaning and hot water, now rent for facilities has become the rule rather than the exception.

The enormous amount of money available in some sports has not stood the test of time in all sports represented in the Olympic Games. Sponsorship money mainly goes to those sports that obtain the biggest media exposure. In Germany this is football. In the Boris Becker and Steffi Graf years, tennis also played a major role; with their decline the interest in tennis has also declined. With the post-modern emphasis on fun and instant gratification the traditional individual sports, such as gymnastics, swimming, and athletics, are losing much of their popularity. American sports, like baseball, American football, and inline skating, are increasing in popularity, while women's gymnastics has turned into aerobics.

Yet, despite a growth in the number of commercial sports enterprises, particularly for fitness, well being and aerobics, the DSB is still increasing in membership; it is the largest membership organisation in the FRG, bigger than the trade unions or the churches.

The size of an organisation is no guarantee of success. While previously all Olympic sports were supported by federal and state money, a greater degree of accountability is having its consequences. To centralise Olympic efforts, Olympic training centres were formed in 1987. The inclusion of the GDR meant that their top facilities were available, bringing the total number up to twenty. The number of centres is now being reduced as some have not been successful, and sports being financially supported in full are being cut.

The successful model of football – with little if any government interference, a pyramid system, talent selection by the top clubs, payment for clubs at the bottom for the talent they produce – is still unique. All the rest rely on government money – more than in 1914, but still according to the same rules co-ordinated through the same ministry.

The diversity of the sixteen German states, the willingness to co-ordinate and to encourage, but not to rule, have given the DSB the strength to adapt to all times and major trends. Sport today is the twentieth biggest industry in Germany, with more people employed in it than in the banks and the petro-chemical industry. About 1.5 percent of the gross national product comes from sport and related exterprises, a slightly smaller percentage than in Great Britain since much more is done in Germany by volunteers, unpaid or underpaid people. It falls far short of the 2.4 percent of Italy. In absolute terms it is around 36 billion DEM (about 18 billion Euro). While sport as a major part of the service industry is rapidly increasing in size and in number of people employed, the traditional industries are shrinking. There is, however, one major trend which is changing the perspective of sport.

The German sports system has traditionally been a vast, voluntary, non-profit organisation with plenty of unpaid helpers. Their number is gradually decreasing, while membership is still increasing. This means that membership fees are going up rapidly as the non-profit clubs have to hire full-time staff, while previously voluntary officials, helpers and coaches were in charge. The club basis is, however, sound and solid. Sports grounds and playing fields are in good shape in the western part of the country, as the old rules of the *Golden Plan* are still applied. A *Golden Plan East* has not been passed, but with the help of federal money the size and quality of sports space in the former GDR is also being improved.

When will there be equal conditions in sport and recreation between East and West? On the whole, income in the East is still only 85 percent of the West, the unemployment rate is almost twice as high in the East than in the West, now called the "old" and the "new" states (*Länder*). The German Sydney Olympics team contained 35 athletes who were born abroad, 160 were born in the former GDR, and 232 in the former FRG, showing that proportionally the GDR-phenomenon is still present. 61.4 percent of all medals won by Germans in Sydney 2000 were still the result of the GDR system. A "GDR team" would still have come eleventh in Sydney, while a FRG team would have come 21st. The results also show that Germany is willing to give a German passport to an athlete much more readily than to an ordinary migrant worker.

In the East there are still more 'hungry' athletes who do not have too many opportunities to rise to national or international prominence except through sport. In Italy, 130 years after Italian unification, one can still see the differences between the former states. Is the German *mezzogiorno* in the East? Nobody knows how long this will be visible in Germany. Sport, as the only area in which the GDR was superior to the FRG in the application of research and elite sport, has an opportunity to be the first sphere in which equal living conditions between East and West will be achieved.

Literature

Buss, W. and Becker, C. (2001) (eds), *Der Sport in der SBZ und frühen DDR (1945 – 1965).* Schorndorf: Hofmann.

Czech, M. (1994), *Frauen und Sport im nationalsozialistischen Deutschland. Eine Untersuchung zu weiblichen Sportrealität in einem patriarchalen Herrschaftssystem.* Berlin: Tischler.

Fenner, A. (1999), The first German *Fräuleinwunder.* Early development of women's athletics in Germany, in: E. Trangbaek and A. Krüger (eds), *Gender and Sport from European Perspectives*. Copenhagen: University of Copenhagen, 97-114.

Krüger, A. (1987), 'Sieg Heil' to the most glorious era of German sport: Continuity and change in the modern German sports movement, in: *International Journal of the History of Sport* 4 (1987), 1, 5 – 20.

Krüger, A. (1991a), 'We are sure to have found the true reasons for the American superiority in sports'. The Reciprocal Relationship between the United States and Germany in Physical Culture and Sport, in: R. Naul (ed), *Turnen and Sport. The Cross-Cultural Exchange*. New York/Münster: Waxmann, 51-82.

Krüger, A. (1991b), There goes this art of manliness. Naturism and social hygiene in Germany, in: *Journal of Sport History* 18 (1991), 1, 135-58.

Krüger, A. (1993), Germany and Sport in World War II, in: *Canadian Journal of the History of Sport* 24 (1993), 1, 52-62.

Krüger, A. (1995), 'Buying victories is positively degrading'. The European origins of Government Pursuit of National Prestige through Sports, in: *International Journal of the History of Sport* 12 (1995), 2, 201-18.

Krüger, A. (1997), Forgotton Decisions. The IOC on the Eve of World War I, in: *Olympika* 6 (1997), 85-98.

Krüger, A. (1998a), A Horse Breeder's Perspective: Scientific Racism in Germany. 1870 – 1933, in: N. Finzsch & D. Schirmer (eds), *Identity and Intolerance. Nationalism, Racism, and Xenophobia in Germany and the United States*. Cambridge: University Press, 371-96.

Krüger, A. (1998b) The Role of Sport in German International Politics. 1918 - 1945, in: P. Arnaud & J. Riordan (eds), *Sport and International Politics. The Impact of Fascism and Communism on Sport*. London: Spon, 79-96.

Krüger, A (1999a), 'Once the Olympics are through, we'll beat up the Jew'. German Jewish Sport 1898 – 1938 and the Anti-Semitic Discourse, in: *Journal of Sport History* 26 (1999), 2, 353-75.

Krüger, A. (1999b) Breeding, Rearing and Preparing the Aryan Body: Creating the Complete Superman the Nazi Way, in: *International Journal History Sport* 16 (1999), 2, 42-68.

Krüger, A. (1999c), Strength through joy. The culture of consent under Fascism, Nazism and Francoism, in: J. Riordan & A. Krüger (eds): *The International Politics of Sport in the 20th Century*. London: Spon, 67-89.

Krüger, A. (1999d), The Homosexual and Homoerotic in Sport, in: J. Riordan & A. Krüger (eds), *The International Politics of Sport in the 20th Century*. London: Spon, 191-216.

Krüger, A. (1999e), A Cultural Revolution? The Boycott of the European Athletics Championships by the West German Team in Athens 1969, in: CESH (ed): *Proceedings Fourth Annual Conference*, vol. 1. Florence: ISEF, 162-6.

Krüger, A. and Riordan, J. (eds) (1996), *The Story of Worker Sport*. Champaign, Ill.: Human Kinetics.

Leistungssport, [Special edition Sydney Results] 31 (2001), 1.

Ofstad, H. (1989), *Our Contempt for Weakness. Nazi Norms and Values – and our own*. Gotheburg: Almquist & Wiksell.

Tannsjo, T. and Tamburrini, C. (eds) (2000), *Values in Sport*. London: Spon.

Teichler, H. J. and Reinhartz, K. (eds) (1999), *Das Leistungssportsystem der DDR in den 80er Jahren und im Prozeß der Wende*. Schorndorf: Hofmann.

Toepfer, K. (1997), *Empire of Ecstasy. Nudity and Movement in German Body Culture, 1919 – 1935*. Berkeley: University of California Press.

The Soviet Union and Eastern Europe

James Riordan and Hart Cantelon

Introduction

Communist sports policy in Europe is dead. It lives on in China, Cuba and North Korea. It was not everywhere identical; nor did it feature highly in terms of national priorities in the less economically advanced communist nations, such as Albania, Vietnam and Cambodia. Nevertheless, it did contain certain discernible similarities that marked it off from sports policies elsewhere in both the economically developed and the less economically developed world. It is these similarities that this chapter examines, as well as the implications of the rapid *volte-face* in sport in virtually all the erstwhile communist states following the revolutions in 1989 throughout Eastern Europe.

The rapid collapse of Soviet-style communism in Eastern Europe and of the nine nations there that subscribed to it (with variations in Albania and Yugoslavia on the totalitarian or *state socialism* model) provides an opportunity to examine the communist sports policies and the impact they had on popular perceptions about sport.

One reason for virtually universal interest in communist sport was that its success, particularly in the Olympic Games, drew considerable attention and admiration. The Soviet Union and the German Democratic Republic (East Germany) provided exciting competition with the USA and West Germany, as did other East versus West, communist versus capitalist sports competitions.

A less remarkable, though perhaps more far-reaching, aspect of communist sport, however, was the evolution of a model of sport or *physical culture* for an industrial modernising society. Sport was employed for utilitarian purposes to promote health and hygiene, defence, labour productivity, integration of a multi-ethnic population into a unified state; what might be called *nation building*. These states sought international recognition and prestige through sports competition. They were admirable objectives. After all, with the exception of East Germany and, partly, Czechoslovakia, communist development was initially based on a mass illiterate, rural population. And subsequently, it was this model that had some appeal for nations in Africa, Asia and Latin America.

In most communist states, therefore, sport had the quite revolutionary role of being a catalyst for social change, with the state political leadership as pilot. In any case, after revolution or liberation, there was rarely a leisure class around to promote sport for its own purposes, as there was say, in Victorian England.

Furthermore, partly under the influence of Marxist philosophy that stressed the interdependence of the mental and physical states of human beings, many communist states emphasised the notion that the physical was as vital as the mental in human cultural development. Physical culture was important both for the all-round development of the individual and, ultimately, for the collective health of society. In the classic statement on this subject back in 1917, the year of the Russian Revolution, Mao Zedong actually placed physical culture *before* mental culture:

Physical culture is the complement of virtue and wisdom. In terms of priorities, it is the body that contains knowledge, and knowledge is the seat of virtue. So it follows that attention should first be given to a child's physical needs; there is time later to cultivate morality and wisdom (Zedong, 1962:p.3).

Major Priorities in Sport Policies

Sport, or rather physical culture, then, had particular social and political significance in the development of communist societies. This is all the more so because the place of sport had been more central in their social systems and controlled and directed by the state. The following would seem to be the main state priorities assigned to sport in communist development.

1. Nation-building

All communist states faced problems of political stabilisation and of economic and social development. Some were confronted with the serious problem of national integration of ethnically-diverse populations into a newly unified state. A key issue here is that of nation-building: the inculcation of political loyalties to the nation as a whole. The bounds of kinship, race, language, religion, and geographical location were to be transcended. Not only was this a key problem facing post-revolutionary Russia (and China and Cuba), it has been equally relevant to post-liberation industrial modernising states in Africa and Asia.

What better than sport to help the regimes in such societies promote the building of strong nation states? After all, sport with its broad relevance to education, health, culture, and politics, and its capacity to mobilise people (predispose them towards change), may uniquely serve the purpose of nation-building and help foster national integration. Arguably, sport extends to and unites wider sections of the population than probably any other social activity. It is easily understood and enjoyed. Organised sports competition transcends social, economic, educational, religious, and language barriers. Sport is cathartic, permitting some emotional release (reasonably) safely. It can be relatively cheap and it is easily adapted to support educational, health and social welfare objectives.

And it is here that the sports introduced by Westerners at the turn of the century in Russia, Poland and the Baltic states, parts of East and Central Europe, have some advantages over the indigenous folk games of these regions. The latter are often linked to annual festivals in the various local communities. Indigenous sports have, therefore, served mainly as a means of expressing selected ethnic or communal identity. Organised competitive sports have served as a means of expressing a national identity. So it was modern sports that the communist nations took up and promoted.

2. Integration

Bound up with nation-building was the state-desired aim of integrating a multinational population, often in transition from a rural to an urban way of life, into the new nation state. Many communist societies were loose confederations of diverse ethnic groups: different races, languages, traditions, religions, stages of economic growth, prejudices. Consider the former USSR (the old Russian Empire with some modifications).

The USSR was a multinational federation of over 290 million people comprising a hundred or more nationalities. The country was divided into 15 Union Republics (now independent nations), each based on separate ethnic groups, and many other administrative divisions (autonomous republics, autonomous regions, territories, national areas). In Soviet schools children studied in as many as 87 different languages and daily newspapers came out in 64 languages.

The Soviet government quite deliberately took Western sports from town to country and from the European metropolis to the Asiatic interior, using sport to help integrate the diverse peoples into the new nation and to promote a patriotism that transcended petty nations and ethnic affiliation.

In Soviet history, for example, even before the Civil War (1917-21) was over, the new Soviet regime organised the First Central Asian Games in the ancient Islamic centre of Tashkent, in October 1920. This was actually the first time in history that Uzbeks, Kazakhs, Turkmenians, Tadzhiks, Kirgiz, as well as Russians, Ukrainians and other Europeans, had competed in any sporting event together. As Rodionov made clear later, "the integrative functions of sport are immense. This has great importance for our multinational state. Sports contests, festivals, spartakiads and other forms of sports competition have played a key role in cementing the friendship of Soviet peoples" (Rodionov, 1975:7).

As we shall see below, the integrating functions of sport are just as clearly evident when the competitive elements are added: in the case of the USSR these became important from the end of the 1920s. Both internally and externally sport was used to mobilise people in ways which actively contributed to the raising of group consciousness and solidarity, goals explicitly favoured by the leadership.

3. Defence

Since many communist states were born in war and lived under the constant threat of war, terrorism and subversion, it is hardly surprising that defence was a prime consideration. Sport, therefore, was often subordinated to the role of military training. In some countries the system was best described as the *militarisation of sport*. The role of the military in sport was further heightened by centralised control of sports development. Even before the Russian Revolution, however, Russia had military personnel playing a prominent role in sports administration, largely because of the country's geopolitical situation and history of foreign invasion. It has to be remembered that the Soviet Union had extensive borders with twelve foreign states—six in Europe and six in Asia. Further, even in relatively recent times the nation lost immense numbers of people in wars. For example, tsarist Russia lost 4 million persons in World War I and a staggering 44 million Soviet citizens were killed in World War II, far and away the greatest human war losses in history.

In the Soviet Union, as well as certain other communist states (e.g. North Korea and Cuba), the sports movement was initially the responsibility of the armed forces and even recently was dominated by instrumental defence needs of military or paramilitary organisations. All the communist nations had a nation-wide fitness programme with a bias towards military training, modelled on the Soviet *Prepared for Work and Defence (GTO)* system——originally taken from the standards set by Baden Powell for the Boy Scout *marksman* and *athlete* badges and significantly called by Powell *Be Prepared for Work and Defence.*

Even in a relatively industrially advanced country like East Germany, albeit a *front line state*, it was the Soviet military-oriented fitness system that was employed, particularly for young people. Childs writes about the former GDR sports system:

The performance objectives of the sport and physical educational programmes are based on the requirements of a graded sports badge, the pattern of which was adopted from the Soviet Union . . . Initially this badge carried the imposing title of 'Ready to Work and Defend Peace' and was heavy with militaristic and ideological requirements . . . (it has since become) 'Ready to Work and Defend the Homeland' (Childs, 1978:78).

All communist and some non-aligned states had a strong military presence in the sports movement through armed and security forces' clubs. This connection provided military sinecures for more-or-less full-time athletes and, at times, established direct military supervision over sport and physical education, such as in the USSR in the periods 1918-22 and 1940-46. There was also an international link through the Sports Committee of Friendly Armies, set up in Moscow in 1958.

In many communist states, therefore, the armed and security forces provided much of the funding and facilities that enabled people to take up and pursue a sport, especially full-time and in sports involving expensive and/or scarce equipment (ice hockey, soccer, gymnastics, weightlifting, equestrianism). The military clubs thereby helped to ensure that as many people as possible were physically fit, mentally alert and possessed the qualities (patriotism, will-power, stamina, ingenuity) regarded as being of particular value for military preparedness (and for internal policing against dissidents and deviants). Furthermore, military organisation of sport appeared to be an efficient way of deploying scarce resources in the most economical fashion and using methods of direction that were more effective coming from paramilitary than from civilian organisations.

4. Health and Hygiene

Of all the functions of state-run sport in communist societies, the promotion and maintenance of health was to be given greatest priority. But with the Cold War importance surrounding international sports success, funding for high performance athletes often surpassed that allocated to the overall health and hygiene of Soviet citizens. Nonetheless, a healthy active lifestyle was important enough to place sport under the aegis of health ministries in many communist states.

In so far as sports development was based for much of Soviet development on a population at a comparatively low level of health, and as it served as a model for most other communist societies, it will be instructive to examine briefly that experience.

When the Russian communists (Bolsheviks) took power in October 1917, they inherited a semi-feudal, 80-percent peasant and illiterate empire of over a hundred different ethnic groups. The country was in a state of war-ruin and chaos. It was a land with an overwhelmingly inclement climate, where disease, epidemics and starvation were common, and where most people had only a rudimentary knowledge of hygiene. The Bolsheviks well knew it would take a radical economic and social transformation to alter the situation significantly. But time was short, and able-bodied and disciplined men and women (children too) were needed urgently, first for the country's survival, then for its recovery from the ravages of war and revolution, its industrial and cultural development, and its defence against further probable-seeming military attacks.

Regular participation in physical exercise, therefore, was to be one means—-relatively inexpensive and effective—-of improving health standards rapidly and a channel by which to educate people in hygiene, nutrition and exercise. For this purpose a new approach to health and recreation was sought. The name given to the new system was *physical culture*.

The pre-revolutionary and Western conception of sport and physical education was thought to be too narrow to express the far-reaching aims of the cultural (mental and physical) revolution under way. Physical culture was to embrace health, physical education, competitive sport, and even civil defence and artistic expression. The acquisition of that culture was said to be an integral process that accompanied a person throughout life.

As Nikolai Semasko, himself a medical doctor and the first Health Minister (also concurrently Chairman of the Supreme Council of Physical Culture), made plain in 1928:

Physical culture in the Soviet understanding of the term is concerned not with record breaking, but with people's physical health. It is an integral part of the cultural revolution and therefore has personal and social hygiene as its major objective, teaching people to use the natural forces of nature—-the sun, air and water—-the best proletarian doctors (Semashko, p 37).

In other words, physical culture was to be a platform of a national healthcampaign, encouraging people to bathe, to brush their teeth regularly, to eat and drink sensibly, to employ a rational daily regime of work, rest and sleep (hence Semashko's 1926 slogan of *Physical Culture 24 Hours a Day*—eight hours' work, eight hours' sleep and eight hours' recreation). Even more than that: at the cessation of World War I and the Revolution, the country found itself in the grip of a typhoid epidemic. Further, it had long suffered from such near-epidemic diseases as cholera, leprosy, tuberculosis and venereal disease. It suffered, according to Semasko (1928), from "dreadfully backward sanitary conditions, the ignorance and non-observance of rules for personal and public hygiene, leading to mass epidemics of social diseases such as syphilis, trachoma, scabies and other skin infections" (Semashko, 1928, p 24).

Physical culture, therefore, in a country impoverished by war and industrial under-development, was to help combat serious disease and epidemics. The therapeutic value of regular exercise, for example, was widely advertised in the intermittent anti-TB campaigns of the late 1920s. But physical culture was not confined only to improving *physical* health; it was regarded as important in combating what the leaders defined as anti-social behaviour in town and country. If young people could be persuaded to take up sport and engage in regular exercise, they might develop healthy bodies *and* minds. Thus, the Ukrainian Communist Party issued a resolution in 1926, expressing the hope that "physical culture would become the vehicle of the new life. . . a means of isolating young people from the baneful influence of the street, home-made alcohol and prostitution" (Landar, 1972, p.9). The role assigned physical culture in the countryside and the peasant population was even more ambitious. It was:to play a big part in the campaign against drunkenness and uncouth behaviour by attracting village youth to more rational and cultural activities. . . . In the fight to transform the village, physical culture is to be a vehicle of the new way of life in all measures undertaken by the authorities—in the campaign against religion and natural calamities (Landar, 1972:11).

Even in the 1980s, the name of sport was still being invoked to combat alcoholism and religion (Nekrasov, 1985:37-39).

Physical culture, then, stood for *clean living*, progress, good health and a rational world view, and was regarded by the state authorities as one of the most suitable and effective instruments for implementing their social policies, as well as for the social control mechanisms implicit in the programme.

As industrialisation got under way at the end of the 1920s and intensified with the first of Stalin's Five Year Plans (1929), physical exercise also became an appendage, like everything else, of the Plan. At all workplaces throughout the country a regime of therapeutic gymnastics was introduced with the intention of boosting productivity, cutting down absenteeism through sickness, injury, and drunkenness, reducing fatigue, and spreading hygienic habits among the millions of new workers who had only recently inhabited bug-infested wooden huts in the villages.

By the time of the second Five Year Plan, the most dedicated of industrial workers were called Stakhanovites, after the mining exploits of a Donets coalminer, Alexei Stakhanov, who was able to extract sixteen times as much coal per day as the normal standard output. This industrial movement rapidly came to define, more generally, an authority-preferred life style of *worker athletes* (healthy workers) and *athletic workers* (high performance athletes) and was the basis of the Soviet health-oriented system of sport. It was imposed upon or adopted freely by every other state that took the road to communism.

5. *Social policies*

There are many facets of social policy relevant to sport that concern communist states. Some have been referred to above: combating crime, particularly juvenile delinquency; fighting alcoholism and prostitution; attracting young people away from religion, especially from all-embracing faiths that impinge upon large segments of social life. One aspect of the use of sport for social policies is the concern that it can make some contribution to the social emancipation of women.

The strong motivation here was less a concern for equality among the sexes as the desire by leaders for national recognition through international sports success. The attention paid by some East European nations to women's sport sometimes contrasted with the relative neglect in both the more *enlightened* nations of the West and in developing states. As an East German sports official, Otto Schmidt noted, "While other nations can produce men's teams as good as, if not better than, ours, we beat them overall because they are not tapping the full potential of their women" (Schmidt, 1975:12-13).

The impact of women's sport is even greater—-though emancipation is far more protracted and painful—-in communities in which women have, by law or convention, been excluded from public life and discouraged from baring face, arms, and legs in public. Some multi-ethnic communist countries quite deliberately used sport to break down prejudice and gain a measure of emancipation for women. This was a conscious policy in communist states with a sizeable Muslim population, like Albania, the USSR and Afghanistan. In reference to women of Soviet Central Asia (bordering on Iran, Turkey and Afghanistan), a Soviet sports official (Davletshina) asserted that "sport has become an effective and visible means of combating religious prejudice and reactionary tradition; it has helped to destroy the spiritual oppression of women and to establish a new way of life" (Davletshina, 1976:62).

It is a sobering thought that had the grandmothers of such Soviet Uzbek gymnasts as Nelli Kim or Elvira Saadi appeared in public clad only in a leotard, they would almost certainly have been stoned to death. Such was the fate of a young Russian named Umarov. His companion, an Uzbek girl Aigul, was seriously injured in the same attack. Their crime? In October, 1921, they had ventured into historic Tashkent to persuade women to take part in a sports parade to mark the second Central Asian Olympiad (Sviridov, 1958:16-17).

It was mounting Western official (as well as Western women's) awareness of losing out to communist nations that arguably contributed to the encouragement, *inter alia*, of heightened interest in women's sport and employment of training methods for women commonplace in Eastern Europe. But the influence has sometimes been the other way. For example, it was the Western women's example that overcame the prejudices of some (male) communist leaders against such sports as women's soccer, rugby, ice hockey, weight lifting and long distance running.

6. International recognition and prestige

For all young countries trying to establish themselves in the world as nations to be respected, even recognised, sport may uniquely offer them an opportunity to take the limelight in the full glare of world publicity. This is particularly important for those nations confronted by bullying, boycott and subversion from big powers in economic, military and other areas. This has applied as much to the Baltic states in regard to Soviet Russia as it has to Cuba and Nicaragua in regard to the United States. This has put particular responsibility on athletes from communist nations in that they have been seen by political leaders as *sweat suit* ambassadors, encouraging a sense of pride in their team, nationality, country and even political system. But such a role is not without its consequences. As already mentioned, high performance sport siphons off valuable resources from less visible *sport for all* initiatives. And not all communist athletes accepted the role of national representatives, nor did the *ordinary citizen*, as witnessed by the post-communist outbursts in post-1989 Eastern Europe. The role that sport has played in communist foreign policy is dealt with in more detail below.

Sport and Foreign Policy

Ever since the first communist state came into existence in 1917, communist leaders made explicit the dependence of external sports relations on foreign policy. It could hardly be otherwise in countries where sport was centrally directed and employed in the pursuit of specific socio-political objectives, including those of foreign policy. We have already seen that sport was a political institution run by the state, and that overall sports policy was laid down by the communist government. Decisions of national import concerning foreign sports policy—-such as participation in the Olympic Games or in particular states disliked by the ruling Communist Party—-were made, therefore, by the Party and government. On occasion it was a supranational body, like the Warsaw Pact, rather than a sovereign government, that decided policy, as in the case of the Soviet-led boycott of the Los Angeles Olympics in 1984. Notwithstanding, for those communist states in Eastern Europe that had been closely tied to the USSR, it was often the Soviet Politburo that imposed a *fraternal* sports policy upon them.

That is not to say that all communist leaderships acted in accord or collusion. China, Yugoslavia and Romania took part in the Los Angeles Games in the face of Soviet opposition. Cuba and Marxist-governed Ethiopia acted in solidarity with North Korea in boycotting the Seoul 1988 Summer Olympics, while all other communist states (save Albania which boycotted all Olympic Games up to Barcelona in 1992) competed. Finally, one only need have witnessed any competition between East Germany and the USSR to sense the intensity of rivalry that existed between Warsaw Pact nations.

The role of sport in communist foreign policy varied in importance over the years, reflecting both shifts in domestic and foreign policies and the rapidly changing world situation. In the years from 1917 to 1948-49, when the Soviet Union either constituted the sole communist state in the world or held undivided sway over the communist movement, it was Soviet policy that dictated communist involvement in world sport. But following the Soviet break with Yugoslavia in 1948 and the communist revolution in China in 1949, the Soviet monopoly was broken.

Since the end of World War II, a major aim of several communist states was to attain sports supremacy over capitalist nations, particularly through the Olympic Games. Where other channels have been closed, success in sport would seem to have helped such countries as the USSR and East Germany as well as many other states in the industrially developing world to attain a measure of recognition and prestige internationally, both at home and abroad. Sport here is unique in that for all communist societies, including the USSR, it was the only medium in which they were able to take on and beat the economically advanced nations. This took on added importance in view of what their leaders traditionally saw as the battle of two ideologies for influence in the world. It is not surprising then, that in 1948, the Central

Committee of the USSR Communist Party made wholesale changes to the sports organisation so that "Soviet sportsmen, in upcoming years will surpass world records in all major sports (Resolution, Central Committee, All-Union Communist Party (b), 27 December, 1948). One year later the influential monthly *Kultura i zhizn* claimed that "the increasing number of successes achieved by Soviet athletes . . . is a victory for the Soviet form of society and the socialist sports system; it provides irrefutable proof of the superiority of socialist culture over the moribund culture of capitalist states" (Kultura i zhizn, 1949:5).

Despite occasional setbacks, there is ample evidence to show that the economically advanced socialist states went a long way to achieving their aim of world sporting supremacy, especially in the Olympic Games. Socialist states provided two of the top three nations in the Summer Olympics since 1968 (except 1984, when they provided two of the top four despite the overwhelming communist boycott of the Los Angeles Games) and in the Winter Games since 1972. Even in the Barcelona Summer Olympics of 1992, when the USSR had already broken up (it performed as the *Unified Team*, which excluded athletes from the three Baltic states of Latvia, Lithuania and Estonia) and other East European countries were in disarray, the Unified Team beat its nearest challenger, the USA, while the two communist nations, China and Cuba, came fourth and fifth respectively.

The Soviet Union dominated the Olympic Games, summer and winter, ever since it made its debut in the summer of 1952 and the winter of 1956. In fact, the greatest challenge to USSR domination came from the German Democratic Republic which gained more medals than the USA in the 1976 and 1988 Summer Games, and more medals than the USSR in the 1980 and 1984 Winter Olympics. The only interruption to communist victory was in 1968, when the USSR took second place to Norway in winter and to the USA in summer, and in 1984, when the major communist sporting nations boycotted Los Angeles.

The example of East Germany, with a population of under 17 million is particularly instructive. An overriding problem facing the GDR after the 1939-45 War was that of gaining international acceptance as an independent state. Its leaders further had to contend with attempts to impose Soviet institutions and values upon the country, on the one hand, and Western hostility, subversion and boycott, on the other. The manufactured rivalry with West Germany became a testing ground for proving the viability of either capitalism or socialism in all spheres, including sport.

International sporting success was seen in East Germany as one means, perhaps the most accessible and *popular*, of gaining acceptance of the regime and enhancing its image at home and abroad while other channels were closed. It was not easy. In the Winter Olympics of 1960, for example, the USA refused to issue visas to East German athletes to travel to Squaw Valley where the Games were being held. Such denial of visas was made 35 times by the USA and its NATO allies between 1957 and 1967. In other instances, when East German athletes won competitions, the awards ceremony was cancelled; and oftenWestern officials refused permission for the GDR to display its flag and emblem.

But its leadership persisted and quite demonstrably poured funds into sport to try to establish the nation as a world power to be recognised and reckoned with. As Party Chairman Erich Honecker made clear:

Our state is respected in the world because of the excellent performance of our top athletes, but also because we devote enormous attention to sport in an endeavour to make it part of the everyday lives of each and every citizen (Honecker, 1976:133).

It is impossible to understand East German sport without seeing it in the wider context of, first, the striving to establish the nation as the equal of its fellow German state, the Federal Republic of Germany and, second, trying to achieve both political and sporting status in the world, above all within the Olympic movement and the United Nations. It is a measure of the success of those objectives that final acceptance by the IOC came in 1972, for the Games held in West Germany (Munich), to be followed in 1973 with membership in the United Nations. Both were the result of 25 years of intensive diplomatic activity, sporting and political.

Although the IOC had recognised the East German National Olympic Committee in October 1965 and granted it the right to enter a team separately from West Germany in the Mexico Olympics of 1968, it was only in Munich in 1972 that East Germany for the first time competed with its own national team, flag and anthem. This sporting autonomy and success led to mounting diplomatic recognition of the country throughout the world. While West Germany was overwhelmingly successful in the 1950s, the gap closed in the 1960s, then East Germany forged well ahead in the 1970s and 1980s. It is worth mentioning in passing that the united team of Germany came third in the 1992 summer Olympics, though with 20 medals fewer than East Germany had won at the Seoul Olympic Games in 1988.

The success of East Germany in cultivating elite athletes is apparent in the fact that during the 1980s, in Olympic and World Championship terms, calculated in per capita medals, the country won one gold medal for every 425 000 citizens, by contrast with approximately one gold per 6 500 000 citizens in both the USSR and USA. In short, that means that an East German with sporting talent and ability was 16 times more likely to reach the top and gain an Olympic or World gold medal than a Soviet or American citizen.

With the dismantling of the Berlin Wall in 1989 and the collapse of communism in Eastern Europe, much has been written about performance enhancing drugs and East German sports success. There is no doubt that the GDR training programs for its athletes included a highly organised and systematic steroid programme. But it would be incorrect to suggest that this is the sole reason for the sports success of its athletes. What distinguished East Germans from the rest of the world's athletes was not that some (not all) competed having taken steroids; it was that the East German programme was a planned one. And what also must be remembered is the importance that compulsory physical culture played in East German life, the considerable number of highly trained coaches and volunteer instructors who worked in the country, and the vigilance paid to finding and training those with sports potential.

For East Germany, therefore, to quote the West German book *Sport in der DDR*, we have seen how:

Sport has played a vital role in breaching the blockade which, at the time of the

Cold War, kept the GDR out of virtually all international relations outside the communist states. Because GDR sport attained international standards and in many areas actually set those standards, world sports organisations were unable to ignore the country (Schmidt, 1975:12-13).

This was an important step towards helping East Germany break out of its political isolation, gain credibility for the communist government with its own people, and be recognised as an independent state. Hence the high priority that the authorities accorded the development of sport and international sports performance.

The communist countries, therefore, were keenly aware of the advantages that are thought to accrue from sporting, and especially Olympic, success, and so prepared their athletes accordingly. They believed that the Olympics brought more exposure and prestige, and were, in the view of some communist leaders, *the* measure of a nation's viability.

To sum up, with its control of the sports system, the communist leadership was able to mobilise resources to use sport to perform what it believed to be salient political functions in foreign policy. It is, of course, impossible to measure the impact of sport on the behaviour of states—to discover whether sport can, in fact, ever affect policies, let alone minds and hearts.

All that can be said is that sport would no longer seem to be (if it ever was) the neutral, apolitical medium that some people once considered it to be. The sporting gains of communist policy towards developing and neighbouring countries were evident and tangible. There were some successes in the *hearts and minds* campaign among such nations, but the staunch friendship and solidarity remain open to question: for example, very few developing states showed solidarity with the Soviet-led boycott of the Los Angeles Games in 1984, or indeed, with the Soviet armed involvement in Afghanistan. Some might argue, further, that Western commercial sport had more of an impact on the popular imagination in Africa, Asia and Latin America than had communist- and Olympic-style sports. It may be that, as far as communist influence was concerned, communist policy was most effective where Marxist-Leninist assumptions were accepted, in a handful of communist states themselves. Like the space programme, it seemed more important in establishing national pride and ideological hegemony, though it appears to have had markedly less impact outside of states that were not already Marxist-Leninist; and in the late 1980s and early 1990s even that bastion crumbled.

Some Conclusions

The rapidity of post-totalitarian change in all areas, sport included, in East and Central Europe and the one-time Soviet Union would seem to indicate that the elite high performance sports system and its attainments, far from inspiring a national pride and patriotism, tended to provoke apathy and resentment. This appeared to be more evident in those states—Poland, GDR, Hungary, Romania, Bulgaria—which had *revolution* and an alien sports system and values thrust upon them contrary to their indigenous traditions. A similar mood is apparent, too, in the Baltic states and Islamic areas of the old USSR. Sports stars were seen as belonging to a private, elite fiefdom within the overall domain; they were not part of a shared national achievement, let alone heritage.

Such an attitude is important to keep in mind for all nation states that would attempt to promote both *sport for all* and high performance sport in national policies. It is difficult to be all things to all citizens. The financial and coaching outlay necessary to train Olympic and World champions suggests that, all too often, the recreational participant is neglected. Participation is important for all and when the high performance athlete is seen to get ever more of scarce resources (financial, use of facilities, and instruction), resentment is often the result. For many citizens of Central and Eastern Europe, this was exactly their perception of the communist sport system.

That is not to say that in societies of hardship and totalitarian constraint, and in the face of Western arrogance and attitudes that were sometimes tantamount to racial and/or cultural prejudice, the ordinary citizen obtained no vicarious pleasure in her/his champion's or team's performance. But overall, the dominant attitude was one not entirely different from Western attitudes to sports and heroes that were not *theirs* (e.g. the ambivalent attitude by many Western workers towards Olympic show jumpers, yachtsmen and fencers; the resentment of over-paid professional performers who expect more money while providing less in terms of sporting skill and affiliation to the community).

Notwithstanding, in countries like the now defunct Czechoslovakia and Yugoslavia, as well as the Slav regions of the old Soviet Union (the Ukraine, Belorus, Russia), the patriotic pride in sporting success and heroes would appear to be authentic. One reason for this may be that the socialist revolution of 1917 in the old Russian empire, and of 1946 and 1948 in the cases of Yugoslavia and Czechoslovakia, came out of their own experience and had some popular support.

In these states, the sports system grew up with and was integral to the building of a strong nation-state which generated its own motivational forces and patriotism. It was not strictly the communist ideology that motivated athletes or that Marxism-Leninism was responsible for Olympic success. However, both did imply centralised state control and the planned application of resources, allied to state priorities and the direction of labour. Policies of pervasive social welfare in which sport was an essential feature in constructing the infrastructure of socialist society provided conditions that were more conducive to discovering, organising and developing talent in specific sports than those of the more disparate and private Western systems. And like almost all professional occupations in the planned economy, the privilege and monetary rewards granted high performance athletes were far less than that forthcoming to those sports entertainers in the fully professionalised and commercial sports of the West: soccer, basketball, boxing, ice hockey, motor racing, tennis and baseball.

Today, the inheritors of the sports system that evolved during the communist years are faced with a choice of how sharply they should break with the past and how quickly they should adopt a pattern of sport based on market relations and the image of athletes as commodities to be bought and sold. *Westernisers* in Eastern Europe, with public support nourished on a rejection of the communist past *in toto*, and aided by those Westerners eager to tap the sporting talent trained under the communist system, wish to see the old communist states join the *free* world, abandon socialism, central planning and social provision.

It is possible that sport in such states will become a hybrid of the worst of both worlds, retaining the grinding bureaucracy of the old and adding only the exploitation and corruption of the new. The final product may well not inspire admiration, and its advocates should keep in mind that post-Soviet market capitalism "has been by every measure far more destructive of people's daily and long-term security and well-being than any Communist Party policy since the Second World War" (McMurtry, 1998:208). Much the same could be said of the larger *reform* processes underway.

Such a radical shift in policy is ill-conceived for communist sport was not utterly and entirely bad. Based on an entirely different economic system, it provided ready-made rivalries. *The Russians are coming* was a clarion call for competition that would be predictably excellent. The old system was generally open to those with talent in all sports, probably more so than in the West. Would, for example, the many highly skilled tennis players from Central and Eastern Europe, most from modest family circumstances, have reached their level of expertise had they been born in a Western society? The old system provided opportunities for women to play and succeed, if not on equal terms with men, at least on a higher plane than Western women. It gave an opportunity to the many ethnic minorities and relatively small states in Eastern Europe and the USSR to do well internationally and to help promote that pride and dignity that sports success in the glare of world publicity can bring. Nowhere in the world has there been, since the early 1950s, such reverence by governments for Olympism, for Coubertin, for Olympic ritual and decorum. One practical embodiment of this was the contribution to Olympic solidarity with industrially developing nations: the training of Third World athletes, coaches, sports officials, medical officers and scholars at colleges and training camps. Much of this aid was free. None of it was disinterested, directed at those states whose governments generally looked to socialism rather than to capitalism for their future. But it also went to those who were clearly exploited, as was the case with the Soviet-led campaign against apartheid in sport and the success in having racist South Africa banished from world sports forums and arenas.

In Eastern Europe and the erstwhile USSR, the international challenge is today diluted through lack of state support. The free trade union sports societies, as well as the ubiquitous paramilitary (Dinamo) and armed forces clubs, have given way to private sports health and recreation clubs. Women's wrestling and boxing, meant to titillate the paying spectator, attract more profit than women's chess and volleyball. Women's gymnastics has given way to aerobics and one wonders how many young aspiring ballerinas now ply their dancing skills in Western strip bars.

The various ethnic groups (Czechs and Slovaks, Croatians and Serbs, Armenians and Ukrainians, Baltic nations) prefer their own independent teams to combined effort and success. And right across the Central and Eastern European plain, as far as the Ural Mountains, sports and every other form of aid is at an end. The Third World students (in medicine and engineering as well as in sport) have had to go home as their support grants have run out. The ex-communist states have become competitors with other poor nations for development aid from the West. And such aid, as the

International Monetary Fund dictates, comes at a cost. Aid is forthcoming with the liberalisation of prices, rapid privatisation, removal of food and housing subsidies, and the whole-scale dismantling of the social welfare system.

Already a new sports nationalism is emerging, with the newly-independent states eager to wave their flags and sing their anthems in the full glare of world television. Ironically, many of their top athletes are *unavailable* for the national teams, plying their trade as migratory sports workers for professional clubs throughout the Western world. For these athletes, as for many of their fellow citizens, to work is to eat. In the immediate post-communist period, the one-time communist nations have decided that bread is more important than circuses.

Literature

Cantelon, H. (1981) *The Social Reproduction of Sport: A Weberian Analysis of the Rational Development of Ice Hockey Under Scientific Socialism in the Soviet*
Union. Unpublished Ph.D. Dissertation. University of Birmingham, England.

Childs, D. (1978) "Sport and physical education in the GDR", in J. Riordan (ed), *Sport under Communism*, London, Hurst.

Davletshina, R. (1976) "Sport i zhenshchiny", in *Teoriya i praktika fizicheskoi kultury, 3*. Moscow.

Edelman, R. (1993) *Serious Fun: A History of Spectator Sport in the USSR*.
Oxford: Oxford University Press.

Ehrich, D., Heinrich-Vogel, R. and Winkler, G. (1981) *Die DDR Breiten- und*
Spitzensport. Munich: Kopernikus Verlag.

Honecker, E. (1976). *Report of the Central Committee to the Socialist Unity Party of Germany*. Berlin.

Kultura i zhizn (1949) November 1, 11. Moscow.

Landar, A. M. (1972). "Fizicheskaya kultura, sostavnaya chast kulturnoi revoyutsii na Ukraine", in *Teoriya i praktika fizicheskoi kultury, 12*. Moscow.

McMurtry, J. (1998). *Unequal Freedoms: the Global Market as an Ethical System*. Toronto: Garamond.

Nekrasov, V. P. (1985) "Fizicheskaya kultura protiv pyanstva", in *Teoriya i praktika fizicheskoi kultury, 9*. Moscow.

Peppard, V. and Riordan, J. (1992) *Playing Politics: Soviet Sport Diplomacy to 1992. Greenwich, Connecticut:* Jai Press, Inc.

Riordan, J. (1977) *Sport in Soviet Society*. Cambridge: Cambridge University Press.

Riordan, J. (1991) *Sport, Politics and Communism*. Manchester: Manchester University Press.

Riordan, J. (ed.) (1981) *Sport Under Communism: USSR, Czechoslovakia, GDR, China, Cuba*. London: C. Hurst.

Rodionov, V. V. (1975) "Sport i integratsiya" in *Teoriya i praktika fizicheskoi kultury, 9*. Moscow.

Schmidt, O. (1975) *Sport in der Deutschen Demokratischen Republik*. Bonn.

Shneidman, N. (1979) *Soviet Sport: Road to Olympus*. Kingston/Montreal: McGill-Queen's Press.

Sport v SSSR, 6 (1981). Moscow.

Sviridov, G.I. (1958) "Dzhakson ostalsya v Rossii", in *Fizkul'tura i sport, 5: 16-17*. Moscow.

Zedong, M. (1962) *Une étude de l'education physique*. Paris: Maison des sciences de l'homme. (Originally published in Chinese in 1917).

France

Thierry Terret

In spite of the growing globalization and increasing hegemony of the dominant forms of sport, the recent history of sport in France possesses characteristics that stem from its unique incorporation into social and political structures. Indeed, in comparison with many other European countries, one cannot describe the French sports landscape during the last half-century without analyzing the transformations – and permanencies – caused by at least two elements: on the one hand, sport has always been considered part of the "welfare state", rather than part of the private sphere; on the other, sport is believed to have ethical and educational values which have to be protected from many trends (drugs, professionalism, violence). There is undoubtedly a certain naïvety in such attitudes, yet they are largely shared by people in both the sporting and the political worlds. The conflicts observed up to 1998 over the organization of the Football World Cup, confronting the French State with FIFA and the organizers were just one example. However, these characteristics did not always take the same form. Sport has for a long time been marginalized by the authorities who favoured practices whose values seemed more in tune with society's expectations. Until the 1930s, the great weight of both medical and military traditions resulted in pitting gymnastics against sport, putting a brake on the development of the latter. The legitimacy of gymnastics was also based on its early history, leading historians to look for the roots of this French specificity in the consequences of the Revolution of 1789.

To be sure, the history of sport and gymnastics in France dates well before the French Revolution of 1789. A long military tradition had consistently had close links with physical activity, in the form of tournaments, jousting, fencing, horse riding (Jusserand, 1901), in particular among the ruling classes. Townspeople and the peasant population also had a long tradition of dancing and games of strength and dexterity. However, it must be acknowledged that during the Middle Ages and even during the Renaissance, the body was, generally speaking, rather ignored or suspected of being too easily inhabited by the Devil or prone to illness. Doctors and priests did in fact concern themselves with the body's education well before educators and gymnasts.

By the Revolution, however, the cult of lethargy was overtaken by a new need for movement. So legitimacy of physical exercise grew at the same time as education, medical, military and festive practices underwent important changes.

1 – From the *Ancien Régime* to the Third Republic: the days of gymnastics (1800-1875)

Although dancing, fencing and horse riding teachers had an aristocratic clientele and special-purpose schools, most of the 19th century in France was notable for the advent of gymnastics. After the Enlightenment, rationalism, which was in full bloom in the country, was most convincingly expressed in a society that had moved to new factory production. The body was seen in a radically different light. Space and time became precious elements which had to be controlled. From then on, physical exercise was seen as a very real tool with which to control behaviour. Military and medical institutions seized upon this immediately.

Initially, medical doctors provided a mass of recommendations in treaties on hygiene whose range of concern progressively increased. What characterised this advice could be summed up by two concepts: moderation and precision. This only made sense if one had a perfect command of these recommendations. So books on hygiene proposed extensive catalogues of exercises. What Londe researched in 1827 (Londe, 1821), for example, was a rational and exhaustive typology of the effects of external objects on the various functions of the body. The environment was no longer hostile by definition since the human being was able to adapt and react. Doctors were, in particular, unanimous in regarding air as a medium to temper the body. Strategies appeared which associated air, cold or hot water, with a range of effects according to their qualities. The *bourgeoisie* was particularly receptive to the ideas of Jean-Jacques Rousseau, providing their children with an education in relationship with the parents themselves. These images of an internal power, as a potential which was waiting to be actively promoted, were reinforced by scientific discoveries, such as the mechanisms of the cardiac pump by Harvey, studies of the digestive system by Réaumur and Spallanzani and, especially, of respiration by Lavoisier, who isolated oxygen in 1777. Georges Vigarello's writings show how much this last discovery transformed the meaning of breathing and, consequently, the meaning of physical exercise: "neither a simple mechanism to cool blood, nor a simple principle of bellows assisting the heart, breathing became a direct source of energy and force (...)."

The culminating point of these developments was reached at the beginning of the 19th century. It was also a time when the memory of the *épopée* of Bonaparte was still very strong. There was a general fear of degeneration of the race and a need for hygienists to better control people's behaviour. The wish to do away with coercive control over the populace was accepted by politicians who shared the same project of social body regulation. Indeed, the procedures of control and surveillance were part of a consensus between the political institution and the medical institution whose legitimacy increased considerably following the fatal epidemics of cholera in 1835, 1865-1866 and 1873-1874. Thus, schools, military barracks, hospitals and prisons became laboratories for hygienists, with a common goal: to control energies, to prevent any social overflows or deviancies. This aim overtook the simple promotion of health, while inviting people to control simultaneously every action and every thought. The ideal of the honest man, hard-worker, good citizen and good father was looked to.

Consequently, the medical and military tradition converged to promote analytical gymnastics, where movements were clear cut, placed in precise series and taught by a master whose main concerns were obedience and collective discipline. Admittedly, these new conceptions of exercises were not always completely accepted. Francisco Amoros, for example, a Spanish refugee in France, did not restrict himself to abstract gymnastics. He proposed using apparatus to produce more universal movements. His method, written in 1830 (Amoros, 1830), had immense success in France with the armed forces. At the same time, he also had a considerable influence on private and commercial structures which were more and more coming into being. In 1834, Amoros even created a "civil and orthopaedic gymnasium", then the *Gymnase Normal Militaire et Civil de Grenelle*, which denomination demonstrated the integration of medical, military and educational logic. Amoros's influence was decisive in the writing of a text which for a long time provided the basis for both military and school gymnastics. *Instructions pour l'enseignement de la gymnastique* was published in 1846, two years before Amoros's death. Finally, Amoros's ideas were diffused in 1852 in *L'Ecole Militaire de Joinville-Le-Pont*, set up by one of his students, the Commander d'Argy. This military school was created to train future military instructors several of whom later became gymnastics teachers at school.

In the second third of the 19th Century, at the time when the *Ancien Régime* gave way to the Second Empire, the military gymnasium became a model for many private gymnasiums built in the large cities. The first ones were often launched by Swiss (for example, the well-known Clias) or Germans. Many of them tried to associate their name with both a place and a method. As Jacques Defrance has pointed out, to write a book or to join with a local medical doctor often gave the credibility needed to save and rule the company. In the middle of the century, certain gymnasiums, like those of Triat or Eugène Paz in Paris, were famous places where men and women, originating from the same high social milieu, devoted time to practice more or less invigorating exercises.

After 1870, another section of society reacted to the defeat by Prussia. Workers, craftsmen and *petits bourgeois* came together in gymnastics *sociétés* (societies or companies were used for gymnastics, 'club' was used for sports) whose goals were less commercial and individual, and more nationalist and collective. These *sociétés* were very structured, benefiting from the support of both military and civil authorities and they were governed from 1873 by a national body: the *Union des Sociétés de Gymnastique de France* (USGF). They promoted activities which were politically acceptable and compatible with the patriotic and Republican voluntarism to which they explicitly referred. In this sense, they took part in the process of diffusion of recognised values, such as discipline, respect for hierarchy and rules, the cult of physical effort and solidarity. Military ranks, salutes, songs and hymns, systematic sets of regulations and flags constituted a framework which gave physical exercises their meaning. In gymnastics, human pyramids and other collective performances always preceded individual involvement. Anonymity and humility in physical expression were to forge a feeling of unity and being part of the group. In these *sociétés*, whose members were mostly from the middle and lower classes, gymnastic exercises were essentially a collective endeavour. Consequently, the question of quantification of movement hardly appeared. On the contrary, details of movements of the body (or body parts) were subjected to the greatest attention, prioritising uniformity and individual abnegation vis-à-vis the duties imposed by the nation. The meetings were consequently great festivals where the programmes combined collective performance and group contests. Political, military and philanthropic notables did not hesitate to watch — and be seen at — these events, as *good society* recognised in the gymnastic institution the social integration of Republican values.

2 – The beginning of the Republic: sport, gymnastics and military training (1870-1914)

In the context of revenge against Prussia, "the teaching of gymnastics, so useful for the physical development of young people, is essential today as a consequence of both our military organisation and obligatory national service" (*Journal Officiel de la République Française, 1879*). Indeed, even before the fundamental laws set out by Jules Ferry made schooling compulsory, the law of 27 January 1880 made gymnastics compulsory in all state schools for boys. From 1869, the *Certificat d'Aptitude à l'Enseignement de la Gymnastique* (CAEG) gave a common standard of competence to gymnastics masters, but the majority of them were still educated in the Joinville military School. In this Republican project, school gymnastics became military training which favoured drill, order and discipline. A series of simple co-ordinated movements constituted the skeleton of the physical education curriculum, while songs sung during the exercises embodied ideological values. However, the goals of school gymnastics were "to prepare and predispose the boys for their future work as workers and soldiers, the girls for housekeeping and women's work" (*Arrêté, 1882*). Female education was not directly related to forging men needed by the country. But, without giving up the patriotic and *revancharde* ambitions accorded to boys, it was intended to train and develop women's bodies in order to give birth to healthy future soldiers of the fatherland. Indeed, "the woman (was) the basis of the family (...). Health for her (was) a peremptory necessity, even more than for him, resulting in the power of generations which must come from her" (*Journal Officiel, 1879*).

The implementation of military gymnastics for boys at school was particularly obvious in the experiment of the *scholar battalions* between 1882 and 1890. Indeed, on 6 July 1882, "any primary and secondary education state school or any combined state school having from two hundred to six hundred twelve-year old pupils and above was authorised, under the name of *scholar battalions (bataillons scolaires)*, to assemble their students for gymnastic and military exercises during school" (*Décret relatif...1882*).

Formed by companies of at least fifty children, each battalion had its flag, was equipped with rifles, and had the right to a uniform. The school battalions were conceived as an opportunity to forge citizen-soldiers, ready for war as well as for inclusion in active life, at a moment when the political authorities were growing less favourable to a professional army thanks to an army of conscripts which could be trained at school in discipline, respect for hierarchy and weapon handling. The experiment ended around 1890 owing to financial and pedagogical difficulties, and also as a consequence of the crisis which temporarily affected the Army. Looking ahead to the great conflict of 1914, France decided it was better to prepare its young troops by reinforcing school shooting *sociétés*.

This broad movement was partly contradictory in regard to the new orientations given by some doctors and enlightened intellectuals who were more open to scientific progress. In 1884, for example, the discovery of Chauveau and Marey of oxygen flow in the blood stream led to new forms of physical exercise. The muscle, whose form and size were still the main references for gymnastics, from now on became a seat of combustion needed to produce movement. In the last quarter of the 19th century, hygienist attention gradually turned to the functioning and the conditions of functioning of the body rather than its forms and appearance. Thus, on 9 August 1887, the Academy of Medicine published an influential report in which, as recalled by Pierre Arnaud, several recommendations were made to transform the French education system. In this context, it asked a commission chaired by Marey and Démenÿ in 1887-1888 to reconsider school programmes relating to gymnastics. In the same years, Fernand Lagrange succeeded with *Physiologie des exercices du corps* in the contest organised by the Academy of Medicine to promote books written in favour of the diffusion of gymnastics. His work, like the creation in 1881of the first world research centre dedicated to physical exercise — the Station physiologique du Parc des Princes — resulted in new forms of exercise becoming more favourable to intense and outdoor physical activities, while remaining systematically controlled. Games for children, designed by experts, and sports for adults, became essential complements to gymnastics and, beyond it, to the development of everybody's health.

Philippe Tissié founded the *Ligue Girondine d'Education Physique* and launched the idea of *lendits* (outdoor games organised for students over several days) with Pierre de Coubertin and Jules Simon, who also created in 1888 a *Comité pour la Propagation des Exercices Physiques dans l'Education*, with Pascal Grousset, founder of the *Ligue Française d'Education Physique*. Another notable who was extremely favourable to the development of outdoor games was Fernand Lagrange who belonged to the vast current which defended the idea of educational games as opposed to military gymnastics. Nevertheless, both logically merged in the form of an eclectic programme in the *Manuel d'exercices gymnastiques et de jeux scolaires*, published in 1891 and which constituted the actual school programme of gymnastics until 1923.

This movement provided a context in which the first "sports" events truly appeared. It must be admitted, however, that the term itself had existed earlier. But *Le sport à Paris*, the well-known book by Eugène Chapus published in 1854, only described the fashionable distractions of the French capital (horse racing, horsemanship, hunting, boxing, swimming, gymnastics). In France, the first sports activity — in the modern sense of the word — occurred in places where the British merchant community was well implanted, i.e. in Paris and the Channel and Atlantic Ocean ports. In 1872, in Le Havre, some Englishmen created Le Havre Athletic Club. In 1877, British textile traders, established in Paris for commercial reasons, and some French students created together the "English Taylors" club, followed two years later by the Paris Football Club. Other French high-school pupils and students countered bourgeois city life by holding running races on the model of horse races. In 1882, they formed a group within the *Racing Club de France*, and in 1883 within the *Stade Français*. In 1887, Georges De Saint Clair founded the *Union des Sociétés de Courses à Pied* which, two years later, became for more than thirty years the main all-sports national body: the *Union des Sociétés Françaises de Sports Athlétiques* (USFSA).

First organised according to the rules of the British Amateur Athletic Association, in particular the regulations relating to the definition of amateurism, USFSA remained for a long time socially elitist and, thus, was the subject of much reaction and criticism from those who reproached it for its too restrictive conceptions of what a sportsman was. Other organisations subsequently appeared in concurrence – and sometime in conflict – with USFSA. These new bodies gave people the possibility either to develop and diffuse a particular sport – as was the case with mountaineering (*Club Alpin Français* in 1874), cycling (*Union Vélocipédique de France* in 1881), rowing (*Fédération Française des Sociétés d'Aviron* in 1893) – or to make room for a more popular or a more professional practice (for example, the *Fédération des Sociétés Athlétiques Professionnelles de France*). All the same, USFSA increased inexorably from 12 clubs (including 9 collegiate clubs) in 1890, to 50 in 1892 and 1,673 before the First World War. Its elitist recruitment resulted in retaining and reinforcing the social (young middle-class adults), sexual (men only) and economic characteristics of the new leading classes around activities like lawn tennis, track and field, football, swimming, winter sports, for the management of which smaller committees were gradually set up.

Women were excluded from USFSA. At the end of the 19th century, however, French women practised at least three main forms of physical activity. The first and most popular developed in the form of gymnastics *sociétés* in the same patriotic and *revancharde* mould as for men. This military spirit resulted in few women being attracted to join, only a few going to private gymnasiums to benefit from more hygienic practices. The second form of physical activity, which related more to the *bourgeoisie*, was directly influenced by the model of British sport. However, it was inhibited by the press, the political and medical authorities and also the sports organisers themselves, who were unanimous in proclaiming the physical, aesthetic and moral dangers to women from excessive sports activity. Sport appeared incompatible with the roles of mother and wife that society considered as a normal and exclusive life experience for women. The third type of physical exercise was aristocratic and involved highly distinctive practices to which few women had access. However, people from High Society partially escaped criticism by being more open to women's activity and, as testified by the portraits of Baron de Vaux,[1] some women engaged in horse riding, golf, tennis, cycling, shooting, hiking, fencing, dance and swimming.

Nevertheless, sport could not be reduced to a model of male sociability. As gymnastics was a vehicle known and recognised for its Republican and non-clerical ideology, sport was able to serve other interests. In 1908, the creation of the *Fédération Sportive et Athlétique Socialiste* confirmed the birth of worker sport as clearly distinct both from patrician sport and company sport. Before 1914, the success of this movement was poor. All the same, youth interest in sport made it a privileged instrument of the Catholic movement at a time when, at the beginning of the 20th century, tensions between Church and State were at their highest point. Politically, the separation of both institutions was officially voted on in 1905. At the cultural level, Doctor Michaud had used Catholic *patronage* since 1897 as a means of bringing together young people for sport, simultaneously to transmit a spiritual message to them and to bring them back to the Church. Running races took place and were soon to justify, in 1903, the creation of the *Fédération Gymnastique et Sportive des Patronages de*

France (FGSPF). Republicans reacted by creating non-religious clubs, thereby setting up a large network of sports associations for young people. In that way certain sports became the object of strong tensions. Football, favoured by Catholics, was opposed to Republican rugby. For different reasons, the rivalries, which then defied the three largest sport bodies in France – the USGF, the USFSA and the FGSPF – became increasingly stronger, while contributing to a certain democratisation of sport. The law of 1901 granting the right for anybody to come together in an organisation for non-profit purposes gave a legal basis to all clubs and *sociétés* and ratified a movement which developed ineluctably in two ways, competition and leisure, as testified by the example of cycling.

Cycling had already twice been a fashionable activity, the first time between 1818 and 1820, under the *Ancien Régime*, the second time between 1861 and 1870 under the Second Empire. Under the Third Republic, in particular between 1889 and 1903, it experienced a new period of prosperity. The first two phases were aristocratic and eccentric; the third appealed to the *petite reine* ('little queen') in the Parisian, then the urban *bourgeoisie*. In the 1890s, "the bourgeois became cyclist and tourist (...). The productive and rural countryside could also be consumed and admired. The bicycle brought closer the townsman to his ideal of nature while enabling him to explore rural France" (Gaboriau). In 1890, the *Touring Club de France* was logically created to diffuse tourism by means of the bicycle. France had 3.5 million bicycles before the Great War, many practitioners initially considering it a means to discover new space and landscape, and not a way to strengthen their lungs, according to the normative suggestions of the hygienists.

At the same time, this tourist sport was counterbalanced by long and extremely popular races. In 1891, Bordeaux – Paris (580 kilometres) and Paris – Brest – Paris (1200 kilometres), in 1903, the Tour de France created by Henri Desgrange, owner of the newspaper *L'Auto* which already had a circulation of 100 000 in 1909, confirmed the rise of the sport.

Can we affirm that sport was then fully accepted by everybody in France? The answer can hardly be yes. For example, the playing of sport at school remained exceptional and confined to some private institutions. The political authorities simply tolerated it; its organisations continued to be torn by internal dissension and, even in the fatherland of Pierre de Coubertin, the Olympic Games – including those held in Paris in 1900 – were seen only as a spectacle not very different from the performances of acrobats and strongmen who attracted people to village squares. Evoking the Olympic Games of 1912, Géo André recalled after the War that, "France did not want to parade; nothing was ready, not even a tricolour flag. To avoid a diplomatic incident, we were obliged to carry on (...). It was a humiliation, which preceded for two years that of the Great War (...). It did not profit us. The indifference of our elected bodies to the question of sport was so scandalous that our enemies could easily remain convinced of our decline" (André, 1919).

3 – Between the two wars: towards a reorganisation of sport (1914-1936)

The consequences of the Great War for the sports economy (facilities), structures and behaviour were numerous. The most obvious outcome was the institutional change which followed the Armistice. The USGF maintained its social credit level in spite of the disappearance of the spirit of revenge. The USFSA, however, internally torn by the question of amateurism, victim of an excess of centralism and attacked by Catholics over football, no longer resisted the tide of modernisation which was sweeping the country. A *Comité Français Interfédéral* had been created since 1907 by the FGSPF to control the spread of football. In 1919, it set up a French Cup whose success resulted in the decline of the USFSA. Indeed, more and more sports officials advocated structures that were more flexible and autonomous in regard to every sport. During the USFSA's General Assembly of 25 January 1919, Frantz Reichel finally succeeded in forcing a vote on a motion allowing the more independent functioning of every sports committee within the overall organisation. Footballers decided to cut off all ties with leaders who seemed more anxious to maintain their prerogatives than to promote the sport. Thus, they were the first to use the new set of rules and, as early as 7 April 1919, they created the *Fédération Française de Football*-Association. Subsequently, in little more than a year, several sports bodies were founded on the same model for field hockey, athletics, winter sports, tennis, swimming. This soon resulted in the demise of the USFSA.

Moreover, general opinion was quite favourable to sport. Even the political authorities began to be interested in it, after considering the importance given to sporting success by the Americans during the Inter-Allied Games of 1919 in Paris, and the Olympic Games of Antwerp the following year. The *Service des Œuvres Françaises à l'Etranger* (SOFE) was created alongside, in 1919, its "Tourism and Sport" section, having the specific mission to promote the image of France abroad through sport.

Economically, however, the priorities were elsewhere in such a period of rebuilding the nation. France still had no national stadium, only in Lyon where one had been built during the War. It did not enter any local, regional or national official's mind to implement a sports facility policy. Sport remained a private matter and factory owners built most of the existing facilities, for instance, cycle tracks, tennis courts, golf courses or even swimming pools. Paris, in charge of the organisation of the Olympic Games of 1924, refused until the last moment to accede to the requests of the French Olympic Committee, obliging the organisers to find a replacement for the decaying facilities of the *Racing Club de France*. The story repeated itself some months later when Chamonix was chosen to stage an international winter sports event which was later called the First Winter Olympics, or in 1938, when France hosted the football World Cup. The country had become more and more interested in sport, but neither the State, nor the sports organisations themselves, were ready to support its development. Consequently, the French team did not particularly shine internationally, with some notable exceptions in activities which were of an older tradition or which had a more important "pool" of athletes: water polo, rugby, weightlifting, fencing, equestrian sports. Even the figure of the sporting hero, hardly conceivable at the beginning of the century, became possible. Jean Bouin having been killed in the war, the best-known champions at that time were Jules Ladoumègue, who soon became convinced of the benefits of professionalism, in athletics, James Couttet in skiing, Jean Taris in swimming, Suzanne Lenglen and the "Four Musketeers" Lacoste, Borotra, Brugnon, Cochet in tennis, and Georges Monneret, Maryse Bastié and Helène Boucher in mechanical sports.

These images were made even more immediate by the conjuncture of three phenomena. On the one hand, professionalism, for long accused of being the main disease in sport, reappeared in the Thirties. After a period when money was clandestinely used, in particular in team sports, athletics, cycling and boxing, the first professional football team was launched in Sochaux in 1929, and resulted in a professional championship soon after in 1932, with twenty clubs. In 1934, professional Rugby League divorced from Rugby Union, still theoretically amateur. On the other hand, newspapers also discovered the sports phenomenon and contributed to the creation of myths. Sports specialist daily newspapers, such as *L'Auto,* or weekly magazines, such as *La vie au grand air,* had already existed before the Great War. From now on, they had to compete with newspapers like *Le Miroir des sports* and others, whose popular success increased phenomenally. Lastly, in particular after 1930, a new architectural conception of sporting facilities led to the building of stadiums devoted to the spectacle, which intensified identification with the champion or the team.

These trends were not shared by all, however. First, sport suffered a massive and determined attack from a very important part of the medical community, which accused sporting contests of leading to specialisation, and consequently, to deformations of the body, in opposition to the concept of balanced, all-round exercises traditionally advocated by doctors. Faced with such opposition, Coubertin defined sport as "the voluntary and common cult of intensive muscular exercise (...) which can continue until the risk of injury". Such a definition appeared strongly to contradict the requirement of moderation and physiological control (Boigey, 1923). In addition, universities were still opposed to any link with games or with pleasure, because these values were not compatible with those promoted by the school system. Much criticism also came from sportsmen themselves, like Géo André, who thought that to "teach" or coach sport would destroy its very fundamentals. Educators and teachers shared some of the arguments of the hygienists and they focused, in addition, on the moral risks that sport could potentially pose when it became a "market of the muscle", as denounced by Georges Hébert in 1925 in his celebrated book, *Le sport contre l'éducation physique.*

In these conditions, schools remained hostile to the integration of sport with physical education. The first project, symbolically entitled *Règlement de la méthode française,* was written by Joinville in 1919, in order to "adapt (PE) to the national temperament". Following the reflections of George Démenÿ, this text taught "how to discipline movements and learn muscular habits better adapted to everyday life" (Reglement general d'education physique..., 1925). The "gymnastics of development", which was a compulsory part of school PE, did little to involve pupils in sports activities. Indeed, sport as part of the lesson itself was only 'proposed' for the oldest pupils, those whose parents' social position would give them access to the high school which, at that time, was very distinct from schools for the masses. A few initiatives were taken on the fringes of school, with the creation of sports collegiate organisations, the *Union Sportive du Premier Degré* (USEP) for primary schools in 1929, the Office du Sport Scolaire (OSU) for university students in 1934. Even popular articles by Georges Hébert (1875-1957), inventor of the "natural method", were unable to change the first choice of Swedish gymnastics. Hébert, who was recognised neither by the military authorities of Joinville, nor by those of the State, developed his work in private organisations, in particular in the *palestras* for girls and, later on, in the *Champs d'ébats*.

Indirectly, the Great War also had major consequences for the worker sport movement and female sport. The first, having only a thousand members before 1914, became more institutionalised after the Armistice with the creation of the *Fédération Sportive du Travail* (FST), which was affiliated to the Second Communist International. However, both national and international political contexts put a brake on this brief unity. Indeed, a scission between French communists and socialists occurred in 1920, having several immediate effects for worker sport. The FST became a member of Red Sport International, i.e. of the Third Communist International, and a dissenting organisation was set up under the authority of the SFIO (French socialist movement): *Union des Sociétés Sportives et Gymniques du Travail*. When the danger of fascism became evident, the two structures joined together in 1934 and formed the *Fédération Sportive et Gymnique du Travail* (FSGT), which had more than 40,000 members.

The case of female sport also testified to this institutional recasting which affected French sport, as well as to the transformation of people's thinking. At the turn of the century, sportswomen were still mainly recruited from the middle class, where access to better social conditions, a sometimes more open education, as well as a certain financial autonomy, resulted in the first sports activities including women. General hostility, however, remained high and forced women to create organisations which were distinct from those ruled by and for men. The *Ondine de Paris* was probably the first female club to appear, in 1906, followed by the well-known *Fémina Sport* in 1912 and *Académia* in 1915. Neither the USGF, nor the USFSA was ready to recognise women and accept their presence. Faced with opposition from these two sports bodies, women created the *Union Française de Gymnastique féminine* (UFGF) in 1912, followed four years later by a rival *Fédération des Sociétés Sportives Féminines*, whose President was the famous Alice Milliat.

The First World War had contributed to modifying representations of gender, showing that women could replace men and ensure their functions at work. However, in the 1920s, Pierre de Coubertin was still claiming that "there will not be a female Olympiad" and many doctors remained reticent about the idea of female sport. They nevertheless were forced to observe significant developments in women's physical activity, within the traditional gymnastics, with the transformation of the UFGF into the *Fédération Française Féminine de Gymnastique et d'Education Physique* (FFFGEP) in 1921, as well as within the framework of the more active FSSF. The latter had only two clubs in 1916, but had grown to 70 in 1921 when the FSSF became the *Fédération des Sociétés féminines Sportives Française*. Faced with the hostility of Coubertin, Alice Milliat launched the idea of a "Female Olympiad", which was finally held in Monte Carlo in April 1921; then came the idea of the "first female Olympic Games" whose first attempt took place in Paris at the Pershing Stadium in April 1922, with 300 women from five countries. Alice Milliat also took the initiative to create the *Fédération Sportive Féminine Internationale* of which she became President in 1921. Her efforts resulted in the acceptance of women into the Olympic Games in 1928. At the French level, most of the national sports bodies finally accepted women in the inter-war period, with some notable exceptions, such as the French Cycling Federation and the French Rugby Federation.

On the fringes of these structural changes, a naturist movement developed with its own distinct characteristics. A more educational activity concerned children in "outdoor schools". And physical recreation spread to the seaside with growing success, benefiting from the creation of many clubs and the self-promotion of numerous trainers. Finally, private gymnasiums for body-building, gymnastics and physical culture multiplied in the cities, and advertised for members to reinforce their muscular potential according to the recommendations of trainers, the most famous of whom had been Edmond Desbonnet from the end of the 19th century.

4 – From one Republic to another: French sport under state control (1936-1959)

After June 1936 and the setting up of the Popular Front, a large democratic movement developed in France, symbolically illustrated by several social laws, like the two-week annual paid holiday. This new policy cared much more about sport and physical education, which was then seen within a larger framework, including leisure and popular culture. For example, the government refused to build a *Grand Stade* in Paris for the football World Cup in 1938 and, more generally, it rejected all sports specialisation in favour of what later would be called "Sport for All".

The ministers Jean Zay (National Education), Léo Lagrange (Leisure and sport) and Henri Sellier (Health) joined together to promote a new notion of physical education, which was more modern, as it would include sport. In the same spirit, the creation of a *Brevet Sportif Populaire* (BSP) was intended in 1937 to implement a sporting self-evaluation system which was expected to make a broad impact on people's health. As Léo Lagrange claimed in the foreword to the BSP's guidelines, "it must result in involving young people in a movement towards physical education and sport training". This diploma, which was not specifically addressed to students, was integrated in schools in 1938 as a physical education test as part of the compulsory examinations at the end of the final year.

Compulsory education was increased to the age of fourteen, and all classes of primary and secondary schools had a weekly half day for outdoor activities in 1937. Being distinct from the physical education lesson itself, this half day was probably the first real occasion in which sports training could reach all students. The idea of a significant increase in the weekly amount of time given to PE of up to five hours was also a consequence of medical concerns at a time when tuberculosis was causing serious concern. Finally, intercollegiate sport also developed, the OSU being extended to high-school students in 1938 when it became the *Office du Sport Scolaire et Universitaire* (OSSU), a structure which was, however, controlled mainly by the State.

Many of the Popular Front projects did not have time to be implemented. After a few months, a new government took over. This, in turn, was not for long, inasmuch as the country capitulated before Hitler's troops in 1940. The Vichy government of Marshal Pétain then tried to repair the "errors" of the past, criticising in particular excessive intellectualism which had led to defeat, and advocating the giving of French youth a taste for action. The body cult became a national cause and presupposed control of both individuals and organisations. In 1940, a Commissariat for General and Sports Education (EGS) was set up under the direction of the former tennis champion, Jean Borotra. His first action was to reform physical education by reinforcing its position of up to nine (then seven) hours a week, while launching a plan for the training and recruitment of physical education teachers, giving a central role to the 'natural method' of Georges Hébert. Two billion francs were planned for the building of sports facilities, even though only a few would be built in those difficult days.

Devotion to action and outdoor activities supported the development of all youth movements, including that in sport. Paradoxically in such a dark period, the number of sports practitioners had never been so high. That is why the Government needed better to control the associations and, consequently, defined a Sport Charter in December 1940. This text restricted professional sport and brought the school closer to sports clubs. It also placed the sports movement under the direct authority of the State. For athletes, an oath became the rule: with the extended arm salute, the oath exalted discipline and honesty towards the fatherland. At club level, approval of the State became obligatory, just like, for every sports national body, affiliation to the National Sports Council, an old structure founded in 1908. Moreover, a council of sports leaders was directly chosen by the State from now on.

Such control procedures were not always applied: Borotra was dismissed in 1942, then put in prison. He was replaced by Colonel Pascot, whose docility towards the hierarchy and administrative zeal made sport a part of the State collaboration system.

After 1945, the world of sport and physical education did not escape a purge – at least at the administrative level – that spread across the country for several months (a special commission for '*épuration*' was set up in October 1944). A General Direction for Physical Education and Sports was created, soon ruled by a senior military man from Joinville, Gaston Roux. Demographic and medical concerns (responsible for the baby boom) and economic requirements for rebuilding France resulted in neglect of sport. In fact, the State authorities shared two beliefs: the educational values of moderated sport and the new prestige given to the country by its champions.

The first conception was the more widespread. In conformity with the ideals of the Popular Front, sport was still perceived as an attribute of the welfare state. Consequently, everything had to be done to protect it from the *bourgeoisie* and Big Business, and to preserve its values. At a time when juvenile delinquency was increasing, it was assumed that the principles of painful and tough training, or the values of noble competition, could be transferred to everyday life. This belief made sport a "discipline of life", in particular for activities to which the statute of "basic sports" was ideologically given (swimming, athletics, gymnastics). A consensus on this was shared by teachers, the state authorities and even the National Council of Resistance: sport should be a self-accepted discipline whose control by individuals would become a step to better citizenship. Physical education was redefined in 1945 and 1959, giving a growing place to sport, while still being subject to medical objectives. Such a status presupposed, of course, that "real" sport could be protected from the "sirens of the stadium". With the Ordinance of 28 August 1945, for example, State subsidies and even the right to set up a national team were reserved only to those sporting bodies which had signed a special agreement with the State. In addition, medical control was made compulsory in 1945 for sports competition, the State partially assuming its cost. Finally, for safety reasons, certain professions were, from now on, governed by new texts which formally described the professional competencies and required diplomas to teach or train: for instance, for mountain guides (1948), skiing instructors and swimming teachers (1951), and judo instructors (1955).

These examples clearly indicated the preferences of the authorities. Sport was seen as a remedy for the nation's weakness; it consequently had to be controlled. However, during the first years following the *Libération*, the State had to treat this need for sport as a national obligation with major transformations of the sports system.

The development of French sport in the post-war period initially confirmed certain tendencies which had appeared earlier. On an institutional level, a few changes had been observed since the creation of national bodies in charge of basketball (1932), volleyball (1936) and handball (1941). At another level, however, violence, corruption, lack of democracy in the clubs, drugs and boycotts came more and more to the fore. Sporting reality was fully opposed to the values associated with it by political leaders. Moreover, these contradictions were still more obvious since sport was strongly 'mediatised'. Sports displays were not yet systematically televised, but sport benefited from excellent coverage on radio. *L'Equipe*, arising out of the ashes of the newspaper *L'Auto*, which had been accused of collaboration with Vichy in 1945, also became, from February 1946, one of the world's most renowned sporting periodicals. Thus, the media contributed to give sports events an audience never reached before. Descriptions of races and matches by journalists became dramas from which it was hard to escape. France had its sport heroes: Bobet, who won the *Tour de France* in 1953, the boxer Marcel Cerdan, winner in the United States, but who died tragically in 1949, the marathon runner Alain Mimoun, whose victories had a particular resonance in such a period of decolonisation (he was born in Algeria, but claimed that France was his fatherland). Journalists stressed the drama of sporting events when, for instance, Germany, the enemy of yesterday, won the Football World Cup in 1954, when cyclists in the *Tour de France* were attacked after crossing the Italian border in 1949, when an accident at the 24-hour Le Mans race resulted in the death of 79 people and injured nearly a hundred more in 1955. Especially, the debut of the USSR in the Helsinki Olympic Games in 1952 led to an emphasis on the role of sport as a vehicle of nationalism and a reflection of international tension. It is true that France had already taken these notions into account for a long time; but the context of the Cold War brought them to a head and had an effect on the expectations of sports people, spectators and political leaders.

The history of worker sport also reflected these changes. Under the Popular Front, the FSGT had increased considerably and had more than 100 000 members in 1687 clubs before the War. After having survived the years 1939-1944 without suffering too much from the political climate and state control, the FSGT was able to attract even more people after the *Libération,* but its rise was suddenly halted by the tensions of the Cold War. In 1951, another political scission between socialists and communists led to the creation of the socialist UST, while the FSGT remained in the shadow of Moscow.

From now on, women were better integrated into male sporting structures, and although they remained excluded from some sports, their participation had increased greatly since the thirties. There were already more than 26 000 sportswomen in 1943. However, public attitudes had barely changed and sportswomen were generally viewed with some condescension or contempt, as attested to in the book by Marie-Thérèse Eyquem published in 1946, *La femme et le sport.* Micheline Ostermeyer, three times Olympic champion in throwing events in 1948 and, simultaneously, first prizewinner at the Academy of Music (piano), played a role in showing that traditional feminine values could be compatible with sporting excellence.

Nevertheless, the forties and the fifties were not favourable to French sport, including school sporting activities. Sport was not completely recognised by the new government statute, and the number of sports practitioners even decreased, in particular after 1949, although sporting bodies had 2.3 million members in 1955. For the State, the priorities were to reconstruct the nation and to end the crisis in its colonies. The economy led to certain priority choices and sport lagged behind, as clearly shown by policies towards building sports facilities, whose poor state was recognised by every sports and political leader. In 1951, the Le Gorgeu commission was charged with evaluating the need for sporting facilities; it confirmed that 64 billion Francs would be necessary over the next five years for sports facilities. But the budget for 1952 only envisaged 885 million! The war in Indo-China, then the Algerian drama, were too costly to facilitate any extra budget for sport. The first hope only appeared after 1958, with Maurice Herzog , who was put in charge of a new *Haut-Commissariat aux Sports.*

5 – The De Gaulle years: a new sports policy (1960-1969)

When, in 1959, De Gaulle took charge of the new Fifth Republic, his ambition for France was to make it a world power, independent of the United States, and one which would excel economically as well as culturally. Sport was part of such a programme: De Gaulle asked the Anapurna winner, Maurice Herzog, to take charge of sports development. In 1948, France had obtained 32 medals in the London Olympic Games. In 1960, in Rome, it gained only five medals: this humiliation was highlighted by the press and was taken as a reason by Herzog to plan a large programme of reforms.

In physical education, the sixties were initially characterised by a reorganisation of sport at school. The half day of outdoor activities literally became a "half day of sport" in 1961, while the OSSU was transformed into an *Association du Sport Scolaire et Universitaire* (ASSU) whose role in the spotting and training of athletes was emphasised. In 1962, then in 1967, "sport and physical activities" ('sport and physical activity' was and is officially used to underline the distinction between sport in clubs and sport in schools) became simultaneously the goal and the exclusive means of physical education at secondary school. From now on, school had to prepare future athletes and future leaders: "Physical education must be the echo, on an educational level, of the increasing importance of sport as a fact of civilisation (...). (It) is practiced according to rules and generates behaviour which coincide with the values normally accepted by society". Teachers were influenced by work done within the FSGT and by several "educational sport" experiments, like the "Sports Republic" of Calais. They consequently accepted this cultural change that they had largely anticipated. The reform was also well received because school attendance became compulsory up to the age of sixteen in 1959, considering that teenagers were more attracted by sport than by gymnastics. This radical inversion of the place of sport in French society was remarkably illustrated by the *Doctrine du Sport*, written in 1965 by 200 authors under the authority of the *Haut-comité des Sports* and the National Sports Council.

With a considerable budget, Herzog was able to push through a very large sports plan and socio-cultural construction as the second plank of his reforms. The sporting elite was supposed to come from the masses: consequently, the first law programme (1961-65) gave 1500 stadiums and gymnasiums and 1000 swimming pools to the country. Although Herzog left the government in 1964, a second law programme (1965-1970) built on this exceptional financial effort.

Many texts were also published for people prepared to train and supervise groups, for example with the creation of a specific statute for primary school physical education counsellors. In the same way, technical advisers were paid by the State and were allocated to most national sports bodies. In return, the control of sporting structures was tightened by a special "delegation of powers" and various subsidies. In 1963, the obligation to be State-certified applied to all sports at a certain level: "No one can teach or instruct physical education or sport for money, either as a main or as a secondary occupation, either in a regular way, or seasonally or haphazardly, and no one can take the title of professor, monitor, assistant-monitor or master of physical education or sport or any similar title without conforming to certain conditions."

The whole system finally made sport a large public service where sporting activities at school, Sport for All and elite sport were covered by the same programme. In parallel, local city leaders started to be more conscious of their role. The Municipal Offices of Sports (OMS) came together in a national official structure in 1958.

The effects of this policy were particularly strong as France, profiting from economic expansion, entered fully into a society of leisure where sport tookits place. The sporting spectacle became accessible to all through television or the specialised press which, with *L'Equipe*, was blossoming. Not only that, French people were simply actively enjoying sport more and more. A quarter of the population claimed they were engaging in sport in 1967. With a major transformation of society, women made up a no less negligible part of these results since, with 22%, they were not far from the male indices of sports participation. In Olympic sports alone, women had 220 630 participants in the late 1950s, compared to a total of 1 228 336 in 1963; they made up 693 142 out of a total of approximately 2 million sports participants in 1970. This general democratisation, which profited not only Olympic sports, could also be seen at school where USEP members rose to more than half a million in 1965, while those of the ASSU rose to 380 000 in 1968.

Internationally, France initially tried to maintain a diplomatic balance with its colonies. Having thought for some time, in particular after 1945, that sports development in the colonies could simultaneously ensure a better integration of athletes in the nation and bring top athletes to the national team, French leaders changed their mind after 1960. France was often reduced to the role of organiser, for example, of the *Jeux de la Communauté Française* (Tanarive, 1960), then the *Jeux de l'Amitié* (Abidjan, 1961, Dakar, 1963), as preludes to future African Games.

In charge of the organisation of the Winter Olympics at Grenoble in 1968, France wished to gain moral, material, symbolic, political and economic profit from the event. Its first idea was, essentially, to stimulate the traditional skiing economy and to help the city of Grenoble to reach the same level as other skiing cities in terms of infrastructure. However, the Games became progressively the focal point of several hopes at local as well as national level, such as the prestige of the nation, stimulation of the French winter sports equipment industry, winter tourism in general and in the Alps in particular, the revival of French sport, the building of a modern image of Grenoble. The objectives came to focus on the sale of French snow to fortunate foreigners. The triple gold medal winner Jean-Claude Killy, and the victories of the sisters Goitschel produced an enthusiasm for such projects. However, subsequent assessments of Grenoble's success, in particular at an economic level, did not live up to expectations.

6 – The present: sport and leisure between market and association (1970-2001)

The beginning of the 1970s was marked by the rise of "Sport for All", which a number of developments contributed to. After May 1968, young adults were not so attracted by traditional sport clubs. Ten years later, a dual movement appeared. On the one hand, alternative practices developed outside the sports institutions, including sometimes activities which were apparently related to sports activities, like road races. This rejection of the traditional system (clubs, hierarchy) had a strong impact on the rise of outdoor activities in which to enjoy nature and adventure was central (windsurfing, cross country skiing, climbing, rambling) and, later on, street sports (skate boarding, roller skating). On the other hand, all-round fitness activities (gymnastics, aerobics, body-building) had increased success. The movement started as early as the sixties and grew stronger in the seventies. For example, membership of the French Federation of Physical Education and Voluntary Gymnastics went from more than 40 000 in 1970 to 333 505 in 1984. Then the movement truly took off during the eighties, less through the pressure of American culture than as a result of a Sunday televised series entitled "Gym-tonic". Soon after, fitness centres mushroomed; but today they are mainly under the monopoly of firms like Mouving and the Gymnase-Club.

Paradoxically, the participation of French people in the traditional sports system has not significantly decreased, since there were more than 13 million members in nearly 150 000 clubs. In 1985, as many as 73.8 % of the French population was taking an active part in sport, while only 19.3% were members of an organised sports body.

The participation of women has undoubtedly had something to do with these results; indeed, women's sports participation went from 32% in 1983 to 64% in 1994. By contrast, 72% of men took an active part in sport. However, the nature of the activities is strongly correlated with gender. Thus, French women especially practiced gymnastics (25 %) in various forms, from aerobics to sophrology, swimming (23%), walking (22%), whereas men chose cycling, tennis and football as their top three active sports.. Certain activities remained, on the other hand, only slightly feminised, in particular football, rugby, boxing and cycling. In addition, the increase in female sports participation has for the past thirty years concerned mainly non-institutionalised and non-competitive activities. Indeed, while the number of women who were members of a club was about four million in 1992, women constituted only 26% of the membership of Olympic sports bodies (1.7 million). Compared with the whole of the French population, 6% of women competed actively in sport, as opposed to 17% men. Lastly, the difference between males and females increased with age.

The rise of competitive and leisure practices has led to a sports market in certain activities. The sports market was brought under control by the establishment in 1985 of a sports instruction diploma, distinct from the diploma in sport and physical education for teachers, so as to ensure at local level the implementation of sports policies which city authorities wish to develop. In 1992, the state introduced general standards that all instructors, advisers and operators in physical education and sport had to meet..

The role of the state in the promotion of sport has not diminished over half a century. It was been embodied and redefined twice in law, in 1975 with the Mazeaud law and in 1984 with the Avice law. The nation's responsibility was spelled out and a new contract between State and sporting organisations was prescribed. These laws expressed a permanent feature of the state's desire to control sport ever since the Popular Front. Sports policies were always attempts to prevent sport from being left to the market or to private or any other sports administrators. At a time when Europe was taking a new shape within the European Community, this 'state sport' position put France in an unusual situation. With the decentralisation laws of the Mitterrand years, the importance of local communities, in particular those of the cities, was mounting, resulting in a more geographically dispersed network of sports facilities. In addition, the economic crisis of the eighties led to a social crisis and many local politicians tried to limit its effects on young people in the suburbs by supporting local sports events and building community sporting facilities.

As far as physical education is concerned, state control has remained very strong. The curriculum has hardly changed since 1967 in spite of the many texts published after 1985 intended to define exactly what had to be taught in sport and what place had to be given to such physical activities as outdoor activities (climbing) and dance. On the other hand, physical education teaching was formalised in 1977 by a university degree, and universities were integrated through the institutionalisation of a new scientific body of knowledge called "STAPS": Sciences and Technologies in Physical and Sport Activities. In addition, special sports studies classes were created at the beginning of the 1970s to enable students to follow their academic studies while training under privileged conditions.

The country's involvement in sport is also apparent in its desire to organise international events. For the third time in its history, France hosted the Winter Olympics in 1992, at Albertville, and then the football World Cup in 1998; this resulted in an amazing popular fervour and made it possible to build the *Grand Stade* which had been awaited since 1938.

The most popular sporting figures of these years were Guy Drut, Olympic champion at 110 metres hurdles and a future Sports Minister, Alain Prost, Formula 1 World Champion, Bernard Hinault in cycling, Thierry Rey and David Douillet in judo, Jacques Secrétin in table tennis. Then there was the French football team which had great success in the 1980s under its captain Michel Platini, and in recent times under Zinedine Zidane, or certain clubs like Saint-Etienne, in the mid-1970s, whose exploits in the European Cup were followed by the whole country. French sportswomen were no longer being ignored by the pubic; they too were becoming part of myth, for example, Jeannie Longo and Felicia Ballanger in cycling, Isabelle Letissier in sailing, Marie Claire Restoux in judo, Murielle Hermine in synchronised swimming, and Marie-Josée Pérec in athletics. The *Tour de France* in cycling, the Five Nations tournament in rugby, the Roland Garros tournament in tennis are events followed by millions and confirm the preference of French people for certain sports: football, rugby, boxing, tennis, Formula 1 motor racing — all sports supported by television.

Conclusions

Such a presentation of sports history on the scale of a country and over such a long period ineluctably leaves key aspects in the shade, for example the paucity of political, economic and social data. We have also ignored the geographical diffusion of sporting practices, as well as the history of techniques and technologies which shed much light on the more global history of sport. A comparative analysis of certain sports would also have allowed us to adumbrate the periods and main explanatory factors that we have only mentioned in passing. Instead we chose to dwell on the particular relationships that the French State has maintained with systems of physical exercise, first gymnastics, then later, sports. Analysis of such instruments of sports diffusion as schools and universities, or the efforts devoted to encourage mass as opposed to elite sport confirms the importance of French sport as part of a welfare State whose values have to be under the control and part of the responsibility of the State. The new context of globalisation, as well as economic realism, is weakening this position. Nonetheless, it is still an excellent indicator of the history of physical activities in France.

Literature

Arnaud, P. (1985) *Les athlètes de la République*. Toulouse : Privat

Arnaud, P. (1994) *Les origines du sport ouvrier en Europe*. Paris : L'Harmattan.

Arnaud, P. and Camy, C. (1986) *La naissance du mouvement sportif associatif en France*. Toulouse : Privat.

Arnaud, P. and Riordan, J. (1998) *Sport et relations internationales*. Paris : L'Harmattan.

Arnaud, P. and Terret, T. (1993) *Le rêve blanc. Olympisme et sports d'hiver*. Bordeaux : Presses universitaires de Bordeaux.

Arnaud, P. and Terret, T. (1995) *Education et politique sportive*. Paris : Ed. du CTHS.

Arnaud, P. and Terret, T. (1996) *Histoire du sport féminin*. Paris : L'Harmattan, 2 tomes.

Arnaud, P. and Terret,T. (1996) *Education physique, Sports et Arts. XIXème-XXème siècles*. Paris : Ed. du CTHS.

Amar, M. (1987) *Nés pour courir. Sport, pouvoir et rébellion*. Grenoble : Presses universitaire de Grenoble.

Callède, J. P.(2000) *Les politiques sportives en France. Eléments de sociologie historique*. Paris : Economica.

Dauncey, H. and Hare, G. *(1999) France and the 1998 World Cup. The National Impact of a World Sporting Event*. London: Frank Cass.

Davisse, A. and Louveau, C. (1998) *Sport, école, société. La part des femmes*. Paris : L'Harmattan.

Defrance, J. (1987) *L'excellence corporelle*. Rennes : coédition Presses universitaires de Rennes – éd. AFRAPS.

Gaboriau, G. (1995) *Le Tour de France et le vélo. Histoire sociale d'une épopée contemporaine*. Paris : L'Harmattan.

Gay-Lescot, J. L. (1991) *Sport et éducation sous Vichy*. Lyon : Presses universitaires de Lyon.

Holt, R. (1981) *Sport and Society in Modern France*, London.

Hubscher, R., Durry, J. and Jeu, B. (1992) *L'histoire en mouvements. Le sport dans la société française (XIXe-XXe siècle)*. Paris : Armand Colin.

Irlinger, P., Louveau, C. and Métoudi, M. (1987) *Les pratiques sportives des Français*. Paris : INSEP.

Terret, T. (2000) *Education physique, sport et loisir. 1970-2000*. Marseille : Ed. AFRAPS.

Rauch, A. (1981) *Le corps en éducation physique*. Paris : Presses universitaires de France.

Vigarello, G. (1993) *Le sain et le malsain*. Paris : Seuil.

[1] Baron de Vaux, *Les femmes de sport*, Paris, 1885.

Spain

Teresa González Aja and Patrick Stumm

Introduction
"Continuity of change" can be considered as one of the fundamental characteristics of contemporary Spain. This does not always mean evolution; it is more that games, sport or spectacles have been strongly conditioned by the political and social changes that have affected Spanish history. It is therefore difficult to give a chronological account of Spanish sports history, because the evolution is not continuous and is linked to political issues.

However, contemporary Spanish sport history can be differentiated in three general ways. First, from the ancien regime to the Civil War. Second, focusing on the whole period of the Franco dictatorship. Finally, there is the transition to democracy and the present, when, in 25 years, Spain has made an enormous advance to recover Spanish sport and to play a more important role in international sport.

1. From the Ancien Regime (mid-18th Century) to Civil War (1936-1939)
Some sporting and physical activities in contemporary Spain can be traced to the 18th and 19th centuries, during the ancien and new regime. The ancien regime represents the previous status of the revolution and has to be understood as a rapid process that caused a series of modern transformations that otherwise would have taken centuries to achieve. The "revolution" is usually interpreted as a process that rescued Spanish society from absolutism and established liberalism and a sort of democracy with effects not only for politics, but for the whole social environment. The vital step to the new regime refers traditionally to the year 1808, when the French troops of Napoleon entered Spain.

The ancien regime coincides with the 18th century and is connected with King Carlos III (1759-1788) who for many was a reformer and personification of the maturity of the century. One of his principal amusements and that of his son, the future Carlos IV, was hunting – owing to the boring court atmosphere of military life. However, the King´s arrival in Madrid in December 1759 heralded a series of transformations in the image of the city, its structure and organisation, as well as daily life to which he accorded huge importance. Even if Carlos III prohibited many aspects of social life, like smoking, immoral conversation, playing billiards or cards, which had been a game only for kings, Madrid changed at the end of the 18th century to one of the liveliest cities in Europe, conceived as an "open" city, especially in terms of leisure. The carnival arose in Madrid, the authorities organised masquerades, dances and wine drinking establishments for amusement. The famous Spanish painter Francisco Goya (1746-1828) showed a proud, insolent and provocative Spain. In Goya's works the amusements are hunting scenes and popular parties. Extremely modern in its conception was Goya´s opinion of the new times, shown in paintings like "The Crazy Skater" (El loco de patines) or the cyclist in "Crazy Modern Times" (El loco tiempo moderne). One of the major popular amusements was the "national festival" of bullfighting. In the 18th century, the nobility began to abandon bullfighting in favour of horse riding, horses now being considered "noble". The new monarchy, which had been originally French, did not appreciate bulls as amusement at all; they considered bullfighting a terrible and cruel spectacle. So the main bullfighters were no longer nobles. but the lower classes, village people and professional bullfighters. The Bourbon rejection of bulls manifested a clear concern for the types of amusement to be provided for the Spanish public. It was in this context that Gaspar Melchor de Jovellanos proposed establishing instructions for physical education in the school system and all villages, as well as the training of teachers and the founding of educational establishments, so that young people would be able to compete in championships. The invasion by French troops and the beginning of the "War of Independence" in 1808 facilitated this implementation, which would never have been easy in other circumstances. Liberal groups could turn the uncertain times to their own advantage, which antagonised the privileged classes of the ancien regime. The nascent liberalism picked up the concern for education, but now used it more for transforming the political system. In the new ideology the concepts of popular sovereignty, education and public opinion were now intimately interconnected.

The War of Independence, with all its consequences, took Spain into a deep reformation process in regard to politics, institutions, the economy and society. Spain passed from the ancien to the new regime and, in 1814, it was, theoretically – together with the United States – one of the most liberal countries in the world. During the first third of the 19th century, however, difficulties in the Spanish economy were developing and the political administration was failing. The atmosphere that surrounded the life and customs of the time were now seriously affected. The economic and political crisis divided Spaniards and created a climate of civil war and conflict between the ancien and new regime until the year 1823, when King Fernando VII re-established the character of the ancien regime. Fernando's decade appeared to be ordinary, but amusement activities were not the same.

The 19th century continued with an interest in physical education, which is associated with the figure of Francisco Amorós (1770-1848). He closely associated physical activities with gymnastics. Amorós was, from 1800, in the military court of Carlos IV and, in 1807, after having published some educational works, he had an important influence on the regal environment. He created an institute, called "Pestalozziano", in Madrid and Carlos IV also entrusted to him the education of his 12-year-old daughter Francisca de Paula. Considered as the founder of physical education in Spain, Amorós, was closely linked to the "Pestalozziano" movement. The first "Pestalozzi" school had been founded in 1803 in Tarragona, where the spirit of educational renovation allowed the use of the Pestalozzi (1746-1827) method as a model to renovate educational practice in schools. The Real Institute Pestalozziano had a progressive military orientation and, in November 1806, it changed its name to Real Military Institute Pestalozziano.

However, the teaching situation in Spain was still parlous. So a group of noblemen of philanthropic spirit decided to introduce the monitor method or mutual teaching for physical education. It allowed that a single teacher, without having special training, could instruct a large number of students if the class had been homogeneously distributed into groups. In other words, a student could lead the class as instructor.

The first person to apply the method of mutual teaching in Spain was a military man of Irish origin, Juan Kearney, who had been a student observer at the "Real Institute Pestalozziano". The liberals, who had power during the Liberal Triennium, continued the chaotic situation; their practical impotence was shown by the instructors having to resort to mutual teaching method.

Between the years 1850 and 1870 some gymnastic centres had been created in which, regrettably, the instructors were mainly acrobats or vaulters. D. Francisco of Aerie Becerril, Count of Villalobos (1817-1867), who had been an admirer of Amorós, published a book in 1842 with the title *A Glance about the Gymnasium, The Utility* and *Advantage of Science*. He founded one of the first Spanish gymnastics centres in Madrid and was also professor of gymnastics (1867) for the Prince of Asturias, the future King Alphonse XIII.

Alphonse XIII was a born sportsman and enthusiast. As well as hunting and polo, he practised pigeon shooting, motor racing and skating. In 1883, he set up the Central School for Teachers of Theoretical and Practical Gymnastics (Escuela Central de la Ensenanza de Actividades Fisicas teoreticas y practices) and, in 1887, the school, which belonged to the University of Madrid and which admitted both male and female students (an unusual feature of the era), was inaugurated. This school was, however, closed for economic reasons in 1892. In 1887, the first vacation schools arrived in Spain, at a time when the National Pedagogic Museum (Museo Nacional de Pedagogia) of Madrid organised the first summer school. It created its own Free Teaching Institution: the Economic Society of Granada (Sociedad Economico de Granada); the Barcelona Society of Friends (Sociedad Barcelones de Amigos) of País did the same in 1893.

At the end of the 19th century, influenced by the modern English sports movement, a Spanish sports system with clubs and federations began to be established. Besides the establishment of gymnastics and education centres, there were also sport clubs for polo (1870 in Jerez), sailing (1873 Málaga), rowing (1821/1878 Barcelona/Tarragona), mountaineering (1876 Barcelona), athletics (1889 Madrid), golf (1895 Madrid) and motor racing (1897 Barcelona). The first Spanish sports federations were for "colombofila" (clay pigeon shooting) (1894), cycling (1895) and gymnastics (1899).

Football became the most popular and national sport during the 20th century. In 1882, football had made an appearance as teachers and students of the Free Teaching Institution and those of Irish Schools in Valladolid and Salamanca were the first to practise this sport. However, it was played in élite schools where games were encouraged, in contrast to the majority of schools, institutes and colleges, where physical education was practically unknown. Later on, the Rio Tinto Company promoted football, as it had British capital and, therefore, had some British employees.

In 1889, the first football club "El Recreativo de Huelva" was founded and, in 1913, the Spanish Football Federation came into being. Football was introduced in Spain, as it was in Europe and South America, for pedagogical and economic reasons. The big clubs of today were created owing to the joint efforts of Spaniards and foreigners (e.g., the Swiss Hans Gamper founded FC Barcelona in 1899; Athlétic de Bilbao came into existence in 1898; Real Madrid in 1902, Atlético de Madrid in 1903).

King Alphonse XIII promoted sporting activities and sponsored some clubs and Spanish events. In particular, he showed a considerable interest in the celebration of sports events and especially in the Olympic Games by presiding over the Committee for the Candidacy of Barcelona to host the Games in 1924, even if the Barcelona bid was unsuccessful. The link between the aristocracy, sporting activities and the IOC was well established. This is evident in the case of Marquis of Villamejor, who was nominated as member of the IOC and was succeeded in 1922 by Baron de Güell. This trend had already become manifest in 1920 and it intensified during Primo de Rivera's dictatorship. This changed in 1931, in the Republic, when the aristocracy was an idle and isolated caste and the King was unpopular.

The Republic tried, for political reasons, to democratise and proletarianise the Olympic movement which was closely linked to the ruling and aristocratic classes. The Spanish government was not in favour of its athletes participating in the Berlin Olympic Games of 1936 and refused to give subsidies which the Spanish Olympic Committee had requested in order to participate. It considered the Games tainted with political ideology to which it was clearly opposed. However, the government wished to celebrate alternative Games in Barcelona, which had been promoted by various communist, socialist and Jewish groups. The so-called Popular Olympics attracted a total of 4500 entries from many nationalities, including British, Swiss, Dutch, Norwegian and French. The opening ceremony was planned for 19 July 1936 but, on 18 July, the military uprising in Morocco broke out, thereby precipitating the Spanish Civil War. So the Popular Olympics were never held and most of the foreign athletes who were already in the country were evacuated or stayed to fight in the Civil War.

If the Civil War prevented the holding of parallel Games to the Olympics, it also put an end to attempts by the Second Republic to implement educational programmes that would permit qualitative and quantitative changes in public education. Until that time, the country's political, economic and social situation had not permitted any attempt to establish a strongly structured state school system. Physical education had only been introduced in small élitist circles.

Interest in physical education during the 19th century was intended to renovate the school system and establish the movement of "new" education. The new school was meant to bring about a basic reformation of national schools. The Free Institution of Education had most success and tried to develop an innovative model of a scientific character for all levels of education which extended into the 20th century. The Institution valued physical education in an extreme way, so that it seems to have "dissolved" into general education. Muscular education was carried out indirectly with the locality, with the school opening up its facilities, school materials and the general regime of teaching, and directly with exercises, gymnastics, games, walks, excursions and holiday camps.

However, all the evolution and experience sport and teaching came to an end in 1936 when the Civil War began. Franco's new political system changed Spain at all levels of society until his death in 1975.

2. Establishment of the Franco Regime (1939) up to Franco´s Death (1975)

Until his death in November 1975, General Franco continued to be, as was proclaimed on his coins, "Caudillo of Spain by the Grace of God" and answerable, according to his apologists, only to God and history. Although in the last years he distanced himself from direct intervention in daily politics, it is certainly true that no important decisions could be taken without his consent. Right to the end, thanks to what was called the "Francoist Constitution" he kept power to appoint and dismiss ministers, a power which he used whenever he saw fit. The period, which began with the end of the Civil War, was marked by the personality of this man who considered that the liberalism of the 19th century had been the cause of the final eclipse of Spain's greatness. He therefore carried out a systematic purge of men and ideas. The regime of freedoms characteristic of the previous system was replaced by a regime in which one had to obtain authorisation to undertake any type of activity. Furthermore, the media and the teaching system were used to inculcate ideas and values which would ensure acceptance of the new regime. The only values taken into account were religious and patriotic ones. In order to inculcate them suitably in the younger generation, the Church and the Falange were incorporated into the teaching system.

With these premises it would appear logical to use sport to serve the political ideal. An attempt was made to follow the Nazi German model. But several aspects should be borne in mind: Franco was never willing to build a totalitarian state with only one party after the Italian or German model. After the powers of the Axis were defeated, Franco understood the need to abandon the Fascist image of his regime. And with regard to the specific sports question, Franco was never willing to spend money on it, unlike Hitler or Mussolini.

On 22 February 1941, Franco signed a decree which created the National Sports Delegation of the Traditionalist Falange (Delegocion Nacional de Deporte de Tradicionalistas de Falange) and of the National Syndical Offensive Juntas (JONS – Joventud de Ofensiva Nacional de Sindacos). The decree entrusted "the direction and promotion of Spanish sport" to the Falange.

The Falange had been founded in 1933 by José Antonio Primo de Rivera, son of the military dictator of the 1920s. The party's ideology adopted many concepts from Fascist Italy: the defence of Christian values against the peril of Marxism, a totalitarian state which would create a classless society promoting the interests of the workers, and an imperialistic destiny at the expense of weaker races.

The Falange was a small body until the outbreak of the Civil War; but during the conflict its membership increased – in a similar way to that of the Spanish Communist Party – to nearly two million, many of whom fought against "the Reds" in the different Falangist militia. However, the rise of the Falange was thwarted by two fundamental blows which would give rise to eternal political frustration: the execution of José Antonio Primo de Rivera in Alicante Prison in November 1936 and Franco's incorporation of the Party into the "ambiguous" Movement, together with the monarchist and the Carlist, in April 1937. This is the Party which was entrusted with sport by Franco through the creation of the National Sports Delegation (NSD) (Delegocion Nacional de Deporte). The NSD was presided over by the National Delegate of Physical Education and Sports, who was also President of the Spanish Olympic Committee (clearly contravening IOC rules which declare that national committees should be strictly non-political), and responsible for sports medicine, legal, transport, press and propaganda sections, which made up the department of military sport and general sport in the Movement. He was also head of the department of national federations, and his control over the different federations was total. The NSD appointed not only the presidents and vice-presidents of the various Spanish federations, but also the members of their boards of directors and, in addition, the presidents and vice-presidents of all the regional branches of these federations. As if this was not enough, Article 4 of the Decree conferred on the NSD the right to veto the decision of any federation with which it did not agree. With all this it completely controlled the whole of Spanish sport. As Cazorla Prieto states: "all the social organisations of sport were subject if not to an absolute state or para-state control, then to a rigid discipline imposed by the public authorities, which practically stifled any trace of social protagonism".

The new organisation was to be a delegation or agency of the General Secretary of the National Movement, the only political party permitted, an uncomfortable alliance of Falangists, monarchists and Carlists. Its mission was to use the international sports ambit to exhibit Spanish virility and "passion", the same as the Italian and German regimes had done between 1930 and 1940. Therefore, any possibility that sport could have a certain degree of independence from the new political power was discarded from the outset. The NSD introduced a series of Falangist customs and symbols into sport; for example, they changed the customary red shirts of the national football team to blue, and instituted the Fascist salute by athletes at the beginning of competitions. The post of national delegate was occupied by war heroes, Falangists and politicians on their way up, and it is thus not surprising that the NSD failed in almost everything that it tried to do. It certainly failed in its attempt to make Spain a nation of athletes and to play an important role in international competitions. The very few Spanish sports successes, especially those of the football team Real Madrid, were the product of a massive importing of foreign stars, who were mainly recognised as such abroad. The failure of the NSD was in appointing people whose capacity for sport administration left much to be desired (with the exception of Samaranch), but who were totally loyal to the regime. Furthermore, the scant investment which Franco considered suitable for sport meant that the NSD had to exist on money collected from the football pools.

The brilliance of Real Madrid, a handful of outstanding individuals or the success in an insignificant international sports area, like clay pigeon shooting and hockey on roller skates, could partially conceal the poor level of sport in Spain in general. In six Olympic Games in which Spain participated during the Franco years, it won only one gold medal, two silver and two bronzes. Franco was not willing to make any sort of economic investment in sport.

Furthermore, coeducation disappeared, the physical training of both sexes became totally different. The boys would do rigid, virile exercises of a marked military nature. The girls would practise Swedish and rhythmic gymnastics and the popular dances characteristic of Spanish regions.

Also the old summer holiday camps were replaced by camps or hostels organised by the Youth Front, the Female Section or the trade unions for Education and Rest. The ideology of these camps was far from hygienic postulates which had given birth to the holiday camps and put them closer to the practices of the Hitler Youth, emphasising their marked Fascist character.

During the Francoist period football played an important role in daily life and its impact and development depended on different periods of Franco´s dictatorship.

At the beginning, during the 1940s, the national team was hard put to find countries to play against. Football was an important element in the hands of the new regime established as a vehicle for Fascist attitudes and propaganda. A good example of this is the image of the two teams which played the first final of the Generalissimo´s Cup in 1939, Seville and Racing El Ferrol; they lined up before the match with their right arms raised in the Fascist salute, enthusiastically singing the "Cara al sol" (Facing the Sun), the Falangist battle hymn, echoed by the crowd which filled the stadium, and which also stood and sang, arms raised. During this epoch Fascist concepts were applied to the game. The Falange wanted to show the world the impressive power and potential of their "New Spain". There aim was to create a Spain in which everyone would play one sport or another, while the nation's best athletes demonstrated their superiority in international competitions, especially the Olympic Games, thus gaining the admiration of the world.

However, in the hungry Spain of the 1940s, all the yearnings for greatness of the Falange were destined to a most resounding failure. Both in terms of the practice of sport by the general population, and in international competition, like the Olympic Games, the results were pathetic.

After the defeat of the Axis powers in 1945, to a large extent Spain was considered by the rest of the world as the last bastion of Fascism, and it was subjected to the diplomatic and economic boycott of the United Nations. Franco understood that to free himself from this purgatory, he needed to change the image of his regime, which meant eliminating many of the Falangist symbols of Fascist origin. However, at a structural level the Falangist influence would still take many more years to eliminate. Thus, it was the rule that two Falangists were obligatory on the governing board of every club; this was maintained until 1967. The mythology which the press applied continued to be essentially of Fascist origin. The tone adopted by the media was vigorously patriotic and exaggeratedly triumphal.

In the 1950s, Spain became a country in which a great deal of importance was given to sport, but not in the way that the Falange would have liked. While the few athletic tracks and facilities that did exist were seldom used, the masses swarmed to the impressive new stadia, which were built by private football clubs with very little help from the NSD, to admire imported foreign stars. Football would be useful to the regime, to improve its external image abroad. Especially, Real Madrid is considered to be the team which most helped the regime to improve its image abroad. In the 1950s, Real Madrid won the European Cup five times in a row and was the best propaganda for Franco's regime. The President of Real Madrid (1943-1978), Santiago Bernabeu, had been a good friend of Franco since childhood. Bernabeu was conscious of the role of Real Madrid, which had been seen as ambassador of the regime and the country; both were considered one and the same thing inside and outside of Spain.

In the 1960s, sports politics was focused more than on football. In 1961, the first National Sports Institute of Physical Education (INEF – Instituto Nacional de Educacion Fisica) was founded. However, the sport infrastructure and formation was still pretty poor. The lesser Spanish sport, athletics, had to use football grounds for competitions and training. Football still dominated Spanish sport. Also basketball, motor racing and bullfighting, which had been a powerful tourist attraction, became important and were an excellent ambassador for the regime.

Undoubtedly, it was football which did most to improve the international image of Francoist Spain. Other big clubs played not the same attractive football and, from a political point of view, did not play the ambassador role. In the context of the problems of regionalism, which arose during Franco's dictatorship, clubs like Atlétic Bilbao or FC Barcelona made a series of important political gestures which manifested their opposition to Franco´s regime. In the Basque country opposition was more physical than intellectual (above all because of actions taken by ETA); in Catalonia a vast intellectual movement arose against Franco, but there was a remarkable absence of violence. This has been related to the playing style of the different teams. While the characteristic features of the two Basque teams were physical power and aggression, in FC Barcelona (the Catalan team) they were talent and imagination.

The link between football and regionalism in the Franco era has a very simple reason. The Basques and Catalans had supported the Republican cause in the Civil War, so Franco tried systematically to destroy, or at least neutralise, all the institutions which showed even the most remote traces of regionalism or separatism. The Basque and Catalan languages were officially, and at times, brutally suppressed, being forbidden in schools and in all official institutions. The national flags were also banned, as were many other regionalist manifestations.

3. Democratisation and Decentralisation (1976-1985)
When Franco died in 1975 political power was taken by King Juan Carlos I, who declared his intention of forming a democratic state. In the transition process of 1976-1978, former Francoists and the reconstituted political parties made important decisions about the future formation of Spain. One of the first changes regarding sport was the conversion of the NSD into the Council of Sport ("CSD: Consejo Superior de Deportes") on 27 August 1977. The CSD appointed a General Assembly of Sport in December 1977 in order to discuss the future of sport and its integration into Spanish society. The informal committees proposed adapting international sporting standards of an active sport policy and also eliminating the idea of sport in Franco times as a

"spectacle hobby" and "social drug" for society. Therefore, they created democratic structures which had to be made accessible to all individuals and groups. Sports practice had to be reinforced by a constitutional law and also be obligated to the state for financial suppor. As a result, this agreement influenced the basic formation of the Spanish structure of sport. When democracy was legally constituted in 1978, it was the first time in Spanish history that sport had been given a constitutional law at national level (Article 43 III – Spanish Constitution). However, sport was not an explicit and guaranteed right of Spanish citizens, it was more public protection by the state, instead of free associations, which became a guaranteed and fundamental right of Spanish society (Article 22 – Spanish Constitution). Sports clubs and associations were subject to democratic rules, membership was voluntary and the prescriptive public intervention low.

The Spanish constitution set up a decentralised state in order to give the regions more autonomy, in particular the Basque and Catalan counties with their separatist tendencies. However, the general delimitation of authority has created political conflicts to this day. Some regions are demanding more autonomy and political independence. Extremist violent groups, like the Basque organisation ETA, endanger the political climate and life of the young Spanish democracy. In 1982 there were approximately 63 cases of political conflicts between the state and the regions and they have continually bedevilled Spanish life; there were as many as 420 'terrorist acts' in 1989. Spanish sport has also had conflicts of authority and is characterised by a double regulation. Sport as a cultural matter has been integrated into the decentralised political system, in which the three political levels (national, regional, local) work together and divide up sporting matters. The 17 Spanish regions receive explicit power in sport, according to Article 148.1.19 of the Spanish constitution. Other regional sports authorities cover education, research, health and economic legislation. The state power of sport is not only reserved for international relations, national laws and civil-, labour-, and market-legislation. Some regions have tried to interpret authority further and reclaim national sport decisions for themselves. The national programme of the CSD to promote Spanish competitive sport (Centro de Iniciación Tecnicó Deportiva) from 1979 to 1982 had to be abandoned owing to regional interests. Catalonia regarded the national sport selections of athletes as an individual area of authority. The Supreme Court decided that the regions had exclusive sports authority only within their territory and any national matter belonged to the state. Inaccurate delimitation of authority and the absence of priority regulation of national rights led to further political tensions and a double regulation in many areas. Therefore, many sports decrees and laws at national and regional level can be found in Spain. The national sport laws, however, have always been more important and decisive for sports development.

In 1980, a new sports law (General de la Cultura Física y del Deporte) replaced the national sports law of 1961. It mainly regulates the nature of clubs and associations which are regarded as private legal entities, that have to regulate their internal democratic structure independently. The free law of association in the constitution had been restricted and only one sports association can be established for each sport modality, and clubs have to join them if they want to enter competitions, thus leading to a monopolisation of the associations.

The CSD carries out the registration of the national sports federations, according to Article 22.3 of the Spanish constitution, and is in addition responsible for their financial funding. The tasks of the state and international sports policies now became formally and physically separated. The Spanish Olympic Committee (COE) is explicitly responsible for Olympic sport and the CSD for national sport and general international relations. However, the teaching of physical education in schools is still irregular and Spain has only two sports institutes (INEF Madrid and INEFC Barcelona-Lleida), in which there are teachers and lecturers of different qualifications. Therefore, the state decided that everyone active in sport, including coaches and lecturers, has to complete a uniform education. Training almost entirely takes place at the INEF Madrid and allows people with experience and qualifications to complete their education in less than five years. The sports law of 1980 also laid down the integration of further sports institutes at universities, calling them "faculties of physical activities and sport" (Facultad de Ciencias de la Actividad Física y del Deporte).

In the 1970s very few local sports organisations and sport structures existed. After the first local elections were held in 1979, and the Socialist Party PSOE (Partido Socialista Obrero Español) had won in 1,100 communities, local sport started to become more important. Sport facilities in the communities have not only been concentrated on traditional competitions, they have followed the popular international campaign for "Sport for All" as their specialism. In consequence, the communities have made a huge investment in sport and leisure and built a lot of sports centres. However, the communities did not possess exclusive authority according to the constitution. In 1985, a national sport decree legitimated local authority and obliged the 17 regions to pass authority to their communities. Many local politicians promoted sport because of their initial enthusiasm, but they became more interested in winning the next elections and using local sport in their political interests.

Furthermore, the social importance of active sport increased considerably at the beginning of the 1980s. In 1974, only 17.7 % of the Spanish population practised sport, in 1980 it increased to 25 % and in 1985 to 34 %. The CSD subsidies for the Spanish federation increased from 15 million Euro for 1.5 million athletes in competition in 1978, to approximately 30 million Euro for 2.1 million athletes in 1985. In 1985, 54 Spanish sport federations had been registered; badminton, squash and caving were established in 1983. Other sports could individually achieve some success on an international level (athletics, motor sport, golf, judo, canoeing, basketball and disability sport).

In 1982, Spain organised the Football World Cup, which was one of the first important boosts for Spanish sport. King Juan Carlos I sponsored the organising committee and the King´s family has – traditionally – until today an important involvement to sport. His children are involved in sailing and one daughter is married to an important Catalan handball player. However, beside the modernisation of football stadiums, new sports had an opportunity to be demonstrated in the cultural programme of the Football World Cup of 1982, e.g. golf. The organisation was quite successful, yet the World Cup was a "disaster" for the nation because the Spanish team lost in the second round.

In 1980, Spain obtained a key international sports political position: the Catalan Juan Antonio Samaranch became President of the International Olympic Committee (IOC). After the young Spanish democracy had averted a military coup in 1981 and the Socialist Party had won the general election with an absolute majority on 28 October 1982, many observers regarded this moment as the real beginning of Spanish democracy. The Socialist Party also had majorities at regional and local levels and influenced further sport policies decisively, especially by interpreting sport policy as active state intervention and support.

4. Expansion (1986-1992)

In 1986, after three attempts (1924, 1936, 1972), Barcelona gained the promise of hosting the Olympic Games in 1992. The decision was made in the third round of the IOC election committee, where the main influence came from IOC President Samaranch, a Catalan, who wanted the Games to be held in his region. Spanish sports policies supported the effort to organise a perfect Games, particularly because of the Catalan separatist movement. Therefore, the unsatisfactory results at the previous Olympic Games, with a total of 27 medals for the whole of Spanish Olympic history, had to be substantially improved. In 1988, the CSD founded – as in other countries – a national programme, called "ADO 1992" (ADO = "Asociacion de Deportes Olímpicos"), to promote and support Olympic athletes. The intense promotion and the combination of public and private organisations were new for Spanish sport. The CSD, COE, Spanish National Television (RTVE = Radio Televisión Española) and 22 commercial companies supported ADO 1992 with 120 million Euro. This money sponsored 743 athletes in 1988 and, later on, 278 athletes out of the 503 Spanish Olympic participants. Even the women´s hockey team, with only 500 athletes in Spain, was able, surprisingly, to win the gold medal in Barcelona, after one year of intense preparation. As a result, the Olympic Games of 1992 have been, until today, the most successful sports event in Spanish history. With 22 medals Spain gained sixth place in the ranking of nations and henceforward earned its place in the world´s athletic elite. The organisation and financial income had gained new superlatives in Olympic history and led to considerable international prestige. High spectator interest and positive satisfaction with the Spanish sports success created a high identification of all Spaniards with their athletes; this led to an improved national consciousness. Although the Ninth Paralympics did not stand so high in the public interest, Spain achieved a successful result, with 107 medals and fourth place in the national rankings. In the following years, four disabled Spanish sports associations were founded (in 1993 for the deaf, mentally challenged and cerebral palsy, and, in 1995 for the blind). In contrast to summer sport, Spanish winter sport is relatively unsuccessful; that might obviously be a result of the warm climatic conditions in Spain. At the Winter Olympics in Albertville, 1992, Spain won its second winter medal in Olympic history, even though there is only one Spanish sports federation representing all winter sports disciplines.

Spanish sports policies have not only focused on improving Olympic sport, they have also supported improvement in the general sports situation. They made higher investment in sports performance and the infrastructure. The subsidies for competitive sport increased annually, in which the ADO programme made up 20 % of the cost. From 1983 to 1995, the CSD invested, together with regions and communities, 480 million Euro in 3000 sports installations. In 1987, they created 15 sports centres for professional athletes. Furthermore, physical education has become a regular subject at school, so there has been a need for more teachers and coaches. In 1982, Granada established the third "faculty of physical activities and sport", followed by Vitoria and Valencia (1986) and A Coruña, Las Palmas and Leon (1987).

The Olympic Games in Barcelona 1992 represented an essential boost for all Spanish sport starting in the late 1980s. The historical equating of sport with football could be ended, even if football is still dominant in the sports landscape and its importance has not decreased. The development of other sports has continued and some of the successes in the 1980s became established sports disciplines in Spain, especially basketball, athletics, swimming, tennis, golf, cycling, motor sport and rallies. The expansion is linked with sporting success. Thus, the cyclist Miguel Indurain or tennis player Sánchez Vicario, have motivated many people to practise their sport. Commercialisation and professionalisation have also affected Spanish sport, which is closely connected with increasing economic production and entry into the European Community in 1985. In 1991, the sports sector took 1.2 % of the national product and had approximately 43,000 job places.

In 1983, the socialist government decided fundamentally to reform the structure of sport and to adapt it to its increasing economic importance. In 1990, after two years of intensive consultation among several groups, the new sports law, called "ley del deporte 10/1990", was ratified. The sports associations were now officially considered as private legal entities and their monopoly position was recognised. Regarding the conflict of authority, this law interpreted the position of the state more strongly and its role in sport as active support and intervention. The law also strengthened the battle against drugs and violence in the stadiums. However, the most important reform for Spanish sport was the creation of professional structures to cut the huge debts of the football clubs. The law introduced professional leagues for football and basketball similar to those of the United States, in which the indebted sport clubs had to transform themselves into "joint stock sports companies", called SAD (sociedades anónimas deportivas). However, the political interest was more concentrated on settling the debts than to install professional structures. Therefore, the law allowed clubs to keep their non- profit form if they had incurred no debt in the last five years or if they had sufficient financial guarantees. So football clubs like Osasuna, Atlétic Bilbao, Real Madrid and FC Barcelona were able to keep the traditional non-commercial form until today (Montes 1999: 308). At the moment there are two CSD accepted professional leagues: the "National League of Professional Football" (LFP) and the "Association of Basketball Clubs" (ACB). Both disciplines had to be separated from a multiple-sport club, but they could still form a club together, which is the case with Real Madrid and FC Barcelona. The professional league is an individual legal entity, in which the clubs are taking key decisions. They are also independent of the

Spanish federation, though they have to be integrated into the respective national federation. The changes in professional organisation contributed to a situation where sport as a spectacle has been more emphasised in its development. The importance of sport as entertainment is no longer only concentrated on football, it has increased in complexity and its commercial level.

There are also increasing sporting trends in society which started at the end of the 1980s. From 1985 to 1990 the level of sports participation was constantly about 34 %, but people were engaging in sport more frequently and in various new forms. Especially aerobics and fitness are in increasing demand, mainly by women. The economic processes of Spanish sport started to adapt not only professional structures for entertainment sport, but also the culture of post-industrial consumption. Not all the new sport disciplines have gained an opportunity to be integrated into the sport system, inasmuch as the main processes are not affecting the clubs. Moreover, with the law of 1990, CSD had made criteria for a Spanish association even more difficult. Sport must be of national and international importance, enjoy competition and be present in more than 50 % of the clubs. So the 1990 law established a new association form, called "aggregation of clubs" (Agrupaciones de Clubes). The form could give rights and duties, especially financial support, if the new sport promoted competition. All the same, the majority of Spanish people connect sport with fun and enjoyment rather than with competition. Since 1968 about 60% of the Spanish population are practising sport without any sense of competition. But the established Spanish sport system is identical with that of modern British sport. The low participation rate in sport during Franco times did not make it necessary to change the traditional sports system. With increasing sport practices, public opinion is growing more important. So the 1990 sports law established another structure to support the new non-competitive sport, called "sport promotion organisation" (Entes de promoción deportiva). Sports clubs or other associations (like neighbourhoods, travellers, etc.) gain the opportunity* to create this organism and receive financial support. The activities have to be linked with sport (in open definition) and should not be competitive. The association barrier nonetheless is still high, the sports promotion organisation has to be represented in six regions with 100 associations and 20,000 members.

5. Stabilisation (1993-2001)

The Barcelona Olympic Games brought a remarkable expansion in Spanish sport. In 1993 to 1996 an economic and political crisis took place. The national debt and unemployment rose considerably, so public budgets were forced to save money in order to meet Maastricht criteria and admission into the European Monetary Union. Investment in sport was no longer as generous as before and the ADO programme had to face difficulties in its extension. In 1996, the total amount for ADO was only 78 million Euro and, in Atlanta (1996), the money covered 301 Spanish athletes out of 479 Olympic athletes. Spain gained 17 medals and 13th place in the medal table.

In 1996, the right wing party "PP" (Partido Popular), a former Francoist party, won the election to the Spanish parliament and replaced the 14-year government of the Socialist Party. In 2000, the PP also gained an absolute majority in the parliamentary election. In consequence, sports policies have changed. Especially since 1996, there have been problems. The political leadership of the CSD changed four times in four years and the CSD has focused more on legislation regarding football, quite in the style of old Franco times. The ADO programme continued with less financial support and, in Sydney, Spain gained only 11 medals and 20th place in the medal table. As a consequence, the PP government seems to be promoting sport more actively. In addition the economic and financial situation has improved in the last four years. The patronage of the 2004 Olympic Games in Athens has now been taken over by Spanish Olympic Committee (COE – Comiteo Olimpica Espanol), but there is still no ADO programme for 2004 established.

In international sports politics Spain has gained more leading positions. In 1990, Spain had 272 representatives at international level, which increased to 363 in 1999 (after calculations of the CSD). The investment and expansion of the sports infrastructure have improved. In 1997, Spain could boast approximately 66,000 sport facilities and 155,000 sports camps for various sports activities. In addition, five new faculties of physical activities and sport were established (1994 Caceres; 1996 Madrid European University; 1998 Toledo, Murcia and 1999 Pontevedra), so that Spain had thirteen faculties of sport. INEF Madrid is now integrated into the Technical University of Madrid (Politecnica), but INEFC Barcelona-Lleida is still an independent institute. Furthermore, in 2001 Spanish sport received approximately 135 million Euro through the CSD, which is an increase of 3.6% over 2000. On the other hand, the reform of Spanish education is reducing the hours of physical education to only two hours per week.

The economic importance of sport has expanded further, which is especially a result of spectator trends. Most event tickets in sport are sold for football (53%) and basketball (21%), but other spectator sports are of interest, like handball, athletics, motor sport and cycling (all about 9%). The highest income, particularly for football and basketball, is from television agreements. Furthermore, professional clubs have the opportunity of going public on the stock exchange from 2002/2003. Besides football and basketball, there are other sports leagues with a high professional level, even if they are not recognised officially as professional leagues by the CSD; they are organised like committees in the respective national federations. That is the case for indoor football (LNFS), handball (ASOBAL), volleyball (ACEVOL), cycling, hockey and women´s basketball. At the moment, the CSD is likely to approve handball and volleyball as official professional leagues.

The importance of participant sport is growing, both in traditional and in new sports. In 1999, 76,806 sport clubs were registered, by contrast with 66,571 in 1990. An empirical study on the situation of the sport clubs does not exist at the moment, but some local surveys in Barcelona and Seville show that sports clubs are relatively homogenous in their constitution. In 1990, Spain had 2,319,038 athletes in competition, which increased to 2.5 million in 2000. At the moment there are 62 national sport federations (28 for Olympic sports) and two "aggregations". The CSD is still concentrated only on sport as competition, even if it does recognise sport as an important institution for improving health and fitness of the population. The CSD´s main aim is to keep the number of national sports federations low, so that expenses through financial funding are not increasing. In 1999, the national sport federation received 55 million Euro in financial subsidies. In 2000, football (578,213) and basketball (275,737) had the highest number of athletes in competition, followed by golf, judo, athletics, tennis, volleyball, karate and handball.

A tremendous success in the field of competitive sport is "Paddle" (Padel), a sport similar to tennis and squash. Originally Paddle was confined to Spain, but it expanded to Latin America, particularly Brazil, Argentina, Mexico and Uruguay. In Spain it started to gain importance in the late 1980s. In 2000, there were 6,143 athletes in competition and 120 Paddle installations. In 1997 Paddle gained acceptance by the CSD as a national federation, despite the higher barriers. The most recent establishment of a national federation has been for Surfing, which had been a federation between 1971 until 1981, but had a fall in athletes in competition. In 2001, the CSD wanted the integration of surfing into the sailing federation as with windsurfing. However, the Basque region had accepted a surfing federation, so the CSD, wanting to avoid political problems, permitted the creation of a Spanish surfing federation.

In Spain, active sport – as already mentioned – is practised more in informal leisure time and connected with fun and enjoyment in terms of motivation. In 1997 approximately 73.5% of the Spanish population engaged in sport without any competition. So the top ten sports being played are different from the number of athletes in competition. In a representative study in 2000, the most practised sport was swimming, followed by outdoor and indoor football, cycling, senior gymnastics, basketball, jogging, tennis, aerobics, hiking and athletics. Besides the increase in aerobics and fitness sport at the end of the 1980s, a higher demand for nature and adventure sports (like climbing, mountain biking, diving, rafting, etc.) can be seen in the 1990s. In research undertaken in 1995 approximately 16% of the Spanish population practised nature sport. The sports sector of nature and adventure sport is offered by private commercial enterprises linked with tourism activities. Besides traditional sports, the Spanish sports landscape has become more complex and differentiated.

Conclusions

This description of Spanish sports history has tried to show and explain the main motivating factors, characteristics and evolutionary processes which have defined Spanish sport from the middle of the 18th century to the start of the 21st century. We have seen how four principal changes and transitions marked political and sporting history: from monarchy to republic, from dictatorship to democracy. The cycles of change were discontinuous and nothing lasted for more than two generations.

The political and social integration of Spain during the present democratic era brings Spain up to the international political and sporting standards of other industrial societies. The continual change in Spain, unique in contemporary history, may now be stabilised; in future Spain is likely to be more involved in European history and its changes.

Literature

Amoros, Francisco, Cantiques religieux et moraux ou la morale en chansons (Paris, Colas, 1818); Manuel d'Education physique, gimnastique et morale (Paris, Roret, 1830).

Blanco (1999),"La ley del deporte de amibito estatal," in Blanco et al, *Manuel de la organización institucional del deporte*, pp 53-76. Barcelona.

Consejo Superior de Deporte (1995), *Legislación del deporte*. Madrid: Ministerio de Educación y Ciencia.

CSD (1996), *La evolucion del deporte en Espana 1983-1995*. Madrid:Ministerio de Educación y Ciencia.

CSD (2000), *El deporte Español ante el siglo XXI, Resúmenes, cifras y propuestas*. Madrid:Ministerio de Educación y Cultura.

Puig Barata, Nuria/ Garcia Figueras, Oscar/ Lopez Perez, Carlos (1999), "Clubs deportivo en Espana," in CSD, *Participiacion deportiva: perspectiva ambiental y organizacional*. Madrid: Ministerio de Educación y Cultura, pp 53-81.

Sambricio, Carlos (1988) "Presentación del Comisario, Carlos III Alcalde de Madrid, Ayuntamiento de Madrid," p. 27. Cited by Desdevises du Dezaert, G. (1989), *La Espana del Antiguo Regimen*. Madrid: Fundación Universitaria Española, p. 137; Jose Ortega y Gasset (1950), Goya, *Colleccion El Arquero*, Madrid.

Serrano, J. A. (1995) "Estudio del asociacionismo deportivo en un sistema deportivo con baja orientacion del deporte hacia el tiempo libre," in *ACTAS del Congreso Científico Olimpico 1992*.

Valls Loret, Jose Domingo (1998) *Derecho del deporte Materiales y textos*. Barcelona.

Italy

Angela Teja and Marco Impiglia

Historical Profile

From the early nineteenth century the myth of the *Nation in Arms* and the *Citizen Soldier* were widely diffused in all Europe, from the French Revolution to the armies of Napoleon. These myths were the basis for introducing physical education into the school system as an essential element of pre-military education. It was assumed that a strong nation needed a strong army, that a strong army needed the citizen to stand up for the nation. All this was to be prepared in the school system. This had democratic connotations as it implied that the soldier-citizen had an interest in his own affairs and those of the nation. Italy was no different. We can, therefore, see that the movement for military physical education is older than the sports system.

Actual sports had their origins in the Kingdom of Sardinia (a state which was composed of the Piemont and the island of Sardinia). The Swiss Rudolf Obermann began to introduce German gymnastics (Turnen) in Turin in 1833 – at first to the Piemont Army. In 1844, Obermann founded the first Italian gymnastics club, the Royal Gymnastics Society of Turin. It was open to all classes and strata of society without restriction. The membership lists included, for example, Carlo Alberto, a simple worker. In this period gymnastics was favoured as pre-military exercise for young men and was enthusiastically supported as it was part of the national fervour for strength and national unity. Enthusiasm was also prevalent for mountain climbing, target shooting, fencing, and horseback riding. Gymnastics was a synonym for fatherland, for pre-military readiness and it was not yet a true sport.

Giuseppe Garibaldi, freedom hero for all of Italy, was very active in a campaign for the promotion of target shooting which he started in the North of Italy. After Italian unification (1861) Turin became the capital of the newly-founded Kingdom. Thanks to the aristocrats who came to the royal court, Turin automatically also assumed a role in the leadership of the new sports movement.

The first physical education classes in school took place in Turin, as the school reform of Casati (1859) had introduced gymnastics instruction into the school system and also the preparation for gymnastics teachers for schools. It was also here that the National Federation for Target Shooting (1861) and the Italian Alpine Club (1863) were founded.

In the mid-eighteen seventies there was a move towards the liberals and the left in the Italian parliament. A political and economic crisis became more obvious as the unemployed masses were very visible and unemployment among intellectuals also rose. In addition, there was a considerable mismatch between the relatively rich North and the poor South. In this process of construction of national unity gymnastics, as a forerunner to sports, was used as part of the superstructure by the dominant classes.

There were mainly two functions for physical exercises:

1. To repair the historical hiatus between the real nation and the legal nation, between North and South, to construct national manifestations for national unity. This assured social and regional integration, similar themes to be discussed, a similar language to be used.

2. To introduce, prepare and conserve military preparation of all Italians. This was done by the diffusion of gymnastics societies and the increasingly active sports associations (a phenomenon at first limited to the cities of the North and the Centre). This was favoured by the introduction of physical activities into the school system, the only method to really bring physical education to everybody and create the basis for a sport culture. The State Law of De Sanctis (1878) introduced physical education into all primary and secondary schools of the Nation, providing a military orientation. The Law of Daneo (1909) assured that all cities had to provide gymnastics halls and sports fields near the school buildings, thereby providing the necessary material precondition for physical education to take place.

The years 1890 and 1915 (when Italy entered the First World War) saw three major changes:
1. English sport was introduced and the gymnastics organisations tried to contain and control the young sports movement for the benefit of national preparation for war.
2. Cycling became by far the most popular sport in all Italy.
3. Milan was becoming the new sporting capital of the Nation.

The gymnastics federation, formally founded in 1869, had only 70 clubs in 1890 with a total of some 8,000 members. These clubs were almost all located in the cities of the North and the Centre of Italy. Their names related to health, patriotism, ethical and social aims, such as *Salus et Robur, Pro Patria, Vigor, Libertas, Forza e Coraggio* (force and courage), *Fratellanza ginnastica* (gymnastics brotherhood). This related to an increasing consciousness among the upper-middle and upper classes of the importance for healthy living and an increase in individual responsibility.

The working class also had an increasing political awareness in these years of growing industrialisation and proletarianisation. Socialism soon became popular with its own aims for the betterment of society through education. Of this physical education became a part and thus the gymnastics societies had also to take charge of a new kind of member.

A considerable dispute erupted over the methodology and character of physical education in Italy. There were basically three different directions:
* Gymnastics according to the German model (*Turnen*),
* Gymnastics without the heavy apparatus, with health as the prime motive and a well-developed body: Swedish gymnastics

* Sport with its emphasis on games heavily under British influence (athletics, football, tennis, etc.).

These new exercises and games were sometimes used in the traditional gymnastics society, sometimes in special sections of the old clubs, and sometimes in newly founded clubs.

Traditional gymnastics formed a united *"anti-sportista"* front to stop the introduction of British sporting games. On the other hand, the new sports drew passionate spectators and helped to enhance a national interest in the new "sports".

In 1898, athletics and football left the Gymnastics Federation, which until then had been the umbrella for those sports, to become autonomous federations. Football, in particular (the gymnastics people had renamed it "calcio", using a name from the Renaissance game of Florence), changed its character. From an entirely upper class game of students and merchants in contact with Britain and other foreign countries, it attracted a worker backing in the years directly prior to World War I. Thanks to its capacity to mobilise local support, to its modern and dynamic rules, calcio was able to take the place of the more static earlier game of "giuoco del pallone". In the course of the nineteenth century, a professional circuit developed. Big stadiums could be built and large crowds of passionate spectators came to support the city team which replaced the earlier representation of the Italian city states.

In 1910, the national team played for the first time and, only three years later, 18,000 spectators attended the match, Italy against Belgium, in Turin. In those days it was not calcio that drew the biggest crowds but bicycle racing. Ten years after establishing the sport (the first "Veloce Club" was founded in Milan in 1870, the Federation *Unione Velocipedistica Italiana* in Turin in 1885), the cycling craze exploded in the 1890s when the "iron horse" ceased to be a bizarre attribute of "sportsmen" and became the favoured means of locomotion of the bourgeoisie. In 1894, Touring Club Ciclistico Italiano was founded in Milan according to the model of similar tourist associations in England and France.

In many cities cycle tracks were constructed with gate money to be paid and betting according to the horse racing model. The first cycle races of any consequence were on the track and not on the road. With the movement came economic interests: bicycles had to be constructed and sold in large numbers in mass production, tyres were used in even greater number, advertisements had to be employed to buy particular brands. This resulted in the publication of the first regular sporting journals: *Il Ciclo* (later *La Bicicletta*, 1893) and *La Gazzetta dello Sport* (1896).

At the beginning of the century, the cost of cycles had gone down and the new status symbol of the upper class became the motor car. This was a time when the working class appropriated for itself the bicycle as its prime mode of transport to work and its prime interest in the sports world. The Sunday cycle tour became the only form of tourism and recreation for the worker at a time when there was still the six-day working week with very little time for proletarian recreation. With the advent of the great cycle road races came the first generation of legendary champions, such as Gerbi and Ganna who earned their place in the memory of people ever since as these were the first workers' champions with a truly proletarian background.

When in 1909 the inauguration of the annual *Giro d'Italia* took place, there were in all about 800,000 bicycles in use in Italy. The *Gazzetta dello Sport* staged this national bicycle race 'kermesse' following the model of *L'Auto* of Paris with its *Tour de France*, to multiply rapidly its sales and convert the journal into a daily publication, surpassing in turn the weekly *La Stampa Sportiva* (1902) of Turin.

When we talk about the relationship between sport and industry (cycling, automobilism, motorcycling etc.), it should not be overlooked that this is mainly a phenomenon of the big industrialised cities like Milan and Turin, which served, however, as a model for much of Italy and attracted many people from the rural areas to the centres. Thanks to the frenetic activities of sports organisations and the sports events staged by *Gazzetta dello Sport* and others, Milan became the new sporting capital of Italy. All principal national sport associations took their seat in the Lombardian capital. Turin, Genoa, Florence and Rome all followed at a certain distance. In the south, with the notable exceptions of Naples and Palermo, there was still great poverty and ill health which meant that sport was the hobby of the 'idle' rich and could not yet catch on as a mass activity. The Italian Socialist Workers Party still considered sport as a useless private activity which took time away from the more important political struggle.

The Beginning of Women's Sport

The beginning of women's sport in Italy at the end of the nineteenth century was motivated from the outside by eugenic theories to assure the healthy and strong body of future mothers. The *Federazione Ginnastica* founded a Central Women's Committee in 1896 to propagate the education of women through conferences and sports and gymnastic games. Not all the member societies responded positively. Sport and gymnastics were to lose their manly, virile, pre-military and militaristic spirit if women were to be allowed to participate, as such character traits were considered impossible for women.

In 1898, the newly founded Central Committee for Physical Education and Gymnastics Games for Schools and the Public decided to have a women's section, and the Roman noble ladies Carolina Rattazzi, Cecilia Scialoja and the Marquise Costanza Gravina were put in charge. They had founded in 1890 the Female Section of the Gymnastics Federation of Rome and now took charge on a national scale.

For them women's sport had to be less fatiguing and violent than men's sport. They favoured archery, tennis and golf and sports which stressed the modesty of women, as best expressed in gymnastics, in hiking on Sundays (even in the mountains), a little of bicycle tourism (no races), a little swimming (no competitions, no men watching), a little athletics (no competitions).

Women were not yet considered equals of men. So, in men's competitions they were to crown the victors, but could not take part in the same meeting. Their own meetings were more of the folklore type with no serious striving for victory. Ballerini, who recorded the story of a female tournament in Rome in 1897 among English ladies, reported that the programme contained sack races, egg and spoon races, cake races, marches to the rhythm of music, a concert with bicycle bells, and similar events. Only since 1908, when the national championships for women took place in Milan, did the situation change. *Insubria Milano* took these championships seriously, won, and started a new era. They gained the right that only women could manage events involving women in sport. So, as of 1911, there were only women judges at women's gymnastic competitions.

During the *Belle époque*, Italy also entered Olympic competition. In Paris (1900), London (1908) and Stockholm (1912) a total of 13 medals were won. In 1904, Baron de Coubertin proposed staging the Olympic Games of 1908 in Rome. To measure up to the more sporting nations of the north of Europe and the United States, an Italian Committee for participation in the Olympic Games was founded three years later. This was the basis for the Comitato Olimpico Nazionale Italiano (CONI, the name still used) which was founded in 1914.

At the beginning of the twentieth century the role of women improved also in the field of sport – slowly but surely. By the end of the First World War, women had gained a status where they could engage in sport just for fun and not because it helped support their potential motherhood. This had a lot to do with the role of women in society. During the War women had taken many places that men had vacated owing to the war effort and their active involvement in the fighting. After the war, men regained their jobs, but in leisure-time activities the new-found self-awareness of their powers helped women to maintain their improved position. In 1921, Italy was among the founding members in Paris of the International Women's Sport Federation, together with the United States, Britain, Czechoslovakia and France, and which staged the first Women's World Championships in Monte Carlo.

Sports advances

When the Inter-Allied Games took place in Joinville-le-Pont (near Paris) in 1919, the enormous difference between the sportsmen of the Anglo-American Armies and the Italian troops became obvious. There were very few Italians who had any sporting background at all. The Italian military leadership became convinced that "sport" was necessary for "modern warfare". With the energy the military put into the propagation of sport, gymnastics lost out and the following years witnessed the victory of English sports in Italy – particularly in the industrial centres of the North and Middle of the country.

In the 1920s football 'went mad'. Huge stadia were built and hundreds of thousands of spectators went to see the matches. The "tifosi", the fanatical Italian sport fans, were born. The Football Federation organised leagues which now covered the whole of Italy. Football surpassed cycling as "business" because of the mass of players and fans every weekend, and it was a close second in the hearts of fans. In motor car racing Alfa Romeo of Milan created national enthusiasm, particularly among the workers, through its victories in international races. Boxing attracted many spectators at ringsides that were at first built in theatres. The Sports Bar was invented, where the sports fan could meet every day of the week. New sports were springing up everywhere and professionalism increased. At the Olympic Games of Antwerp in 1920, Italy won 24 medals, including 13 gold medals. In Paris (1924) there were 16 medals for Italy. It was in this climate of a national desire to do well in sports that the Fascist movement started to make use of athletic success for the benefit of Italy and its fascist government. Success on the sports field seemed to imply that the way the Fascist government handled the manpower of the nation was internationally successful – or at least far superior to anything previous governments had done.

Between 1925 and 1929 the sporting interest of Italians took an enormous upswing which helped the Fascist movement significantly. The Catholic and the workers' sports movements were abolished. Sport, just as much as other fields of public life, was placed under the rule of *totalitarianism*, which meant that you could only practice sport (or any other activity for that matter) in the public sphere if you were a member of an acknowledged association which had to be under the leadership of a fascist leader. The *Opera Nazionale Balilla* (ONB – 1926) combined all activities of young people, the *Gruppi Universitari Fascisti* (GUF – 1911) all university students, and the *Opera Nazionale Dopolavoro* (OND – 1920) all workers in their after-work leisure activities. ONB under the leadership of Renato Ricci was charged with promoting a new generation of Italians with perfect bodies, physical endurance and a moral and fighting spirit close to the heart of the *Duce*, Benito Mussolini.

Together with the second organisation, which reached all university students, the two organisations created many competitions inside the country so that young men could measure themselves in regular competitions – *Ludi Juveniles e Littoriali dello Sport*. *Dopolavoro* occupied itself with the leisure activities of workers. That included also sport and tourism. As athletes could also be workers, this created the potential for a new division in the sport movement. In December 1926, CONI therefore became responsible for all physical education and competitive sport. The Fascist Party (Partito Nazionale Fascista, PNF) appointed the leader of CONI and made him responsible for all sport.

As of February 1927, new statutes declared CONI to be the sports governing body of all sports (Olympic or not). The leader of CONI had the right to appoint the president of any sports federation who, in turn, would nominate his board. Elections were thereby abolished. A Party Office for sport was founded which took charge of all the federations and, almost identical with CONI, had its seat in the Palazzo Littorio in Rome, giving it high government authority. The fascist symbol of the fascias was introduced into the Olympic Rings of CONI, just as in all symbols of all sports federations. At international competitions the fascist symbols were shown and the athletes had to give the fascist salute. The close connection between the PNF and the athletic field can best be seen in the notion that sporting competition and training were considered Party service , and athletes had to wear "la camicia nera", the black shirt, of the Fascist Party.

In December 1928, the "Carta dello Sport" (Sports Charter) was promulgated between the President of CONI and the Secretary General of the PNF Augusto Turati; it stabilised the sports situation, permitting CONI (which had been organised to combine private clubs of a liberal mode) to collaborate effectively with the new fascist entities on a governmental basis (ONB, OND, GUF). This agreement lasted until 1942, when a new Law gave CONI supreme power over Italian sport. Between 1929 and 1933 the offices of all national sport federations were transferred to Rome to assure greater efficiency and a higher degree of centralisation. In the capital city of Rome, a new sports daily paper arose, *Il Littoriale*, founded by the President of the Italian Football Federation Leandro Arpinati. During this time the Italian Sport Medicine Federation was founded in Turin (1929) by Turati, as he wanted to have the best medical treatment and sports-related research for his national calibre athletes.

In the 1930s the fascist regime pursued a sports policy that was entirely nationalistic and was to ensure national prestige through sport. It had two major aims. First, as many young Italians as possible were to take part in sport. This was the so-called fascist generation of the future, including young girls and women, the latter with some reservations. Secondly, Italians should win as many medals as possible at international competitions to show other nations that Fascism was successful and that Italy was a dynamic and modern nation. To ensure these aims many stadia and gyms were constructed all over Italy. This also helped to provide government-sponsored employment to the whole country. In Rome (the Foro Mussolini) and in Orvieto, academies were created to prepare physical educators and instructors for such an enormous sport programme. The government heavily financed (with many millions) CONI which, in turn, supervised the preparation of elite athletes. With the help of the *Dopolavoro* and other fascist organisations, Italian championships took place from the grass roots level upward. This co-operation resulted in GIL becoming part of ONB in 1937, to co-ordinate the organisations even more. It can clearly be seen that by 1935 Italy had joined the more advanced countries of Europe in the diffusion of sport and had achieved an intermediate place among West European countries.

The second aim was achieved even more impressively. In the Olympic Games of Amsterdam (1928), Los Angeles (1932) and Berlin (1936), Italy reaped 76 medals, including 27 gold medals. It had clearly established itself as a world power in elite sports, coming third in Amsterdam, coming second to the USA in 1932 and third to Germany and the USA in 1936. Italy continued to do well in such sports that had always been high on the list of Italians: fencing, gymnastics, cycling, boxing and football. The "squadra azzurra" with the manager Vittorio Pozzo won the World Football Championships in 1934 and 1938. In football, cycling, motor racing, athletics, we still remember such legendary figures as Meazza, Piola, Girardengo, Binda, Bartali, Nuvolari, Carnera, Beccali. The athletic success of such champions made the fascist years prior to World War II the "golden era" of Italian sport and intertwine the myths of the nation, sport and ... Fascism.

The ten years between 1929 and 1939 were also an important period in the development of women's sport as the general sportification of youth did not exclude the female sex. In spite of medical warnings, there was a general conviction that sport was good for women as – within limits – the healthy and sporting body of a women was to be a eugenic advantage as it helped to strengthen the reproductive system. As this was a disputed area, the *Gran Consiglio* of the PNF asked the Federazione Medici Sportivi on 17 October 1930 to come up with a unified "authoritative" statement. The organisation of sports medical practitioners was very reluctant to advocate women's sports. It pointed out that Italian women were first and foremost Italians and should, therefore, avoid any "Americanisation". Many doctors, such as Poggi-Longostrevi, Pende and Crispoldi, expressed their doubts that any sport (athletics, skating, swimming, fencing, winter sports, basketball, tennis, shooting, competitive gymnastics) was good for women. Others were looking more for a compromise and were for rational limits on women's sports, assuming that some sport was necessary for the development of a harmonious body.

With such a mixed recommendation the fascist government adopted a strong physical education system for women and put less emphasis on women winning medals at international competitions. In 1932, the Female Physical Education Academy was opened in Orvieto, the first of its kind in the world. The explicit aim was to assure that the future mother was to be sufficiently fit to give birth to the future race of citizen-soldiers for the Nation. With grandiose choreography, GIL presented masses of young women who were not just supposed to be future mothers and wives, but true sporting athletes, healthy, tough, desiring to take part in all healthy aspects of sport and to win – but at the same time being aware of the therapeutic hygienic possibilities of physical education and sport.

With the fall of the Fascist system, CONI was taken over by the Prime Minister of the new Republic. In June 1944, the Socialist Giulio Onesti became Extraordinary Commissioner of CONI with the explicit task of liquidating it – just like all other fascist organisations dependent on the PNF had been eliminated by the new post-war democratic government. Onesti, however, saved CONI from dissolution, adapted its status to the new democratic conditions and the democratic constitution (1947). He was successful in assuring that CONI was granted a guaranteed organisational autonomy, administrative and financial independence. The instrument Onesti used to assure this was the football pools (*Toto*). As of 1948, matches of the Italian football league were used for this sporting lottery – and all the income was granted to CONI. Thanks to the foresight of Onesti, Italian sports continued to flourish. All through the many crises of the Italian Republic, with its frequent dissolution of Parliament, with many new governments in office, with serious financial difficulties for the state, CONI remained well financed, independent of overt political influence. A percentage of the *Totocalcio* goes to the government, but CONI receives its share without any government action necessary.

This is similar to the situation prior to the War. The government does not finance sport, but it gives it the means to finance itself and thus pays* its regular dues to the state. The "politicizzazione" of sport is now within the sporting organisation: conservative Christian Democrats, Communists, Socialists, Liberals, and those of the Right all act within the sports organisations and have to make use of them for their political aims, but they are not able to blackmail them as sport is sufficiently independent from government or party pressure. In the 1950s, when the supervision of CONI passed to the Minister of Tourism and Public Events, CONI started to use the excess money from the football pools for the construction of more and more sports facilities. This resulted in the Olympic Games of 1960 being transferred to Rome and a building boom for sport facilities in the Roman Capital for that purpose.

The influence of government can also be seen in another sphere. It can almost be said that this runs through Italian sporting politics like a red thread from monarchical times, through Fascism to the new Democracy. There is an equilibrium between competitive sport and all those other public entities which have an interest in the diffusion of sport; public agencies for propaganda and tourism, the military, university centres, commercial interests. They all have to co-operate with CONI. CONI thus assumes a role far beyond its actual responsibility for elite sports and national representation through sports. It speaks on behalf of physical education, the training of physical education teachers (coaches and sport managers), sport as leisure-time activity, and sports in the tourist resorts, just as much as professional sports. An important date in the history of CONI (and its Secretary General Bruno Zauli) in its efforts for physical education in schools was its return into the realm of the Ministry of Education in 1947. In 1952 the *Foro Italico* (ex *Foro Mussolini*) of the *Istituto Superiore di Educazione Fisica* (ISEF) was opened in which the government, in close co-operation with CONI, trained physical education teachers for the school system. It was the follow-up organisation to the Fascist Academies in Rome and Orvieto.

At first (1952), the programmes of the ISEF were approved for secondary schools, but then, in 1955, also for primary schools. Finally the Moro Law of 1958 determined that physical education was an integral part of the school system, that all pupils were to have two hours of physical education per week, that the teachers trained at the ISEFs had the same rights as teachers trained at universities for other school subjects. In 1989, the obligatory classes of physical education became optional in the last two years of the secondary school. In the last year of school there was to be a practical examination in PE to which a theoretical examination was added in 1977. At first, there were also school sports clubs (ended in 1975) which were the basis of the Annual Italian School Championships in all sports. Finally, the statutes of the ISEF of Rome were approved, providing for teaching but also for research into PE and sport. Only in 1999 were the ISEFs included in the universities, so that now the study of sports science and physical education has become a regular university subject and the ISEF of Rome has become the Sports Science Faculty of Rome University. The long-term special role of the ISEFs has been in close association with the special role of CONI and its fascist tradition.

Since the early 1970s CONI has been distancing itself from attempts by various governments (by such actions as the creation of a Minister for Sport) to reduce its autonomy. The so-called "statalizzazione" is seen as an attempt to curb autonomy and to make use of the popularity of sport for party political benefit. A government plan to promote the spreading of sport was also seen as an implicit criticism that CONI was not able (or willing) to promote sport for all, concentrating too much on elite sports. In the last fifty years the percentage of Italians doing sport regularly has increased from 2 % to 26.5 %. This tremendous increase has, of course, not reached all parts of the country equally and so the diffusion was strengthened by government activities. The activities of the government in school physical education is customary in all countries of Europe. To push back the influence of CONI in this field was, therefore, seen by the government as a natural act, while CONI showed some resistance at first as it tried to maintain its monopoly.

It can still be seen, however, that in spite of all the efforts of the government to spread physical education, there is still considerable public resistance to forcing young people to do physical education. Only in the last fifteen years did the various governments really try to insist that physical education ought to have the same status as any other school subject. After many efforts the government finally succeeded in ensuring that the field was treated equal to any other. As much good as CONI did for sport in other areas, it is questionable whether its resistance to have physical education move from a special to normal status was not a hindrance for the development of sport. A special field under the jurisdiction of a special body responsible only for sport (CONI), a model that was cherished by Fascists and Nazis alike, that was used for parts of PE teacher training in the USSR and the GDR, had advantages as long as there was just one physical education model. As soon as there were several models, the liberal preparation and outlook of a general university education seem advantageous. It cannot be shown that physical education teachers prepared under the jurisdiction of CONI did any better in preparing pupils for sport than any teacher trained by a university along more scientific and less practical lines.

In the Olympic Games, from London 1948 to Sydney 2000, Italy won a total of 172 Olympic titles, being in the top ten in the world all the time. The best result was achieved in Rome, 1960, and in Sydney, 2000 (seventh with 13 Gold, 8 Silver, 13 Bronze Medals). Italian efforts are well co-ordinated and elite athletes receive a great deal of help. This has a lot to do with Italian hero worship. The 1950s and 1960s are the years with myths around the most famous cyclists of the world: Bartali and the unforgettable Fausto Coppi, the two most loved champions who showed that Italian success in sport was Italian and not fascist, that Italy was back after the terror of the war. It was the time of the boxing hero Benvenuti, the motor car victories in Formula 1 of Ferrari, in motor cycling of Mike Agostini and, of course, of the football heroes. Boxing and cycling declined somewhat in popularity in the 1970s as there were not enough local heroes, while tennis (Panatta) and skiing (Thoeni) improved their positions. Motor racing (still Ferrari) and football, with the World Cup Win of 1982 (the "azzurri" of Enzo Bearzot), were still on top. In recent years that has not changed much. It is still Ferraris (though with an international team of drivers), skiing has been doing well (Tomba, Compagnoni), motor cycling (Biaggi, Capirossi) and cycling with the advent of Marco Pantani. But the difference between popular spectator sports and popular participation sports is growing even more, with the tendency of young people to play such "new" sports as volleyball, basketball, gymnastics, martial arts, jogging, skiing (with all its modern variations), swimming and "Californian Sports" (aerobics, windsurfing, snowboarding, roller-skating, body building) and East Asian forms of yoga, together with the traditional sports, like football, tennis and cycling.

Female sport had different problems after the Second World War. At first there were attempts to have a completely different system for women's sports than for men's. There were attempts by modern gymnasts, such as Andreina Gotta Sacco (1904-1988), the *grande Maestra* of the ISEF of Rome, who tried to ensure that the Italian tradition of a less "masculine" sport was maintained. Even the Church gave up some of its opposition to female sport, but still did not support it as fully as men's, in spite of the fact that Pope John Paul II invited young gymnasts to perform in the *Sala Nervi.*

Eventually, even school physical education accepted that girls needed some competitions and started to include female school sport groups in their programmes in 1950. Of course, there were many opposing voices, but girls' and women's sport gradually moved forward along the path to equality.

Recently, more and more Italian women have become international sports stars. Such heroines are necessary to ensure that young girls have role models to follow. Women such as Compagnoni and Belmondo in skiing, Vaccaroni in fencing, Simeoni, Pigni and Dorio in athletics are important stages in the progress of women's sport in Italy. But women diversify faster than men and so the success of Pozzo (mountain bike), Sidoti (walking), Fogli (marathon) and Trillini (fencing) demonstrate the rapid progress of Italian women in sport.

Organisation, Finance and Structure

From the beginning the Italian government took a much smaller role in the development of physical education and sport than in most other European countries. In spite of the influence of the Fascist Party, it was not the Italian state that influenced sport (unless one assumes the identity of State and Party under Fascist conditions). The Italian Constitution of 1948 does not mention sport and the state limits its function to:

a. the supervision of CONI through the Prime Minister;
b. maintaining physical education in the school system and the universities through the respective ministers;
c. encouraging physical activity and fitness in the Armed Forces and other government agencies (Police Force, Customs Guards, Foresters etc.) through the respective ministers;
d. assuring that all athletes have proper medical treatment and that all sports buildings are built according to appropriate standards (through the responsible Ministers).

With the laws concerning decentralisation (1977), the supervision of all sporting activities and facilities has been moved from central government to the localities. In reality, this means that the emphasis on sport differs significantly from zone to zone, and that it is impossible to know which city has which function under which local counsellor.

This leaves CONI as the prime mover in sporting matters as it has had the chance to develop a much stronger degree of professionalism. Even if the regions now put a lot of emphasis on the promotion of sport, in each region there is a regional sports association to look after this and closely co-operate with CONI and the associations for the various sports, which again co-operate with CONI. So it is evident that the influence of CONI is much stronger than that of any government agency, as the government has chosen to distribute its powers to many different ministers and regional and local entities.

The third sub-structure important for the development of sport is the sports associations. They are under the supervision of the *Enti di Promozione Sportiva* (EPS) (Agency for the Promotion of Sport) and reach about one third of all active sportspeople. The EPS are the result of mainly local activities of organisations that are not directly or exclusively occupied with sport. When , for example, the local club for senior citizens wants to pursue some activity, it often decides on something related to sport. When the clubs are well connected they receive money for themselves and thus have money to organise sport. They may also receive money to have their own sports facilities. The only condition the EPS has to observe is that the activities they are supporting are "non profit".

CONI, on the other hand, is using some of its money to organise talent contests each year. This is highly criticised by the EPS which stands for a "SPORT FOR ALL" programme and sees the propaganda competition of CONI as an unfair attempt to lure its best athletes and promising stars to a "rival" organisation. This resulted finally, in 1996, in the creation of the National Committee for Sport for All in which CONI, the EPS and the regional representatives for Sport for All have their seat. Since 1997, the government is attempting to co-ordinate all sport and to bring everything under some kind of unified jurisdiction.

It is still CONI which is the unique organism with an exclusive parliamentary legitimation. It also has the exclusive use of the rights to the Olympic Rings in Italy, a property right which in itself has developed considerable value. But its function is limited to the selection, preparation and co-ordination of the Italian Olympic effort, co-ordination of the sports federation responsible for national teams in the respective sports, and finally to a sports ministry, as the government has so far completely delegated its functions to CONI. Only very recently has the government had second thoughts about it, as CONI installations were used to cover up the doping of elite athletes while, at the same time, the government was advocating the strict prosecution of drugs and drug-takers. The Deputy Prime-Minister has been responsible for sport since 1955 on the side of the government – but with very little staff to promote any independent government sports politics.

CONI also constitutes the national sports governing body in that it is the chief federation of the sports federations, in which the latter determine the structure of CONI. It has central bodies and also regional bodies to ensure that at the level of government CONI representatives can talk to a person responsible for the same geographic area. CONI is also acknowledged by the International Olympic Committee (IOC) as its national representative. The IOC members for Italy are automatically part of CONI Central Committee. All Olympic and also non-Olympic sports federations are represented under the roof of CONI. For traditional reasons CONI also has the Automobile Club and the Aero Club d'Italia and similar old sporting bodies as members. The federations have maximum autonomy in financial and administrative matters, CONI only checks their books as an administrative control agency. The sports clubs are members of the sports associations and have their independence, on the one hand, and their allegiance to CONI, on the other. In technical and disciplinary matters the sports federations are not bound by any decisions of CONI.

In recent years, the Sports Charter has become more and more important. In 1997, there were 174 cases in which the courts have dealt with sport, of which ninety were with professional football. In 1998, the figure was reduced to 52 cases in as many as eleven sports, showing that sporting activities are bound by the state as a field where the rule of law exists just as in any other field. Italy is now attempting to regulate doping, as in France and Belgium, with a national law against drugs in sport and the illegal practices of doping.

CONI has power through the federations and the government. Every four years the presidents of the Italian sports federations (Olympic and non-Olympic) elect the CONI President. Their "proposal" is then officially confirmed (or theoretically not confirmed) by the Italian Minister of Tourism and Events (*Ministro del Turismo e dello Spettacolo*). The annual assembly of CONI members also agrees on the budget of CONI and its member federations. Talent selection and the improvement of sporting talent receive an astonishing 25.2 % of the annual budget. In 1997, *Totocalcio* and *Totogol* brought 985,000,000,000 Lire (about 500,000,000 Euro) into CONI, of which 43 percent was passed on to the federations. The government received slightly more than CONI, i.e. 1,132,000,000,000 Lire, in lottery revenue from the same games. If one adds the other revenue that the government takes from sport (tax on tickets, income tax on sports jobs, etc.), sport is providing the government with about 5,000 billion Lire (2.5 billion Euro). The administrative autonomy of CONI is limited through the Prime Minister. Although this control is more or less theoretical, it means that the budget of CONI is controlled by Parliament. In addition to the administrative expenses the budget of CONI is mainly used in the following ways:

a. Construction of sport installations;
b. Preparation and the sending of athletes to the Olympic Games and international championships;
c. Sports in the Armed Forces;
d. Expenses for the Sportbank (*Credito Sportivo*), an agency through which sport installations are pre-financed;
e. Sport aid for youth centres of the talent preparation process;
f. Collaboration with regional sports for all bodies (*Enti di Promozione Sportiva*);
g. Support for the sports insurance company (*Sportass*), insurance for all active club members in all sporting activities and on the way to the activity.

The other main income of Italian sport comes from sponsors. In 1996, 3,500 billion Lire (1.75 billion Euro) came from Italian sports sponsors: about one quarter of this went to television and the rest directly into sports. Traditionally, the sporting press (print and electronic) have been major supporters of Italian sport. In 1997, the three national sporting dailies (*Gazzetta dello Sport, Corriere dello Sport-Stadio, Tuttosport*) sold on average 677,830 copies a day, i.e. 13.6 % of all daily printed copies of any newspaper. On Mondays, an additional one million sport papers are sold. Considering the number of people who read newspapers, it can be estimated that six million people read sports papers on average every day. *La Gazette dello Sport* is the fourth largest Italian daily paper. All newspapers carry sports news, very often on the front page. According to 1989 data (which do not change much), some 50 % of the money the consumer of sporting news spends goes into the buying dailies, 30 % into sports periodicals, 17 % into paid television and only 3 % into the purchase of sports books.

Television is taking an ever greater part of the attention of the sports fan. By international comparison, Italy is quite backward in the use of the Internet, although since 1995 many sport clubs, journals, Ferrari and others have started with their own homepage. The main television stations carry about 3,000 hours of sport each year (the government television *RAI* with its three channels, and the commercial *Telemontecarlo* and *Mediaset*). The major part still comes from RAI (1,861 hours) which carries a daily special feature (*Telegiornalesport* -TGS). The other national chains, Mediaset (597 hours) and Telemontecarlo (635 hours), have less importance. In addition, an increasing number of spectators watch television via satellite, pay TV and pay per view. *Telepiù* carries exclusive events and had 100,000 paying customers for the matches of the National *Serie A and B* in football.

In 1996, the sports sector of Italy had an annual turnover of about 50,000 billion Lire (25 billion Euro), it employed 500,000 people (additionally there were about 600,000 non-paid helpers). The government is able to take 6,000 billion Lire (3 billion Euro) in taxes from the sport sector, which taxes mainly the 39,000 billion Lire (19.5 billion Euro) that the sport consumers invest in sport. Sport is contributing 2.4 % of the gross national product, of which the public sector is only contributing 0.5 %. If we look at it in absolute terms, Italy is fifth world-wide in the amount of money spent on sport, ahead of countries with a bigger total gross national product. With US $ 293 per head of the population, Italy is spending much more money on sports than other countries in Europe – even those that have a higher percentage of population actively involved in sport.

Over the last 36 years the space designated for sports (stadia, gym halls, swimming pools, etc.) has increased fourfold. The last calculation showed that Italy had 143,523 sporting facilities, i.e. 251.7 sport structures for every 100,000 inhabitants. There is a notable difference in the distribution of these sporting facilities, showing that they were built with the support of national and European programmes to support the less developed South. In the North-east it is 346.4, in the North-west 336.4, in the Centre 254.9, in the South 149.3 and on the Islands 129.4. The Val d'Aosta, the Alpine Valley in the very north of Italy, has the largest percentage of citizens actively involved in sport, as members of associations and federations, buying most sporting goods and spending most in sports shops.

The distribution of sporting facilities is also not directly proportionate to the number of active sports people in the different sports: tennis has 18% of the installations, 17% are multi-sports facilities, a large number is dedicated to the Italian game of Boccia and are indoor halls. Football has 14% of the facilities. 3% are swimming pools and less than 1% are running tracks.

Not all the 143,000 sport facilities are in good shape, however. Between 5 and 15% are closed because of the danger involved in their use, 11% are in bad shape owing to insufficient maintenance, 10% are still under construction – although they are being used. Roughly ten percent were built before 1960. This figure does not include the facilities for school physical education classes. Many of these facilities are not being used in the late afternoon and evenings – in some areas of the country this has changed, and sports clubs can use them. Sporting facilities in the urban centres are still a major problem, as there are not enough of them, and very often there is not enough parking space, so that getting to the centres is difficult and costly.

Financing sport facilities through the sports bank (*Istituto per il Credito Sportivo*) is equally difficult, as can be seen by the fact that in 1996 the bank paid out 335 billion Lire (167.5 million Euro) of which 232 billion came from the public sector and 101 billion from the private. As many as 776 sporting facilities were financed through this special bank, which meant that on average less than 700 million Lire (350,000 Euro) was asked for. This also shows that this institution is heavily involved in Sport for All, as elite sports facilities cannot be built with such a small amount of money.

An important component of the sports system is the sports activities of the universities, the armed forces and other government agencies. University sport (*Centro Universitario Sportivo Italiano*, CUSI) has 44 fine sport centres all over the Italian Peninsula and is co-ordinating the voluntary sports of over one million university students. Each Centre has its own sporting facilities which sometimes are as big as the university campus itself. CUSI is in the tradition of Italian university sport which has been very strong from the very beginning. Already in 1922 Italy staged the first international university competition in Rome. Italy has traditionally played an important role in the international university sports federation (FISU).

The other great past of Italian sport can be seen in the Armed Forces. There are many young men who do their national service in special units for elite athletes fully under professional conditions. There is also employment of those athletes whose service is in the national interest. They can stay in the Armed Forces as quasi-professional athletes. There are also similar places in other government agencies, such as customs officers (*Guardia di Finanza*), State Police (*Carabinieri*), City Police, National Forest Service. Roughly three thousand athletes are hired as "soldiers in the national interest", of whom about 250 are in national teams of various sports (*azzurri*) and 45 are Olympians. About 50 % of the medal winners of the Atlanta and Nagano Olympic Games were serving in the Armed Forces, while only about 30 % of the teams were, indicating that the percentage of medal winners among them was substantially higher. Within the Armed Forces, the athletes do not need to worry about their future, there is regular promotion and a secure retirement.

Every military barracks has sports facilities. On the whole, there are more than 1,500 military sports buildings (also used by civilian athletes) where the military can practice its sports. Another two thousand sport facilities come under government ownership for other branches, such as customs and police. In the last thirty years, the military has opened up facilities for youth sections. Here young men (and women) can practice under the expert guidance of military coaches. This is good public relations and helps to avoid isolation of military athletes. The contract between the Minister of Defence and CONI dates back to 1954.

Physical education teachers and coaches are of particular importance for the sports system. They train in Physical Education Institutes (*Istituti Superiori di Educazione Fisica*, ISEF). These special institutes require the same school qualifications for entry as a university, but do not have university status. There were eleven ISEFs in all of Italy with about 20,000 students. The ISEF of Rome, the only one directly under the government, is based at the *Foro Italico*, the HQ of CONI. Meanwhile, these ISEFs have now been integrated into the universities. But the process is far from complete as research has to gain greater importance and university professors have to be found. This is quite difficult in the early stages, as postgraduate academic qualifications (doctorates, etc.) cannot be attained at the ISEFs and motor science has no field of investigation in the universities outside the medical field.

The main research Centre of CONI is the *Scuola dello Sport* (SdS) which was founded in 1966 in the *Centro Giulio Onesti* in Rome, on an area of 210,000 square meters. This centre is highly esteemed in Europe for its international open-mindedness and international coaching courses. It is here that the actual technical brain of Italian sport works. Sports scientists of the former Soviet Union have been working here ever since the demise of the Soviet Union. It is also the centre of documentation, the preparation of audio-visual material for Italian sport, not just for CONI but also for sports federations. It contains the *Biblioteca Sportiva Nazionale*, one of the best European sports libraries with 250,000 books and more than 500 current journals. Since 1977 it is also the home of the Italian Coaching Academy which has so far produced over 200 level-two coaches of the highest calibre. Since 1997 the Rome SdS has developed eight regional sub-branches to prepare level-three coaches all over Italy.

Integrated into the Giulio Onesti sport complex is the *Istituto di Scienza dello Sport* (ISS) which started as *Istituto di Medicina dello Sport* in 1963. It is here that sports medical and other research directly relating to elite athlete takes place. The talent selection process is co-ordinated here. It has an IOC accredited anti-doping laboratory under the supervision of the *Federazione Medico Sportiva Italiana* (FMSI) to make sure that the training of the athletes and the anti-doping procedures are not conducted by the same organisation. CONI has a long history of active struggle against drugs – a struggle that has not always been successful.

CONI is now organising over ten thousand drug tests annually, many of them unannounced. Nevertheless, drug-taking in Italian sport is an continual struggle which has not been won yet.

On the whole, Italian elite sport is quite successful: at the Olympic Games of Atlanta in 1996 Italy was represented by 344 athletes (242 men and 102 women), of whom 65 placed in the top eight (18.9 %), 35 won medals (13 gold, 10 silver, 12 bronze) in 15 different disciplines. In 1997, Italian athletes won 1041 medals at international championships (390 gold, 331 silver, 320 bronze). This included 99 world titles, in 22 sports, and 117 European titles in 21 sports. In 16 disciplines Italian athletes are among the top three in the world, in 35 disciplines they are in the top ten, while in Europe Italy is represented in 24 disciplines in the top three, and in 50 disciplines in the top ten. This shows that Italy has the same potential as the sports powers of Germany, Russia, Great Britain, France and Spain. It is Olympic success every four years at the

Summer Games that ensures (or ends) the tenure of the CONI President. CONI used 7 % of its annual budget for the preparation of Olympic athletes for Sydney; that is roughly 25 million Euro per year. In Sydney this resulted in seventh place for Italy with 13 gold, 8 silver and 13 bronze medals, six medals ahead of Great Britain and on a par in gold medals with France and Germany, while Spain won only eleven medals and placed 25th overall.

Some current data on Italian Sport

According to 1995 data there were 34.2 million Italians doing some kind of sport out of 55 million six years and older (61.8 percent). These data have to be differentiated between those who answered that they at least did sport once in the year (19,450,000) and those who said that they were doing sport at least once a week (14,750,000, or 26.5%). In the North, the total percentage stands at 72 %, in the Centre at 62 % and in the South at only 50 %. Most sport is done by people in cities between ten and one hundred thousand inhabitants, less in the smaller towns and in the metropolis. It is the lower middle class that has the highest participation rate in sports. Men are still doing more physical activity and sport than women, 9 million men are active (33.6 %) and 9.4 million (35.1 %) are doing sports. 10.5 million women are physically active, but only 5.3 million are doing sport. Considering that on the whole women live longer than men and that the level of physical activity of men and women in the categories above 60 years of age is extremely low it is obvious that the activity level of women (18.6 %) is significantly lower than that of men (35.1 %). Of the roughly 15 million Italians who are regularly doing sport, 8 million are members of a sports federation. CONI organisations have 1,673,000 adult members and 3,350,000 youth members. In the age group 6 through 18, about 50 % are or have been physically active and an additional 30 % are or were doing sport, which means that 80 % (with a perfect balance between the sexes) of the younger generation is doing sport in the widest sense. The highest percentage is reached in the age group 11-13 with 70 %, which then steadily decreases

	Sport	Active members	Participants in competitions
1.	Calcio (football)	3 100 000	518 000
2.	Gymnastics	2 400 000	11 000
3.	Swimming	1 600 000	44 000
4.	Tennis	800 000	73 000
5.	Athletics	800 000	22 000
6.	Cycling	800 000	12 000
7.	Volleyball	750 000	187 000
8.	Hunting (shooting)	720 000	6 000
9.	Winter Sports	700 000	57 000
10.	Basketball	450 000	180 000

Table 1.

to 40 % at the age of 18. Six out of ten adolescents were active in some form of competition. Table1 shows the ten sports most actively practised:

Currently CONI has 54 member federations and associated disciplines. This represents a total of 82,628 member organisation (73,049 sports clubs and 9,579 other clubs that only have a sports section). To run these sports there are 548,000 officials, 138,000 technical staff (coaches, etc.) and 94,000 referees, officials and judges. Every Sunday sees some 35,000 sports meets and matches (plus those that have no official character) involving about 1.7 million athletes and some 200,000 referees, coaches and other personnel. This is a huge machinery which runs smoothly thanks to Italian sports organisation. This has given Italy the prestige of a sports world power which is underlined by the international sports matches that take place in Italy every year. In 1997, there were 350 important international events in Italy, including 8 world and 18 European championships.

The democratic strength of the system lies in the widely differentiated structure of sport which has grown over the last few decades. There are now over four thousand centres that report to CONI and serve the local and regional sport communities. CONI has twenty regional and 104 provincial committees, and 800 local offices with over 1,700 honorary officials as the basis of Italian sports.

Eight million athletes (3.7 million inside CONI) are a good number to work with. They form the basis of Italian strength in sport.

In this selection process the *Giochi della Gioventù* (GdG) have played an important role since 1968. Currently about 3 million young people take part in them annually. Now in Olympic Training Centres the best athletes have everything they need. These athletes are enrolled in the *Olympic Club* which ensures them the best coaches and best facilities in the nation. In recent years special schools have started to co-operate closely with CONI to give their youth physical education classes a special emphasis in competitive sport. 56 schools in 30 cities are currently participating in the programme that is organised in close co-operation with 21 sports federations.

Recent developments in Italian sport

In the last four years of the last century, there were a number of profound changes, which certainly influence – for better or for worse – the future of Italiansport. The success of the past, the traditional passion for sport of the Italian people and the creativity of its administrators are still the same, Italians still play a major role in international sport organisations (especially in the Olympics with four members on the IOC). These legacies of the past are all worth keeping intact. Sport will therefore survive the recent changes, but they have shaken the very basis of the sports movement.

In recent years, the financial basis of CONI was shaken considerably. The football pools, *Totocalcio*, did not bring the expected increase in turnover. On the contrary, instead of receiving more money as expected, CONI received much less. CONI applied for the Olympic Games of 2004, again to be held in Rome, but the Games were granted to Athens. This exacerbated the crisis, as with money for the Olympics some of the fundamental expenses of CONI could have been covered, and some of the staff could have been placed at the disposal of the then organising committee. No Olympics, no additional funds. There were a number of drug scandals which put additional doubt on the ability (or willingness) of CONI to handle the crisis effectively. At the same time, the government was determined to show its strength in many sectors, including sport. At the end of 1998, CONI President Pescante resigned – the first resignation of a CONI president in its history.

CONI had to rely on the help of the state to guarantee the salaries of its 3,000 employees, as the income of *Totocalcio* had decreased by 30 – 40 %, while additional staff had been hired. The reduction in income also meant that CONI could not live up to its obligation to the sports federations. To avoid a major crisis, the government stepped in, paid for sending the Olympic team to Sydney 2000, helped pay the salaries of employees and other major projects. This has been the first time in its history that CONI had such a severe financial crisis. The main formal reason was that the new forms of sport betting which were expected to bring in additional income were not accepted by the public: *Totogol*, *Totosei*, and *Totobingol* flopped.

A major discussion has been going on concerning the restructuring of CONI and all Italian sport. As the basis for CONI is a law of 1942 with some modification of 1947 and 1948, it is parliament that has to establish a new sports charter describing the functions and structures of CONI. Considering that the old structure was intact for over half a century, it is not surprising that a lot of thought has been put into the new structure.

The discussion about CONI comes at a time of widespread constitutional discussion about a greater degree of autonomy for the regions. If the newly founded regions have greater cultural autonomy, this ought to be visible in the new sports structure. As the question of the degree of autonomy of the regions is politically disputed between the major parties, any election can change the future structure of CONI (or any sports governing body for that matter).

For the time being there were a number of changes which can be placed under the heading of greater democratic legitimisation:
* CONI's *National Council* was enlarged. This was where the 39 presidents of the sports federations met, where the President of CONI, the Vice President, the Secretary General and the members of the Executive Board were elected. The function has remained the same, but each federation is now represented by five people, the President, two other functionaries, an athlete and a coach (or technical director). In addition the regions are represented and the Ente di Promozione. With about two hundred people voting, a greater degree of transparency, representation, and control seem to be assured.
* The President is no longer a voting member of the Executive Board. As the Board is supposed to control the President, this ensures that the President is not controlling him(or her)self. Athletes and coaches are now also represented on the Executive Board – proportionally to their representation in the National Council.
* Finally, the status of the sports federations has been changed. They have now become financially independent of CONI, relying on public money and on private sector sponsorship.

The whole reform is heavily disputed between CONI and the Ministry for Cultural Affairs now in charge of sport. The whole struggle about the structure of CONI which had not taken place for over half a century is not productive and is hindering the future development of sport. The first elections under the new structure will show whether the new system will work. We are not critical of the new procedure, but the old structure had the advantage of a high degree of stability independent of changes in government – which have been more frequent in Italy than in most other European countries. The new system runs the risk that it will be changed with every change of government. This might endanger the long-term development of sport which depends considerably on continuity.

Conclusions

We have seen that Italy was a relative late-comer on the sports scene. But the state took decisive action and was able to create and then make use of a wide interest in sport. Currently, the state is again stepping in to modernise the structure of sport. The unique situation of enabling the sport system to finance itself entirely through the football pools provided the Italian sport system with a high degree of independence and stability in a country traditionally distrustful of national bodies. The state maintained its influence in many fields of sport and provided excellent conditions for athletes in the Armed Forces. Italy was also ready to learn from the success of other countries and invests heavily in the translation of material from Russia, Germany and the United States. It has modelled its elite sport system on the most effective programmes. The results have shown that Italian elite sport is among the best in the world and has maintained its high position for three quarters of a century.

The success of Italian sport is also acknowledged internationally. At one time Italy was the only country that had four members on the International Olympic Committee, which shows the high esteem its system has internationally. There are very few countries that have a sport system that creates such a percentage of the gross national product (2.4 %) each year. Italy is therefore no longer a country that was coerced into doing sport. We have a wide variety of sports at all levels that are practised – and every year new trends in sport are readily adopted into the multifarious sports scene.

Literature

De Grazia, V. (1981), *The Culture of Consent. Mass Organization of Leisure in Fascist Italy*. Cambridge: University Press.

Di Donato, M. (1984), *Storia dell'educazione fisica e sportiva*, Rome: Studium.

Fabrizio, F. (1976), *Sport e fascismo. La politica sportiva del regime 1924-1936*, Rimini-Florence: Guaraldi.

Ferrara, P. (1992) (ed), *L'Italia in palestra. Storia documenti e immagini della ginnastica dal 1833 scuola e caserma*. Rome: La Meridiana.

Fabrizio, F. (1977), *Storia dello sport in Italia. Dalle società ginnastiche all'associazionismo di massa*, Rimini- Firenze: Guaraldi.

Impiglia, M. (1996), *Campo Testaccio*. Rome: Riccardo Viola.

Impiglia, M. (2000), "The 'fascist holiday'. The afterwork association and the

beginning of mass tourism in Italy (1926 – 1940)", in: Krüger, A., Teja, A. and Trangbaek, E. (eds), *Europäische Perspektiven zur Geschichte von Sport,*
Kultur und Tourismus. Berlin: Tischler 2000, 87 – 101.

Jacomuzzi, S. (1973), Gli sport, in: *Storia d'Italia,* vol. V, Turin: Einaudi, 912-25.

Jacomuzzi, S. (1976), *Storia delle Olimpiadi,* Turin: Einaudi.

Koon, T. (1985), *Believe, obey, fight. Political Socialization of Youth in Fascist Italy 1922-1943,* Chapel Hill: University of North Carolina Press.

Krüger, A. & Teja, A. (1997)(eds), *La comune eredità dello sport in Europa,*
Roma: Scuola dello Sport.

Krüger, A. & Trangbaek, E. (1999)(eds), *The History of Physical Education and Sport from European Perspectives.* Copenhagen: CESH.

Lämmer, M., Renson, R. & J. Riordan (1989) (eds), *Proceedings of the XIIth Hispa Congress Gubbio-Italy, May 26- June 1, 1987,* Sankt Augustin: Academia.

Noto, A. & Rossi, L. (1992) (eds), *Coroginnica. Saggi sulla ginnastica, lo sport e la cultura del copro 1891-1991,* Rome: La Meridiana.

Pivato, S. (1994), *L'era dello sport.* Firenze: Guaraldi.

Teja, A. (1995), *Educazione fisica al femminile. Dai primi corsi di Torino di Ginnastica educativa per le maestre (1867) alla ginnastica moderna di Andreina Gotta Sacco (1904-1988).* Rome: Società Stampa Sportiva.

Teja, A. (1998), 'Italian sport and international relations under fascism,' in P. Arnaud & J. Riordan (eds.), *Sport and international Politics.* London: Spon, 147 – 70.